Social Work in India

About the Editors

Dr. Bishnu Mohan Dash, M.S.W. (Visva-Bharati), M.Phil. (Delhi University), Ph.D. (Delhi University), ICSSR Post-Doctoral Fellow, Assistant Professor (Senior Scale) in Social Work at Dr. Bhim Rao Ambedkar College (University of Delhi). He is also an editorial board member in several national and international journals. He has also authored/co-authored/edited eight books. He has published more than thirty papers in various reputed National and International Journals including Sage, Routledge, Columbia, and contributed chapters for Post-Graduate Course in Social Work (MSW)/Social work and Counselling of Indira Gandhi National Open University, New Delhi. He has presented papers and Chaired sessions in various national/international conferences including Canada, Japan, Sri Lanka etc. He was also member of the Expert Committee in the BSW and MSW course Revision in several universities. He has completed a number of research projects and organized various workshops and seminars and has been a very active academician and researcher in social work. His areas of interest are social work, education, Rural Development and Child Welfare.

Dr. Mithilesh Kumar is an Assistant Professor and Co-ordinator (Teaching) in Mahatma Gandhi Fuji Guru Ji Centre for Social Work, Mahatma Gandhi Antarrashtriya Hindi Vishwavidyalaya, Wardha, Maharashtra. His Area of specializations are Human Rights, Research Methodology and Gandhian Social Work. He Has Written/Edited 8 Books and 19 Research Papers in reputed national/international Journals. He is recipient of Social Work Education and Promotion Award by International Association for World Peace (Affiliated with ECOSOC of United Nations, DPI, UNICEF, and UNESCO).

Siddheshwar Shukla is a Senior Journalist and Social Researcher based in Delhi. His research interests include public policy, public health, food security, and Indic studies. Despite being a working journalist since over a decade he has more than a dozen publications to his credit. He is presently posted as Deputy Editor, The Sikh Times Group in New Delhi, which publishes three daily newspapers – *The Sikh Times* (English), *Qaumi Patrika* (Punjabi) and *Qaumi Patrika* (Hindi).

Social Work in India

Indigenous Approaches and Models

Edited by
Bishnu Mohan Dash
Mithilesh Kumar
Siddheshwar Shukla

CONCEPT PUBLISHING COMPANY PVT. LTD.
NEW DELHI-110059

ISBN-13: 978-93-88937-49-8

First Published 2020

Published and Printed by

Concept
Since 1974

Concept Publishing Company Pvt. Ltd.
A/15-16, Commercial Block, Mohan Garden,
New Delhi-110059 (INDIA)
T: 91 11 25351460, 91 11 25351794
E: publishing@conceptpub.com; *W*: www.conceptpub.com

Cataloging in Publication Data--Courtesy: D.K. Agencies (P) Ltd. <docinfo@dkagencies.com>

Social work in India : indigenous approaches and models / edited by Bishnu Mohan Dash, Mithilesh Kumar, Siddheshwar Shukla.
pages cm
Contributed articles.
Includes bibliographical references and index.
ISBN 9789388937498

1. Social work education—India. 2. Indigenous peoples—Services for—India. I. Dash, Bishnu Mohan, editor. II. Kumar, Mithilesh (Assistant professor of social work), editor. III. Shukla, Siddheshwar, editor.

LCC HV11.8.I4S63 2020 | DDC 361.3071154 23

Foreword

It is a matter of great pleasure to know that Dr. Bishnu Mohan Dash and other scholars have compiled a volume "Social Work in India" to be published in the form of an edited book. This volume contains chapters on various aspects of *Bharatiyakaran* (Indianisation) of social work education. I am confident that the book would work as a strong foundation for Indianisation of social work education in India as Dr. Dash and his team of learned academicians have made a sincere effort to bring in relevant theories, principles, models, approaches and experiences of social service enshrined in our knowledge system. The book is first of its kind as it focuses on Indigenous Social Work literature. Dr. Dash who is spearheading the movement for *Bharatiyakaran* of social work education by organizing conferences, seminars and workshops has also attempted to develop indigenous social work course materials. This volume essentially highlights the Bharatiya models and approaches to social work education.

It is beyond doubt that the entire curriculum of social work education in Indian universities is Euro-centric and its effectiveness in Indian context has remained much questioned. Just like what has happened in rest of Asia, Africa and Latin America, the learned social work professionals, activists, academicians, and reformers in India have been arguing for liberating the social work education from the shackles of colonialism of Europe and the U.S. The Euro-centric nature of social work paradigms, theories and methodologies are being increasingly challenged all through the world. The relevance, adequacy and effectiveness of the Western social work knowledge and methods for addressing the challenges being faced by the people of the Third World are being questioned more often.

In India, due to the dominance of social work academicians and professionals trained in Euro-American perspective, there could be no significant advancement is this direction as the dominant lobbies kept resisting such a move. Those who occupied the decision making positions in academics were either intolerant or inattentive to indigenous knowledge system that they helped any such effort to be nipped into the bud. Therefore, Indian academia, researchers and professionals could not present or develop their own principles and models suitable to indigenous needs but accepted to work as instruments of implementing Euro-American models in the country which has been having a long tradition of social reforms and service for centuries together.

It was due to this trend in Indian social work landscape that no voice could be heard critiquing the Euro-centricism or proposing some Indic alternatives. We know that many professional social workers and educators recognized the need for Indianisation of social work. Through this work Dr. Dash has surely attempted to emphasise the need for renaissance of Indian social work education which would produce a knowledge system based on indigenous stuff. I hope that the book will be an asset to the students, academicians and researchers not only in the discipline of Social Work but also in other social science domains.

Of course we have to go long way and work very industriously towards Indianisation of Social Work education in the country. I am sure the present volume on Social work in India will motivate other academicians and researchers to concentrate on developing literature on the same theme.

Prof. Virendra Kumar Malhotra
Member Secretary,
Indian Council of Social Science Research

Acknowledgements

We express our sincere thanks to Indian Council of Social Science Research (ICSSR) for financial assistance Prof. V.K. Malhotra, Member Secretary, ICSSR for writing foreword. We are also thankful to Dr. Sachchidanand Joshi, the President of *Bharatiya Shikshan Mandal* (BSM) and Shri Mukul Kanitkar, National Organising Secretary for support. We are also thankful to the Vice Chancellor of Mahatma Gandhi International Hindi University, Prof. Girishwar Mishra, for his guidance and inspiration.

We are also grateful to Dr. G.K. Arora, the Principal of Dr. Bhim Rao Ambedkar College, University of Delhi and Prof. Manoj Kumar, Director, MGFG, Centre for Social Work, Wardha for guidance and support.

Our greatest debt remains to our contributors who agreed to share their chapters with us. Special Thanks to Ashok K. Mittal, Concept Publishing Co. (Pvt.) Ltd. for his support in publication.

We feel privileged to present this book in the present form before academicians, professionals, research scholars and students of Social Work. As there is always scope of improvement, we intend to encourage communication for further improvement.

Bishnu Mohan Dash
Mithilesh Kumar
Siddheshwar Shukla

Contents

SECTION II
INDIGENOUS MODELS IN SOCIAL WORK

List of Contributors

Amod Gurjar, Assistant Professor, MGFG Centre for Social Work, Mahatma Gandhi Antarrashtriya Hindi Vishwavidyalaya, Wardha, Maharashtra.
E-mail: *amod04@gmail.com*

Arul Actovin C., PhD Scholar, Department of Social Work, Pondicherry University, Pondicherry.
E-mail: *arulactovin@gmail.com*

Avtar Singh, Associate Professor, Department of Social Work, Dr. B.R. Ambedkar College, Delhi.

Biplove Kumar, Doctoral Research Fellow, Department of History, Sikkim University, Sikaim.
E-mail: *biplovekumar26@gmail.com*

Dr. Mithilesh Kumar, Assistant Professor, MGFG Centre for Social Work Mahatma Gandhi Antarrashtriya Hindi Vishwavidyalaya, Wardha, Maharashtra.
E-mail: mkt1980@gmail.com

Molankal Gangabhushan M., Professor, Department of Social Work, Assam University, Silchar-788011, Assam.
E-mail: *gangabhushan@gmail.com*

Nayanjyoti Hazarika, Rajiv Gandhi National Institute of Youth Development, Sriperumbudur, Tamil Nadu.
E-mail: *nayanhazarika90@gmail.com*

Payal Poddar Singhania, JRF & Ph.D. Scholar, Department of Social Work, Jamia Millia Islamia, New Delhi.
E-mail: *payalpoddar1428@gmail.com*

Dr. Pratap C. Behera, Assistant Professor, Department of Social Work, University of Delhi, Delhi.

Puneet Kumar Ojha, Ph.D. Scholar, Department of Social Work, University of Delhi.
E-mail: *puneetojhabhu@gmail.com*

Rajan Prakash, Research Scholar, MGFG Center for Social Work, Mahatma Gandhi Antarrashtriya Hindi Vishwavidyalaya, Wardha, Maharashtra.
Email: rajanprakashssm@gmail.com

Ranjana Sehgal, Professor, Indore School of Social Work, M.P.

Dr. Sanjoy Roy, Associate Professor, Department of Social Work, University of Delhi, Delhi.

Shashi Rani, Assistant Professor, Department of Social Work, University of Delhi, Delhi.

Shazia Manzoor, Coordinator, Department of Social Work, University of J & K.
E-mail: *s.beigh25@live.com*

Sumeera Nazir, Research Scholar, Department of Social Work, University of J & K.

Sunil Prasad, Ph.D. Scholar, Department of Social Work, Visva Bharati University, West Bengal.
E-mail: *prasad.sunil17@gmail.com*

Ushvinder Kaur Popli, Professor, Department of Social Work, Jamia Millia Islamia, New Delhi.

Prof. Y.S. Siddegowda, Vice-Chancellor, Tumkur University, Tumakuru and Professor, Department of Social Work, University of Mysore.

Dr. Yugal Jha, Associate Professor & Head, Department of Political Science, K.K.M. College, Pakur, S.K.M. University, Dumka (Jharkhand).
E-mail: *yugaljha@rediffmail.com, yugaljha1@gmail.com*

Introduction

Social work education since its inception in India in the year 1936 is still based on the western euro centric knowledge. Even after eight decades of social work education in India, there has been no significant change in the curriculum, research and fieldwork training. As the discipline has its roots in the colonial India, it was obvious that the entire social work curriculum was borrowed from the West. Till date, we are maintaining *status quo* with regard to the social work curriculum both in theory and field training. By and large, social work methods, principles, values and techniques and theories, taught in Indian colleges and universities are purely Western and have been adopted in our country without evaluating its suitability in Indian context. The Western paradigm of social work is not universally acceptable in India which is characterized by multi-ethnic, multi-cultural, multi-lingual and multi-religious society. This diversity is further complicated due to urbanization, industrialization, modernization and globalization. This intricate mix of traditions and modernity makes it almost impossible to construct one overarching formula to fit all. In the international academic forums there is also a growing and continuing debate on indigenization *vis-à-vis* universalization of social work education. Even the International Federation of Social Workers definition emphasizes on indigenous knowledge, along with theories of social work, social sciences, and humanities as the knowledge base of social work profession. In this situation, it is futile to think of single model to be suitable across all regions for social work education and practice. Therefore, it calls for decolonizing the colonial legacy of social work education and need for formulating (*Swadeshi*) indigenous social work models, theories and more particularly developing of Bharatiya model of social work. Our rich cultural traditions, values and ethics needs to be thoroughly integrated in each and every paper of social work syllabi at the Bachelors, Masters, M.Phil. and Ph.D. level to make it relevant in the contemporary Indian society. The present social work curriculum is mostly outdated. There is a dire need to revise the entire social work syllabi thoroughly. The rich social work traditions needs to be integrated in the Indian Social Work curriculum. Of course, there may be some elements of universality and utility in imparting the colonial model of social work education, but applying entirely the Euro-centric models is further going to deteriorate the quality of social work education in India. So, the book has tried to incorporate the significant contributions and developmental models propounded by the great Indian thinkers particularly Swami Vivekananda, Dr. Bhim Rao Ambedkar, Mahatma Gandhi, Vinoba Bhave and Nanaji Deshmukh which are highly relevant in the reconstruction of Indian Society. The Social work values, principles, ethics and practices embedded in the Indian religious texts and scriptures have not been given due recognition and legitimacy in the professional discourse. The book is divided in two sections—Section I : Indigenous Approaches in Social Work and Section II : Indigenous Models in Social Work also highlighted various indigenous practices of rural development and has also highlighted the role of ICT in social work education.

In Section I, **Ranjana Sehgal** in her chapter highlights Nananji Deshmukh's commitments to the development of backward people by promoting self-reliance, renunciation, penance, diligence, and compassion. For him, Bharat live in its villages and hence all development should begin from rural India. Many of his unique and path-breaking ideas can be inspiration to trained social workers and can be replicated. His Model of Social Work, Problem Solving Orientation is based on human being as the centre stage of the development and his life provides material for social workers to do research and establish a connection between social work practice and his model of social work. **Mithilesh Kumar** in his chapter discusses the contribution of Vinoba Bhave in the reconstruction of Indian society that had remained untouched for centuries. In the third chapter while highlighting the Sriniketan experiment, **Sanjoy Roy** has identified and analysed the backdrop and importance of Sriniketan experiment till today. In his chapter while analysing the influences of Gandhian thoughts and philosophy in the social work profession, **Sunil Prasad** and **Actovin C.** discusses the role of Gandhi in preparing the intellectual climate for the growth of professional social work in India. **Biplov Kumar** in his chapter has described the role of Baba Saheb in social reform who has tried to eradicate the monster of caste and untouchability. **Shashi Rani's** paper has traced the philosophical groundings and approaches adopted by Ambedkar and Phule to address the issue of caste discrimination and marginalization of certain communities. Further, she has made an attempt to locate the issue of caste in contemporary times and challenges it is posing in modern societies. The main focus of the chapter is on to revisit Mahatma Jyotirao Phule and Dr. B.R. Ambedkar approaches of Social Justice and its relevance in contemporary Social Work Practice. **Amod Gurjar** has made an appeal to the social work fraternity to Ambedkar's model of community organization and social action as it is tested and result oriented in India. There is need to add this model in social work curriculum in Universities. **Avtar Singh** in his chapter has discussed Ambedkar's role in promoting human rights and seek to fuse moral vision and political practice. In Section II, **Puneet Kumar Ojha** in his chapter has made an attempt to examine Vivekananda's model of human development and its relevance for contemporary social workers. **Y.S. Siddegoda** in his chapter besides highlighting the various challenges of fieldwork has suggested various indigenous suggestions to improve the quality of fieldwork practice in Indian universities. '*Swadhyaya*' movement is one of the indigenous movement which has been promulgated by Pandurang Shastri Athavale (recipient of the Ramon Magsaysay Award in 1996 and the Templeton Award in 1997), who has been a beacon of inspiration to promote the dignity of the individual and human relationships. The goal of *Swadhyaya* is to create a wholesome society through awakened individuals and awakened social institutions that put people at the core of their agenda. The guiding principles for this initiative have taken from the teachings from the ancient wisdom of our tradition has been highlighted by Molankal Gangabhusan in his chapter. Yugal Jha in his chapter has discussed the spirit of traditional institutions of the Chai Champa polity and the republic of great Lichchhivi of the ancient India on the bank of Bhagirathi, Ganges and its tributaries which have been in veneration by the great people of India since centuries. The Panchayati Raj Institution is the repository of all the experiment of participatory democratic continum which had long been into practice in the ancient Indian village— the symbol of self-reliant and decentralized unit of the Indian nation as a whole. In addition to that, it impressed the creative mind of the indigenous leader, revolutionaries, saints, poets and the chain of social political thinkers and reformers to attain the objectives of the establishment of ***Gram Raj***. The latter meant a self-governing village or a village republic and not merely a village panchayat. Such village would at once become "centers of struggle and resistance" during a revolution and would constitute the bricks with which the structure of the free Indian republic could be built. **Ushvinder Kaur Popli** and **Payal Poddar Singhania** highlight the fact that although the development of ICT for learning is a long-term project and to ensure that social work practice upholds the standards and values of social work ethics, it is necessary that social workers are competent and literate in ICTs and the ongoing rapid growth of ICTs has created a context in which social workers cannot resist technology, but must understand the role it plays in everyday life. **Pratap C. Behera** in his chapter tries to touch the philosophical aspects of human rights, tries to link the issues of difference to human rights and elaborates the reasons to take the side of the weak and protect their interests. The chapter deliberates, how human rights issues affecting the *Dalits* to be looked in a perspective and make efforts to adopt empowering models to address the problem. **Sumeera Nazir** and **Shazia Manzoor** in their chapter make an analysis of the multidimensional problems faced by Half-widows in Kashmir which include social, economic, psychological and legal, and emphasizes the role, need and intervention of social workers in alleviating the sufferings of Half-widows. **Nayanjyoti Hazarika's** chapter intends to examine the scope of professional social work in agriculture extension services based on extension services provided by Assam Agriculture University. And an attempt has been made to provide a base to develop the concept of agriculture social work as a separate specialization. The book will be extremely relevant for the students of social work, rural development, sociology, development studies and allied social science disciplines at Bachelors and Masters level.

SECTION I
Indigenous Approaches in Social Work

1
Nanaji Deshmukh
A Champion of Rural Development

Ranjana Sehgal

Introduction

Bharat Ratna, Nanaji Deshmukh, was a multifaceted person, who donned many hats. He was a celebrated politician, an indigenous economist, an educationist, and above all a social worker par excellence. This chapter takes a look into the life and achievements of this great *'samajik shilpkar'*, with a focus on his innovative experiments in social restructuring on the Indian soil. As not much literature is available, I would like to advise the readers to refer to the few books available on Nanaji, especially the six volumes of '*Virat Purush*' for a deeper understanding of his varied and significant contributions to our society. This chapter is a modest attempt, to briefly showcase the life of this great '*Yug Purush*', highlighting his work as a social worker and social activist. Chandikadas Amritrao Deshmukh, lovingly called as Nanaji, was a visionary and a seer in modern-day Indian politics; a rare example of selfless service and sacrifice. He belonged to that rare category of mankind, as described in the first sentence of this Sanskrit *shloka*:

> एते सत्पुरुष परार्थघटका: स्वार्थान परित्यज्य ये।
> सामान्यऽस्तु परार्थमुद्यमरता: स्वार्थविरोधेन ये ।।
> (वे सत्पुरुष हैं जो अपना स्थार्थ त्याग कर दूसरों की भलाई का कार्य करते हैं। वे सामान्य हैं जो अपना कार्य करते हुए ही दूसरों की भलाई करते हैं।)

Nanaji Deshmukh is an epitome of selfless work in the field of education, health and rural self-reliance and transformed many lives, that too, in some of the most backward villages of our country. Had it not been for his relentless efforts, these marginalized groups would have continued to languish in abject poverty, misery and deprivation. This silent crusader is a rare example, who chose social work over politics. Present day politicians, with rare exceptions, come to join politics not as a mission or service, but for self-aggrandizement and enrichment, by means of fair or foul. Nanaji is the shining example of austerity, humility and honesty in the penumbra of such a class of politicians. He was one of the very few people in politics, whose acceptability in the political spectrum was beyond ideology, organization and party politics. Closely associated and affiliated to the RSS, Nanaji was a rare exception who was accepted and revered by all, his ideology notwithstanding. Though close to the highest echelons of power, he chose to selflessly serve the people and was instrumental in carrying out a social restructuring programme in over 500 Indian villages, especially in Uttar Pradesh and Maharashtra. Even as a politician he was a class apart as he upheld the high moral standards he espoused, so hard to emulate for today's political class.

Brief Sketch of Nanaji Deshmukh

Born on October 11th, 1916 into a poor Marathi-speaking Deshastha Brahmin family at Kadoli, a small village in Hingoli district of Maharashtra, Nanaji lost his parents at a very young age and was brought up by his maternal uncle. Though good at studies, it was an uphill task for him to raise money for his education, but he did not allow his poverty to come in the way of his aspirations. He sold vegetables to raise money to pay his school fees and attended the high school in Sikar, on a scholarship by the Maharaja of Sikar.

Dr. Keshav Baliram Hedgewar, founder of RSS, who was a regular visitor to Deshmukh family was highly impressed by the zeal and devotion of Nanaji since his childhood. Discerning the latent social potential of Nanaji, he encouraged him to attend RSS *shakhas*. Nanaji Deshmukh was the first among the enthused youth who joined the RSS. Dr. Hedgewar was instrumental in spurring Nanaji for further studies and even offered financial help, which he declined. Instead, he saved money for the next one and a half years and in 1937 went for higher studies to Birla College (Now BITS, Pilani). After Dr.

Hegdewar's death in 1940, the responsibility of strengthening the RSS came upon Nanaji. He became a full-time *karyakarta*, and taking a vow of celibacy, maintained a lifelong association with the organization. Besides Maharashtra, he went around many states, encouraging and inspiring the youth to join RSS, and was quite successful in his endeavour. Nanaji was asked to go to Uttar Pradesh, to look over the work of Sangh at Agra and it is here, that he met Deendayal Upadhyaya for the first time and worked in close association with him till the end.

Seeing Nanaji's devotion, RSS Sangh Sanchalak M.S. Golwalkar sent him to Gorakhpur (U.P.) as a *pracharak*, where he embarked on a mission to introduce Sangh ideology in eastern UP.[1] This was a great challenge and an uphill task, as Sangh was short on funds. These were difficult times, and Nanaji had nothing, but his willpower and missionary zeal to sustain his endeavour of introducing and propagating the Sangh ideology. With no money to pay for a place to stay, he considered himself fortunate to have been permitted to stay in the Ashram of Baba Raghavdas on the condition that Nanaji would cook food for him, which he readily accepted. Within three years, Nanaji's hard work bore fruits and as many as 250 Sangh *Shakhas* commenced in and around Gorakhpur. From here Nanaji rose to be the Seh Prant Pracharak of the whole of Uttar Pradesh and became a strong pillar of the Sangh.

Nanaji always laid great emphasis on education. When in 1947, the RSS decided to launch two journals *Rashtradharma*, *Panchjanya* and a newspaper called *Swadesh*, Nanaji was made the Managing Director and a stalwart like Shri Atal Bihari Vajpayee was assigned the responsibility of the editor and Deendayal Upadhyaya was made the *Margdarshak*. It was a challenging task as the organization was always hard up for money to bring out the publications, yet it never dampened their spirits, and gradually these publications gained popularity and recognition because of their strong nationalistic content. Mahatma Gandhi's assassination led to the imposition of the ban on the RSS and its publication work came to a grinding halt. In these trying times, in view of the ban, a different strategy was adopted and Nanaji became the brain behind underground publication work by the RSS in those days. He also published the journal "*Manthan*" (introspection) which was edited by K.R. Malkani for many years.

When the ban was lifted from RSS, it was decided to have a political organisation, and thus, the Bharatiya Jana Sangh (BJS) came into being. Nana ji Deshmukh was sent by Shri Guruji to Uttar Pradesh for its expansion and was asked to take charge in UP as its General Secretary. As Nanaji Deshmukh had already worked as RSS *pracharak* in Uttar Pradesh, his groundwork proved of a great help in organizing BJS at the grassroots. By 1957, Nanaji had extensively travelled all over the state and using his organizational skills, established BJS units at each and every district in Uttar Pradesh. It is from here that Jana Sangh became the focal point of political power and a force to reckon with in Uttar Pradesh. A strong multifaceted personality, Nanaji made a valuable contribution to Indian politics by ably discharging his responsibilities true to his own words, *"main apne liye nahin, apno ke liye hun"*. Highly impressed and inspired by the teachings of Lokamanya Bal Gangadhar Tilak, the foundation of Nanaji's political inning was embedded in Tilak's nationalist ideology.

Nanaji can be safely called as the father of coalition Government in India as he was instrumental in building the Janta Party coalition. His politics was so Machiavellian that Indira Gandhi often referred to him as the Chanakya of the modern Indian politics. In Uttar Pradesh, BJS gained strength from Upadhyaya's vision, Atal Behari Vajpayee's oratory skills and Deshmukh's organizational work and emerged as an important player in the state politics. Nanaji crafted an alliance with socialist groups by bringing together Ram Manohar Lohia and Deendayal Upadhyaya. By bringing leaders of different political backgrounds on one platform he gave Uttar Pradesh its first non-Congress Government. In 1967, BJS became the part of United Legislature Party and joined the Government headed by Chaudhary Charan Singh. Nanaji always shared good relations not only with his party colleagues, but also with his opponents. Nanaji was also nominated to the Rajya Sabha.

Being a highly spiritual soul, he preferred to work behind the curtain. He was the initiator of the *Sampoorna Kranti* (total revolution) called by Jaiprakash Narayan and waged a crusade against the emergency in 1975. Nanaji led the underground movement during the emergency in disguise. During Emergency Nanaji went to prison and was in jail for nearly 17 months. In 1977, when the emergency was lifted, in the elections that followed, the coalition party called the Janta Party swept the polls. Nanaji Deshmukh was elected Lok Sabha MP from Balrampur in Uttar Pradesh, but he was never hungry for power and turned down the portfolio of Industry and Rural development Minister offered by Morarji Desai. Nanaji Deshmukh rejected the offer saying that after the age of 60, MPs should stay away from politics and only do social and organizational work. "I want to show that better work can be done without being in power". He stood for true value-based politics and his courage of conviction was so strong that he left active politics when at the pinnacle.

Nanaji was also a great educationist, instrumental in establishing some leading educational institutions of great repute in the country. He established India's first Saraswati Shishu Mandir at Gorakhpur in 1950.[2] He founded the Deendayal Research Institute (DRI) in 1972 to validate the philosophy of *Integral Humanism* propounded by Pandit Deendayal Upadhyaya (1916–1968). It was due to his unstinted efforts that the first ever rural university, namely Chitrakoot Gramodaya Vishwavidyalaya was established in the country and he also became its first Chancellor.[3] Nanaji worked shoulder to shoulder with Deendayal Upadhyaya and did not suffer from grief after the sad demise of Deendayal Upadhyaya. Instead of adopting a positive and constructive approach, established the Deendayal Research Institute (DRI) on his own in Delhi. He embarked upon a mission to propagate Deendayal's philosophy of Integral Humanism and wanted DRI to be devoted to strengthening the movement for constructive work in Bharat.[4] Incessantly, he worked for the development of rural India on the principle of participation of all the public, the government and the civil society. Integral Humanism gave a vision for Bharat that, with an approach to man and his relationship to society that is integral and complementary, could transform Bharat into a self-reliant and compassionate example for the world to follow.[5] Through the institution of 'Deendayal Shodh Sansthan', he devoted himself to transform Deendayal's ideology of Integral Humanism into a reality to usher in composite development of the village. DRI has an association with the following important institutions among others, The Wadia Group, Apeejay Education Society (AES), Indian Council of Agricultural Research (ICAR), Khadi and Village Industries Commission (KVIC), India Development and Relief Fund (IDRF), Madhya Pradesh Council of Science and Technology (MPCST), India Development Coalition of America (IDCA), Department of Elementary Education (DEE), Sir Dorabji Tata Trust, Ayurveda Yoga and Naturopathy Unani Siddha and Homoeopathy (AYUSH) and Sewa International (SI).

On 27 February, 2010, Nanaji breathed his last on the premises of Chitrakoot Gramodaya Vishwavidyalaya which he himself had established. He had willed that his body be donated to Dadhichi Dehdaan Sansthan of New Delhi. His body was sent by road up to Satna, Madhya Pradesh, and hundreds of people and local residents thronged to participate in the last procession in Satna. From Satna, his body was carried by a chartered plane to New Delhi. In New Delhi, his body was kept for few hours at Keshav Sadan (Delhi headquarters of the Rashtriya Swayam Sewak Sangh), and after that, the body was donated to AIIMS with the help of Dadhichi Dehdan Sansthan.[6]

Nanaji, the Social Architect: A Pioneer in Social Reconstruction

Not many politicians would have the courage to do what Nanaji did at the peak of his career. In the year 1980, when Nanaji turned 60, not only did he opt out from the electoral fray but also active politics and devoted himself completely to constructive social work. Renouncing the allurements of politics, Nanaji took the bold decision to quit politics, thus, putting an end to challenging and spotless innings in politics. If it were not for this '*Yug Purush*', many of our villages would have remained untouched by the wave of development. "My main goal was the positive development of society through politics". That didn't work. He tried to create his version of Utopia at Chitrakoot. He was in constant search of finding goodness in mankind. With a deep-seated commitment to the development of backward people defined by values of self-reliance, renunciation, penance, diligence, and compassion, Nanaji Deshmukh gave the development a new dimension. He devoted his entire life to the service of the poorest among the poor. For Nanaji, Bharat lives in its villages and hence all development should begin from rural India.

From childhood, Nanaji did not enjoy any real childhood due to the constraints of poverty. Moved by the impoverishment of his native place and anxious about the fate of people buried in poverty, he was deeply concerned about the condition of the villages of India. Nanaji was an ocean of kindness and did pioneering work in the anti-poverty and minimum needs programme. Other areas of his work were agriculture and cottage industry, rural health and rural education.[7] He was a silent crusader who lived in *ashrams* and changed the fortunes of the villages in many states of India. He led by example and his charismatic persona attracted many people from different walks of life. The veteran who believed that the 'real' India is in its villages used to put in gruelling 16-20 hours of work in a day.

Deshmukh did a lot of social work in Gonda (U.P.) and Beed (Maharashtra). The motto of his project was: "*Har hath ko denge kaam, har khet ko denge paanee*".[8] Through the Jaiprabha Gam Project in Gonda, he made more than 2500 borewell with bamboo and jute to help farmers to irrigate their land. After initial experiments in Gonda (U.P.) and Beed (Maharashtra), Nanaji finally fine-tuned an integrated programme for the development of rural areas that covered health, hygiene, education, agriculture, income generation, and conservation of resources that were both sustainable and replicable. The basis of the project was 'total transformation through total development with people's initiative and participation'. He showed the difference between Social Reform and charity. According to him in charity, you keep giving and in social reform you empower. On this basis, he envisioned his self-reliance campaign to make the 6,00,000 odd villages of India self-reliant.

In 1969, Nanaji visited Chitrakoot for the first time. He was moved to see the pathetic condition of the people in the *karmabhoomi* of Rama, where Rama spent 12 out of the 14 years in exile. He sat by the holy River Mandakini and resolved to change the face of Chitrakoot during his lifetime. While in exile, Rama had started work for the upliftment of the downtrodden in Chitrakoot. With this important historical and inspiring background, Nanaji Deshmukh made Chitrakoot the centre of his social work.[9] He used to remark that he admired *Vanavasi Rama* more than *Raja Rama* and so would like to spend the rest of his life in Chitrakoot among the *vanavasis* and most backward sections of the society. Nanaji believed that when Lord Rama could work for the upliftment of the tribals and *Dalits* in Chitrakoot during his exile, so could he.

In Chitrakoot, Nanaji developed many successful models of skill development, character building, employment generation, water conservation, health and hygiene, self-help, poverty alleviation, which are waiting to be replicated in the country. The project called the 'Chitrakoot Project' or the 'Campaign for Self-Reliance', was launched on 26 January, 2005 in 80 villages around the Chitrakoot area in the border of Uttar Pradesh and Madhya Pradesh. Chitrakoot was the new model of social work, where he wanted to present his Utopian concept of what rural India should be — self-reliant, high income, with zero litigation. He presented the new model of "Sarthak

Grameen Vikas" and took the villagers into confidence for the implementation of this model. On its completion in 2010, the project planned to make the 500 surrounding villages self-reliant and serve as a sustainable and replicable model for Bharat and the world.

Many of Nanaji's unique and path-breaking ideas can be inspirational to trained social workers and can be replicated. He reintroduced the concept of *Gurukul* in Chitrakoot through DRI. He took retired couples, called them *gurumata* and *gurupita* and entrusted them to take full care of the 20-25 students kept in one *gurukul*. Looking after their all-round development, they gave the children in the *Gurukul* love and care like grandparents. Equally, path-breaking was Nanaji's noble concept of "Samaj Shilpi Dampati", literally meaning sculptors of the society. A concept which he introduced in Chitrakoot, inviting young couples from the whole of India to stay and work in villages for a period of 5 years. Taking into account the needs and resources of the villages, their task was to make the villages self-reliant.

He devoted every moment of his life in making the society self-sufficient and self-dependent. He conducted numerous experiments and used social, cultural and scientific knowledge to make 500 villages in Chitrakoot self-reliant. Students and Researchers from all over the world thronged to study Nanaji's unique experiment of composite rural development for the country. He realized the dream of giving employment to every villager, irrigation to every field and shelter to everyone. In DRI, he gave a living example and a model for the nation. He strongly felt that if an individual was sincere and honest about social cause he was undertaking, he can never fall short of resources. When there is clarity about the social work and its objectives, no patriot will create hurdles in the way. Instead, he will devote his life to make such a project a success.[10] While declaring the joint resolution of teachers to celebrate 11th october, the birthday of Nanaji Deshmukh as Indian Social Work Day in the two days workshop on *Bharatiyakaran* of social work curriculum in India organized during 29-30 June, 2018 at Mahatma Gandhi Antarrashtriya Hindi Vishwavidyalaya, Wardha, Maharshtra, Dr. Bishnu Mohan Dash said, "it is a historic moment for social work fraternity in India. We were waiting for this day for more than eight decades". Dash said, Deshmukh is known for his pioneering contribution towards anti-poverty, rural health, rural education, cottage industry, and tribal population in Chitrakoot in Uttar Pradesh. He carried out social restructuring programme in around 500 villages of Uttar Pradesh,

Madhya Pradesh, Maharashtra and Rajasthan. President A.P.J. Kalam had praised for his single-minded devotion to uplift the people (*The Sikh Times*, July 1, 2018). The resolution of teachers for declaring 11th october as Indian social work day has been sent to Government of India for kind consideration.

Praising Nanaji Deshmukh for his single-minded devotion to the uplift of the people, Kalam said what the octogenarian leader was doing at Chitrakoot should be an eye-opener for others and should be taken as model school which he started throughout the country namely *Education For All: Nanhi Duniya and Octagonal Shape of Classroom,* where student feels nearer to teacher. Abdul Kalam the eminent scientist said that when political leaders empowered people, the prosperity of the nation was assured. Kalam said today 30 per cent of the people were living below poverty line and it was essential to make them prosperous first.[11] Last year the birth of this great person was celebrated from the centenary year *Sharad Purnima* on October 5, 2017. He was awarded *Padma Vibhushan* in 1999. He was nominated to Rajya Sabha by the NDA Government in the year 1999 in recognition of his services to the nation.[12]

Nanaji Deshmukh Model of Social Work

- Problem Solving Orientation Model—It is based on human being as centre stage of the development model.
- Learning through planning and observations.
- Religion–Ram Darshan—It is based on social consciousness. Society in which people are aware and conscious about their social duties, and don't rely blindly on others. Examples: number of child marriage, child labour, and dowry cases etc.
- Integral Humanism—It is based on an integrated and holistic development approach, i.e. balance of body, mind, soul, people, and environment.

This balance is achieved through integral humanism that goes towards self-intuition which is based on the traditional knowledge system enriching it with modern inputs. Today's needs are "complementarily" where individual, family, society and nation all are interlinked. To convert dreams into reality, the need of the hour is holistic planning, i.e. come – sit– think – plan together; work – progress—succeed together. Last but not least, total transformation and development of society, through designing and implementing a framework to achieve and sustain self-reliance in villages through the initiative, involvement and empowerment of the villagers with replicable, definable and tangible parameters.

Conclusion

He was the hero of 'Ma Bharti' to people who lived in areas where nobody wanted to tread. Nanaji went into the lives of people and changed them forever. He showed the way how harmonious villages could be created through people's participation at grassroots level. Development cannot be forced upon the villages from outside. Until the villagers accept wholeheartedly development cannot be sustainable. He encouraged the youth to step forward for the development of villages and led rural India to comprehensive development. Nanaji's life provides material for social workers to do research and establish a connection between social work practice and his model of social work. His model of development was in consonance with the needs of villages and was happily accepted by the people. He gave that essential support system which was the need of that time. Though he may not have been a trained social worker, his model of social work finds a reflection in professional social work. His emphasis on self-reliance and self-dependence is an echo of the fundamental principle of social work to help the individual to help himself. Throughout his life, he worked for poor and the fundamental basis for his development model was Integral Humanism, a model based on objectives of self-reliant village with a prosperous family with no poverty, literate, healthy, public amenities, and social consciousness. All these components are interlinked and are hierarchical to each other and follow a lexical order. Having become first Chancellor of Chitrakoot Gramodaya Vishwavidyalaya in Chitrakoot, India's first Rural University, Nanaji implemented the philosophy of integral humanism to improve the living standards of more than 150 villages of Bundelkhand. Most of his unique and path-breaking ideas still continue to be inspirational for all.

Notes

1. Deshmukh, Nanaji (2018), *Viraat Purush Sakshat Nanaji*, p. 40.

2. Swaroop, Devendra and Deshmukh, Yadavrav (2017), Punokathan by Dr. A.P.J. Abdul Kalam p. 3.
3. *The Hindustan Times*, 10th March, 1991.
4. Deshmukh, Nanaji (2018). *Viraat Purush Sakshat Nanaji*, p. 21.
5. *Manthan*, January 1996.
6. *Last Wasiyat of Nanaji Deshmukh.*
7. *Manthan*, October 1987.
8. *Yuganukool Nawrachna*, October 2009.
9. Deshmukh, Nanaji (2018). *Viraat Purush Sakshat Nanaji*, p. 146.
10. *Kamal Sandesh,* Fortnightly Newspaper, March 16-31 (2010).
11. Swaroop, Devendra and Deshmukh, Yadavrav (2017), *Punrokathan* by Dr. A.P.J. Abdul Kalam.
12. *Sakshat Nana ji*, p. 19.

References

Anamika (1977). "Shades of McCarthyism", *Economic and Political Weekly, 12*(38): 1637-1638. Retrieved from http://www.jstor.org/stable/4365931

Banerjee, S. (1978). "Devaluation of Marxism by Leftist Academicians", *Economic and Political Weekly, 13*(14): 605-608. Retrieved from http://www.jstor.org/stable/4366503

BJP's Search for Allies (1995). *Economic and Political Weekly, 30*(24): 1404-1405. Retrieved from http://www.jstor.org/stable/4402864

Bose, S. (2013). From Independence to 1989. In *Transforming India* (pp. 9-56). Harvard University Press. Retrieved from http://www.jstor.org/stable/j.ctt6wppx4.4

Chhibber, P. (1999). "State Policy, Party Politics, and the Rise of the BJP". In: *Democracy without Associations: Transformation of the Party System and Social Cleavages in India* (pp. 159-176). Ann Arbor: University of Michigan Press. Retrieved from http://www.jstor.org/stable/10.3998/mpub.23136.12

Das, B. (1977). "Emergency Provisions in the Indian Constitution: A Study in Comparative Analysis". *The Indian Journal of Political Science, 38*(2): 237-252. Retrieved from http://www.jstor.org/stable/41854792

Datta, P. (1991). VHP's Ram at Ayodhya: Reincarnation through Ideology and Organisation. *Economic and Political Weekly, 26*(44): 2517-2526. Retrieved from http://www.jstor.org/stable/4398252

Deshmukh, N. (2018). *Viraat Purush Rajnitigya Nanaji*. New Delhi: Prabhat Prakashan.

Double Game. (1987). *Economic and Political Weekly, 22*(42/43): p. 1774. Retrieved from http://www.jstor.org/stable/4377613 on September 13, 2018.

Dutt, V. (1976). The Emergency in India: Background and Rationale. *Asian Survey, 16*(12): 1124-1138. doi: 10.2307/2643449.

Education. (2007). In Jaffrelot C. (Ed.). *Hindu Nationalism: A Reader* (pp. 269-278). Princeton, Oxford: Princeton University Press. Retrieved from http://www.jstor.org/stable/j.ctt7s415.20

Kanungo, P. (2006). Myth of the Monolith: The RSS Wrestles to Discipline Its Political Progeny. *Social Scientist, 34*(11/12): 51-69. Retrieved from: http://www.jstor.org/stable/27644183

Kumar, D., Gopalakrishna, R., Singh, A., Ranjan, R., Pandey, S., and Sarkhel, B. (2014). Developmental potency of pre-implant parthenogenetic goat embryos: Effect of activation protocols and culture media. *In Vitro Cellular and Developmental Biology. Animal, 50*(1): 1-6. Retrieved from: http://www.jstor.org/stable/24596431

Kumar, K. (2002). "Winning Values: Secular Education Redefined". *Economic and Political Weekly*, *37*(52): 5152-5154. Retrieved from: http://www.jstor.org/stable/4413002

Manor, J. (1985). "Rajiv Gandhi and Post-election India: Opportunities and risks", *The World Today, 41*(3): 51-54. Retrieved from: http://www.jstor.org/stable/40395715

Rizvi, M. (2005). "Secularism in India: Retrospect and Prospects", *The Indian Journal of Political Science, 66*(4): 901-914. Retrieved from: http://www.jstor.org/stable/41856174

Rudolph, L. and Rudolph, S. (1983). "Rethinking Secularism: Genesis and Implications of the Textbook Controversy, 1977-79". *Pacific Affairs, 56*(1): 15-37.

Shah, G. (1977). "Revolution, Reform, or Protest? A Study of the Bihar Movement: II". *Economic and Political Weekly, 12*(16): 642-655. Retrieved from: http://www.jstor.org/stable/4365503

Singh, N. (1978). "Ujjain Conclave". *Economic and Political Weekly, 13*(50): p. 2023. Retrieved from: http://www.jstor.org/stable/4367171

Sinha, A. (1977). "Janata Elects a Leader", *Economic and Political Weekly, 12*(26): 1001-1001. Retrieved from: http://www.jstor.org/stable/4365708 Retrieved on Sept, 13, 2018.

Swaroop, Devendra, Deshmukh, Yadavrav (2017). *Rashtra-Rishi Nanaji*. New Delhi: Prabhat Prakashan.

Taneja, N. (2001). "National Convention against Communalisation of Education: A Report". *Social Scientist, 29*(9/10): 77-91. Retrieved from: http://www.jstor.org/stable/3517985

Thapar, R. (1977). "Inside the Janata Party". *Economic and Political*

Weekly, 12(30): Retrieved from: http://www.jstor.org/stable/4365786 on September 13, 2018.

Thapar, R. (1977). "The Political Parade", *Economic and Political Weekly, 12*(20): 783-784. Retrieved from: http://www.jstor.org/stable/4365580

Thapar, R. (1978). "Our Political Aberrations". *Economic and Political Weekly, 13*(23): p. 936. Retrieved from: http://www.jstor.org/stable/4366696 on September 17, 2018.

2
Vinoba Bhave and Bhoodan Movement

Mithilesh Kumar, Rajan Prakash

Introduction

Gunnar Myrdal in Asian Drama rightly points out that in South Asia, land is the key to power and status.[1] This was also true at that time for India. As the country got independence the most important problem of the Indian economy remained the landlessness. India was not self-sufficient to feed. The sharp inequality in landholding was not only bearing an adverse effect on the yield, but it also gave way to exploitation. Redistribution of land was the only solution to the issue, which could be done in three ways—

1. The land could be snatched by landless poor, but this method was neither ethical nor practical.
2. The government could intervene in, by making laws. But this posed an important problem as the right to property in the Constitution was the basic right at that time.
3. Landowners could offer a portion of their land to the landless villagers. Being voluntary this was most suited to the time, Vinoba chose it which later came to be popularized as 'Bhoodan Movement.'

Background of the Bhoodan Movement

Vinoba Bhave once went to see the condition of *Harijans*

(Untouchables) in a village in Andhra Pradesh[2], where they were victims of the atrocities of Naxalite extremism. They pleaded to Vinoba that they should be given the land of around eighty acres, so, that they could sustain their family. Vinoba kept this matter before the villagers in the evening prayer meeting. The result was impressive and a prosperous farmer stood up and donated 85 acres of land to him. This was the beginning of the Bhoodan movement. After that, he went on foot in Telangana[3] and received thousands of acres of land and donated to poor.

Sarvodaya

Vinoba did not coin the concept of *Sarvodaya*, nor was he the first to practice it, being a Gandhian he only strengthened it further. In fact, the concept of *Sarvodaya* is much older than popularized by Gandhi himself and, is rooted in Indian philosophical traditions.

Sarvodaya is a Sanskrit word which means 'upliftment of all'. Ideals of *Sarvodaya* are based on the principle of establishing non-violent social order. Its implications are equally in the economic, social and political field. It came to be popularized with the translation of John Ruskin's tract on political economy, 'Unto This Last' by Gandhi in 1908. One of the influence on Gandhi was that of this book which he has described in his autobiography, *'I determined to change my life in accordance with the ideals of the book'.*[4] Gandhi elaborates the concept of *Sarvodaya*, which are based on three basic principles:

1. The good of the individual is contained in the good of all.
2. A lawyer's work has the same value as the barber's in as much as all have the same right of earning a livelihood from their work.
3. Life of a labour, i.e. the life of the tiller of the soil and the handicraftsman is the life worth living.

Gandhi was not a professional philosopher, he adopted what touched his heart and practised that for the welfare of humanity, for its betterment.

The legacy of Gandhi and Indian traditions went beyond with a number of followers promoting it everywhere. Vinoba is chief amongst them with his *Bhoodan* and *Gramdan* movement.

Vinoba Bhave and **Bhoodan-Gramdan** *Movement*

Although Vinoba has used the word '*Dan*' in his movement for *Bhoodan*. He used to demand the land, claiming it the rights of the poor. He used to say — 'Like everybody needs air, water, so do land as the land is the basis of living.' Vinoba also used the word '*yagna*' for *Bhoodan*. Explaining the meaning of the word '*yagna*', Vinoba says that — the work that all people participate in, is called *Yagna*. Whenever a crisis approaches, the *yagna* is performed. The crisis exists today. There is a distinction between labourers and the owner. Crores of people have no means to survive, *Harijan* and others are living the life of untouchability. There are so many religious controversies. In such a condition, *yagna* performed alone will not be sufficient. Everyone will have to take part in *yagna* of *Bhoodan* giving his or her share.

The *Bhoodan* movement was not a predefined, planned, project-bound programme, but the idea grew with the effort. It started with 'Pochampalli' village[5] of Andhra Pradesh and soon came to creating a stir in whole India. The people associated with *Bhoodan* welcomed it with heart. In the very first year, 1,00,000 acres of land got collected. By April 1958, *Bhoodan* had received, as gifts, 5 million acres[6] — a tenth of 50 million acres which the movement had aimed to collect in its first seven years. The *Bhoodan* Campaign was merely the beginning of his long and comprehensive plan.[7] His vision was of world peace based on equality.

It is necessary to understand that Vinoba's purpose was not only to collect land for donation. Whenever he suspected that there is a lacking motivation of *Kings* in the donation, he did not accept it. Pure charity, a thoughtful donation was his desire. He used to say that his three formulae are:

1. Understanding our thoughts if no one gives, we are not unhappy because we believe that what he does not give today will give tomorrow, our idea is that seed will germinate one day.
2. If someone gives, understanding our thought, then we are happy because his goodness is born.
3. If anyone gives land without understanding our thought, with only pressure, we will be hurt. We do not have to collect the

land in any way, but to create the trend of symmetry and *Sarvodaya*.

The *Bhoodan Yagna* was a different thing for Vinoba. The problem of the land was only a means for Vinoba. His thought was that with this, the world will get a new path, the key to developing non-violence and *Sarvodaya*. Hence, he singled it out. He made it clear in his words:

> "The land problem was a basic one and I saw that unless something was done to meet it, it might develop into a big danger detrimental to the security of the nation. I, therefore, thought it fit, first to concentrate my energy only on that question."[8]

Unveiling the mystery of it at another place, he has written — "People who look at the *Bhoodan-Gramdan* as a solution to the land problem, they do not know its glory. They think this land is for solving the problem. But it is only a means. Vinoba wanted a complete change by *Bhoodan*. He has written in one place, why am I doing all this? What is my purpose? It is clear that I want to change, first change of heart, then change of life and later change of society. This kind of triple change is in my mind. This is the reason that Vinoba used to consider *Bhoodan yagna* as a kind of *Satyagraha*. In *Satyagraha*, with hard-working, moral strength, the heart of the opponent is changed. In Vinoba's words— "We understand that the work of *Bhoodan Yagna* is only *Satyagraha* in a sense."

Gramdan

"*Bhoodan* was only in its infancy when a phenomenon occurred. All the landowners of Mangroh village of Uttar Pradesh devoted their land to *Bhoodan Yagna* and earned the distinction of making the country's first *Gramdan*. In this way, *Bhoodan* entered the *Gramdan* with the second stage, strengthening its position. *Gramdan*, even in its modified form, implied radical changes in the power structure of the villages".[9]

Gramdan was not a predetermined, planned and project-bound programme just like *Bhoodan*. *Gramdan* meant that the donation of all the land by the landowners of the village and its equal distribution.

Explaining the meaning of *Gramdan*, Vinoba says that '*Gramdan*'s developed meaning is that whatever he has, dedicates to the village. Otherwise, it would be something to give religion to some people and to take the religion of someone. The religion is that which is applicable to all, the idea of *Gramdan* is perfect in this way. Here is to note that *Gramdan*'s meaning is not a donation of a village, it is a donation to the village. Eradication of poverty was the main agenda of Vinoba's *Gramdan* movement.[10] In the early period of the Bhoodan Vinoba was saying— "There will be no landless people in our village." During *Gramdan*, "Vinoba started saying, There will be no landlord in our village." Through *Gramdan*, Vinoba got a path of *Gram-Swaraj*. He showed the true nature of trusteeship. Vinoba demanded through *Gramdan* that all the landowners should donate all their collective donations.

Although the imagination of *Gramdan* was fantastic. But he would probably ask the people too much. The land of the village could not be sold, neither can be leased. This led to difficulties in getting loans for the wedding and other occasions. This was the reason that *Gramdan*'s concept could not form its broad base. There is a point here that there was a sense of charity in the sacrament of landowners, but the sense of equality was not in it. Owners did permit that the person who is in front of him also receives a similar status. This was also one of the reasons *Gramdan* did not get the desired success. That is why a path was explored which was a middle path between the desired result of *Gramdan* and the actual situation, and this took the form of the '*Sulabh Gramdan*'.

Vinoba began **Sulabh Gramdan** campaign after Raipur Conference of the ABSSS in 1963. These campaigns reached their climax in 1969 at the Rajgir Conference of the ABSSS in Bihar. *Bhoodan-Gramdan* had broadly three phases:

(i) *Prapti* (receipt of gift),
(ii) *Pushti* (follow-up for verification), and
(iii) *Nirman* (course of reconstruction)

Most of the Gandhian organizations were actively engaged in constructive works.[11]

Under *Sulabh gramdan*, 75 per cent of the cultivators in a village were to contribute at least 5 per cent of their land for redistribution among the landless, retaining 95 per cent for their own cultivation with the legal ownership transferred to the village community. It made a distinction between 'ownership' and 'possession'; that is, a person joining *gramdan* might surrender ownership of his entire land in a village without giving up possession of the entire area. The idea of Blockdan, Districtdan and Statedan were later evolutions of *Gramdan*.[12]

The enthusiasm of donors of *Gram* had increased. But people considered it a compromise. This was not an agreement for Vinoba; it was a thought-provoking politics. According to Vinoba, Revolution can be possible by transcending the minds, the spirit of goodwill, self-realization and constructivism. Vinoba believed in a peaceful revolution based on a fundamental change in values, the realm of thoughts and virtues.[13] Any change cannot be a revolution. He used to say, "One who has the wealth of love and thoughts; never indulges in any kind of dispute or despair."[14] This implies that ultimate power lies in the thoughts. Human beings are blessed with thinking ability. The process which goes frozen after some time after going with some people, or which can be processed by millions of people, is a process of revolution. We should understand that the process which is more powerful to spread is a more elaborate process than revolution.

However, there were a lot of difficulties in the way of *Bhoodan, Gramdan* and *Sulabh Gramdan*. The size, people were the big challenge. Under the influence of Vinoba, the oathletter used to fill up, but the legal proceedings were turned down in time. In this way, a very good conception started breaking the dam without getting the destination. By 1974, this movement became lax and it was abandoned in the hope of fate.

The Outcome of the Movement

Vinoba used to say that this movement for me is also a *Satyagraha* whose purpose was to spread the feeling of compassion in society and to establish real *Swaraj* through its medium. There is the talk of public policy in place of politics, equality in place of inequality and justice in place of injustice. Vinoba believed that as soon as the movement progresses, these feelings will be spread among people. In this way, Vinoba wanted to establish village level, non-violent society through the medium of *Bhoodan-Gramdan-Sulabh Gramdan* movement.

This movement has achieved many successes.

1. This movement changed the mind of the mass of people.
2. A lot of lands have been gained through this movement, which is much more than any government effort.
3. A total of 49 lakh acres land of donations were gained in this movement. It was able to occupy 42 lakh acres land in which 25 lakh acres of land was distributed to the landless villagers.
4. In the direction of *Gram Swaraj*, very commendable efforts have been made in this movement.

Prof. T.K. Oommen of Jawaharlal Nehru University, New Delhi has studied Bhovdan movement in Rajasthan.[15] Professor B.N. Prasad of Anugrah Narayana Institute, Patna has tried to find out the fact that how far this movement was successful.

Prof. T.K. Oommen has selected some indicators for the research. which is given below—

1. Whether his movement has changed the economic structure or not.
2. Whether this movement has brought a changing relationship between governance and politics or not.
3. Whether this movement has changed the quality of local leadership or not.
4. Whether this movement has changed the humanity of people for making a non-violent society or not.

For this study, Oommen selected four *Gramdan* villages of Rajasthan and three non-*Gramdan* villages. His conclusions were as follows –

Change in Economic Relations

Prof. Oommen discovered during his research that there has been no change in the concept of collective land. Prof. Oommen during his study also found that the distribution of land was not equal among the people in the village. Apart from this, most of the land gained in the donation was of poor quality or controversial. Thus, it was concluded that—(i) In *Gramdani* village, the loss of personal ownership was not erased, (ii) The collective ownership was not executed. There is no change in the feudal structure of the agricultural relations. In this way, the movement fails in terms of economic change.

Regarding the Change in Relations of Governance and Politics

In his research, Prof. Oommen also found that the participatory democracy has not been existent in the village and still the minority dominance in the decision-making process persists.[16] This power has also centralized here. What Vinoba wanted to change through *Bhoodan- Gramdan*, was public policy in the place of politics, was not successful. Thus, it was the conclusion of Prof. Oommen that this movement was also unsuccessful in making changes in governance and politics.

Quality of Local Leadership

The third objective of the study of Prof. Oommen was that, whether this movement has changed the quality of local leadership or not. The study found that the local leaders were very traditional and they were not fond of doing anything new. Thus, the local leadership was of the *status quo*, and it was concluded that this movement was unsuccessful even with the view of the revolutionary change in the local leadership.

Changes in Value Consciousness

Prof. Oommen has divided the change in value consciousness to three levels.

1. Cultural changes
2. Transitory changes
3. Practical changes.

In his research, Prof. Oommen noticed that practical changes in village emphasize less about value consciousness, but the theoretical and trendy changes appear as clearly as a Caste system— 36.44 per cent of non-village people consider caste system as undesirable, whereas 61.84 per cent of the rural population regards caste as unbearable. Thus, there is a tendency to change the trend of caste. The status of the person on the basis of birth or on the other side — in this matter also the village people look for more change. Non-*Gramdani* people consider birth as the basis of the status of a person, whereas the *Gramdani* people consider the order as a basis of status. Thus, Oommen concluded that the village shows the change in value consciousness in the people and on this basis the movement has been successful. Apart from Oommen, K.H. Prasad has also researched Mushahari, his findings are as follows: 1. The power balance was mainly inclined towards the minority class. 2. Only the owner was strengthened because in the mind of the weaker class it came that changes in my condition can only be done by the grace of the owner. On the basis of research by Oommen and H. Prasad, we can say that the *Bhoodan-Gramdan* movement failed with its current goal. This movement could not achieve its immediate purpose at the level of thought[17], so, now, we will discuss why the movement was unsuccessful.

The reason for the unsuccessful movement

Ganesh Mantry has said that any movement must match the compulsions and the need for success. That is, having a real goal and circumstantial necessity are considered essential[18] elements for the success of any movement. It seems lacking in the movement of Vinoba. Ideologically, the movement was right, but the element of necessity was not contained in it. The proof of this is that the weapon (methods) adopted in *Bhoodan-Gramdan* was not enough, there were no other measures besides public education, heart transformation, love, compassion etc. This movement lacked these, so *Bhoodan-Gramdan* movement failed. As Ram Manohar Lohia said, "Communism is the principle of hatred, but *Sarvodaya* is an insufficient theory of love." Any movement should have a combination of love and purity of thought. Basant Nalvokar says that there was no place for direct action in this movement. Besides, the person who gained it did not have the place of dignity and honour. Everything depended on the grace of the owner. For this reason, this movement failed.

One of the reasons for the failure of the movement is also that theoretically, it was based on mere explanation of spirituality hence could not transform a social relationship that should have been made. Vinoba himself admits that— "I used to think that all kinds of distinctions will be eliminated by *Bhoodan-Gramdan*, but these things have broken *Gramdan-Bhoodan*."

Additionally, it did not get sufficient support from the government.[19] It is not possible to cooperate with the government on one side and to oppose its policies on another. It is said that no revolution can be fought on the shoulders of the government. Vinoba also later admitted that — "We have believed in the state that the democratic state will work but it has not happened."

One of the main reasons for this failure of the movement is its organizational weakness.[20] Vinoba was a talented man, he was of original spiritual vision, he could have thought, could give inspiration, but he was not a good organization building leader. Sachhindanand Sinha has rightly said that, "Vinoba is a Marx, who needs a Lenin in the Indian context." Vinoba did not have a lack of workers; rather he had a lack of organizers.

There was no challenge to other anti-ideological views at the intellectual level. On one side there was a feudal tradition, on the other hand, was the invasion of modern civilization, with the back-up of international capital.

Another reason for the failure of the *Bhoodan-Gramdan* movement was that its legal side was quite weak. The laws made by the state were insufficient. The *Gramdan* law was made in some states, but they were made when the *Gramdan* movement was on the decline. These laws were not made intentionally with an open heart. Therefore, they could not raise the same amount of money. The former Chief Justice of the High Court, Gajendra Garkar also said that "this movement has created a very good atmosphere, but the state did not do what it was expected."

No back support was found for this movement. In order to run a movement, the need for teaching, training is a must. The workers themselves did not have such training. It would be wrong to say that workers lacked loyalty. There was not an intellectual preparation. This movement did not present any clear concept of alternative development. For example, this movement opposed centralization, industrialization, but did not suggest enough alternatives.

It was also considered a demerit that the *Gramdan* movement ignored the cities. Gnanasahab Sahastrabudde once said that, "*Gramdan* movement was for all the villages. The cities were outside its perimeter. There should be universal efficacy in a revolution. So,

Gramdan was a single movement in nature. I will firmly say that even if every village declares *Gramdan*, the land revolution will not be successful." Today the city has become the centre of modern life. No movement can be successful without touching all the organs of the society. *Bhoodan-Gramdan* did not do this.

Broadcast Media ignored this movement. It is also considered a cause of failure infact, the news agencies pay attention to something which is provocative, sensational. Since there was no such thing in the calm revolution of *Bhoodan-Gramdan*, the media ignored it. In addition, this movement became a victim of neglect of intellectuals. There were many reasons behind the infidelity of intellectuals. Their education was initiated in the values of modern civilization and they had a vested interest. *Gramdan* was unfavourable to their selfishness, so intellectuals ignored it.

However, the movement should not be judged in terms of its material achievement but from the fact that it represented one of the major attempts after independence to provide a peaceful solution of the basic problem of Indian Society, the land problem, through voluntary action involving the masses.[21]

The question arises that what should be the measure of success-failure of the movement. Sarva Narayana Das says that — The success of a revolutionary thought and programme is identified by these questions:

Did the human society achieve a new and exhaustive goal?
Did the society find a way to achieve that goal?
Did that method become more convenient or become expansive?
Has the goal come even close?

He says that in the context of *Bhoodan Yagna*, the answers to these fours are found positive. Therefore, at the level of thought, this movement was completely successful; the result may be more or less. It would be wrong to evaluate anything from the result. The main criterion should be whether the end is fair or inappropriate. If the work is right, then it is valuable in itself. Therefore, I agree with the statement of Sarva Narayana Das that, "from above even if it appears that the *Bhoodan-Gramdan* movement failed because it did not get the expected results, but thinking deeply the movement did not fail. Its unprecedented historical success lies in the fact that it has brought the non-violent revolution to the threshold of the nation and showed that it is possible to bring a revolution without any conflict or confrontation. It is a different matter that neither nationalist, nor public, nor intellectuals had any means to sustain it further. The present scenario is the result of returning from that threshold of revolution.

Summary

Vinoba Bhave, who contributed significantly to enlarge the vision of Mahatma Gandhi's philosophy and his ideas[22], was among those social thinkers who worked on the model of the development of the Father of the Nation and through the *Bhoodan* movement, gave a new direction for redistribution of land to the nation. Vinoba travelled all over India to make his move a success. *Bhoodan* movement was the voluntary land reform movement launched by Acharya Vinoba Bhave in 1951. Vinoba Bhave held that the redistribution of land should not be done only through government laws, but it would be a successful attempt through a social movement. In the fifth decade of the 20th century, Vinoba Bhave used ideas like constructive works and trusteeships followed by Gandhi to make the *Bhoodan* movement successful. He also established the *Sarvodaya Samaj* to bring social change[23] in the country through the non-violent way. This movement created such a social environment that gave way to land reform activity in the country. This movement affected the lives of a large number of people[24] and through it million acres of land got collected, which was distributed among the needy landless poor.

Notes

1. Originally said by Gunnar Myrdal in his book *Asian drama: an inquiry into the poverty of nations*. Pantheon. Adapted from George, A. (2016). *Social Ferment in India*. Bloomsbury Publishing.
2. Raju, K. Akella, K., & Deininger, K. (2006). New opportunities for increasing access to land: The example of Andhra Pradesh. *available at site resources. world bank.Org/intindia/resources/raju.pdf.*
3. Panda, P. C. (2007). India's Poverty and Vinoba's Moral Approach to Development, Sudhakar Panda. *Immortal Sarvodaya*, p. 135.

4. Gandhi, M. K. (2016). *An Autobiography or the Story of My Experiments with Truth*. Ahmedabad: Navjeevan Publishing House.
5. Narayan, S. (1956). *One Week with Vinoba*. All India Congress Committee.
6. *India News* (London), 10 May, 1958.
7. *Ibid.*, p. 210.
8. Quoted by Suresh Ramabha, *Vinoba and his Mission,* p. 168.
9. Ostergaard, G. (1989). The Gandhian Movement in India since the Death of Gandhi. In *Gandhi's Significance for Today* (pp. 203-225). London: Palgrave MacMillan.
10. Srivastava, V. Exploring the Idea of Gandhian Trusteeship in Vinoba's Economic Philosophy. *Revisiting Economy of Permanence and Non-Violent Social Order*, 109.
11. Prasad, B. N. (2011). *Democracy, Development and Agrarian Radicalism: A Regional Framework*. A.N. Sinha Institute of Social Studies, Patna, 21(1), 83.
12. Shah, G. (1977). Revolution, Reform, or Protest? A Study of the Bihar Movement: III. *Economic and Political Weekly*, 695-702.
13. Kalindi, Prempanth, 79.
14. Gautam, *Vinoba*, 319.
15. Oommen, T. K. (1967). Charisma, social structure and social change. *Comparative Studies in Society and History*, 10(1), 85-99.
15. *Ibid.*
17. Weber, T. (1994). The Lesson from the Disciples: Is there a Contradiction in Gandhi's Philosophy of Action?. *Modern Asian Studies*, 28(1), 195-214.
18. Pati, S. K., Bhoodan Movement in Odisha with Special Reference to Koraput. *Odisha Review*, 110.
19. Shukla, N. & Iyengar, S. (2011). *Governing of Commons: The Bhoodan Way.*
20. Harris, I. C. (1987). *Sarvodaya* in Crisis: The Gandhian Movement in India Today. *Asian Survey*, 27(9), 1036-1052.
21. Parida, S., *Twenty-Five Years of Bhoodan Movement in Orissa (1951-76)—A Review*.
22. Prasad, G. (1960). *Sarvodaya*—A Critical Study. *The Indian Journal of Political Science*, 21(1), 38-61.
23. Rawat, R. K. (2004). Vinoba Bhave's Conception of" Sarvodaya. *Peace Research*, 36(1), 25-32.
24. Panda, P. C. (2007). India's Poverty and Vinoba's Moral Approach to Development, Sudhakar Panda. *Immortal Sarvodaya*, 135.

References

Bhave, V., and Bhave, A.V. (1960). *Talks on the Gita* (p. 26). George Allen & Unwin Ltd.

Bhave, A.V. (2017). *Revolutionary Sarvodaya (Philosophy for the remaking of man)*. New Delhi: Bharatiya Vidya Bhavan.

Brown, D.M. (1970). *The Nationalist Movement: Indian Political Thought from Ranade to Bhave*. University of California Press.

Gandhi, M.K. (2016). *An Autobiography or the Story of My Experiments with truth.* Ahmedabad: Navjeevan Publishing House.

Harris, I.C. (1987). Sarvodaya in Crisis: The Gandhian Movement in India Today. *Asian Survey, 27*(9): 1036-1052.

Myrdal, G. (1972). *Asian Drama: An Inquiry into the Poverty of Nations* (Vol. 1). Pantheon.

Narayan, S. (1956). *One Week with Vinoba*. All India Congress Committee.

Oommen, T.K. (1967). Charisma, social structure and social change. *Comparative Studies in Society and History, 10*(1): 85-99.

Oommen T. (1972). Charisma, S. *Charisma, Stability and Change : An Analysis of Bhoadha-Gram Dain Movement in India,* New Delhi: Thom son Press.

Ostergaard, G. (1989). The Gandhian Movement in India Since the Death of Gandhi. *Gandhi's Significance for Today* (pp. 203-225). London: Palgrave MacMillan.

Panda, P.C. (2007). India's Poverty and Vinoba's Moral Approach to Development Sudhakar Panda. *Immortal Sarvodaya*, 135.

Pati, S.K., Bhoodan Movement in Odisha with Special Reference to Koraput. *Odisha Review*, 110.

Prasad, G. (1960). Sarvodaya—A Critical Study. *The Indian Journal of Political Science, 21*(1): 38-61.

Raju, K., Akella, K., and Deininger, K. (2006). New opportunities for increasing access to land: The example of Andhra Pradesh. *available at siteresources. worldbank. org/intindia/resources/raju. pdf.*

Ramabhai, S. (1954). *Vinoba and His Mission.*, Akhil Bharat Sarv Seva Sangh.

Rawat, R.K. (2004). "Vinoba Bhave's Conception of Sarvodaya". *Peace Research*, 36(1): 25-32.

Shukla, N., and Iyengar, S. (2011). *Governing of Commons: The Bhoodan Way.*

Srivastava, V., Exploring the Idea of Gandhian Trusteeship in Vinoba's Economic Philosophy. *Revisiting Economy of Permanence and Non-Violent Social Order*, 109.

Weber, T. (1994). The Lesson from the Disciples: Is there a Contradiction in Gandhi's Philosophy of Action? *Modern Asian Studies, 28*(1): 195-214.

Wolpert, S. (2002). *Gandhi's passion: The life and legacy of Mahatma Gandhi*. Oxford University Press.

3

Tagore's Sriniketan Experiment

A Viable Indigenous Model of Rural Development

Sanjoy Roy

Introduction

Rural development has always been an important issue in all discussions pertaining to economic development, especially of developing countries, throughout the world. In the developing countries and some formerly communist societies, rural mass comprises a substantial majority of the population. Although millions of rural people have escaped poverty as a result of rural development in many Asian countries, a large majority of rural people continue to suffer from persistent poverty. The socio-economic disparities between rural and urban areas are widening and creating tremendous pressure on the social and economic fabric of many developing Asian economies. These factors, among many others, tend to highlight the importance of rural development. The policy-makers in most developing economies recognize this importance and have been implementing a host of programmes and measures to achieve rural development objectives. While some of these countries have achieved impressive results, others have failed to make a significant dent in the problem of persistent rural underdevelopment.

Therefore, rural development should be the starting point of development in India, because India is a society with a vast rural area having a large rural population. About 75 per cent of the Indian population lives in rural areas. Education, employment and self-sufficiency will carry them towards advancement and one day this rural lifestyle will merge into the integrated process of development with their own characteristic features along with their acquired modern and scientific techniques as Rabindranath Tagore used to think.

Till now a majority of the total Indian population live in the numerous villages, scattered throughout the country. The rural population in India comprises the core of Indian society and also represents the real India. According to the 2011 Indian census, there are 6,40,900 villages in India and about 68.84 per cent (8,33,087,662 persons) of Indian population lives in these villages with a literacy rate of 68.9 per cent. The rural population in India, actually, provides the real picture of the Indian society. A majority of the rural population in India lives on agriculture and linked occupations in the rural areas. Though agriculture has been the primary occupation of rural people in India since the ancient period, the scenario is changing day by day. Now, many Indian villagers have engaged themselves in various non-agricultural occupations. There is also a common trend of rural to urban migration among the Indian villagers. However, the Indian villages are economically weak. In addition, lack of infrastructural facilities makes their life more difficult. Naturally, the villagers face a lot of problems in their daily life. Recently, the authorities are taking some initiatives to improve the quality of life of the rural population in India.

During Tagore's lifetime, rural India was far more backward. So, he felt it necessary to start his development programme from within the rural Bengal, and even after selecting a single village, the primary objective of Tagore was to make that village self-sufficient in the proper sense of the term which would establish itself as a model village. According to him, all the potentials were inherent in the social structure. Tagore's thought that each and every human being possesses strength, power, courage and capabilities. It is only necessary to revive and reconstruct them. Besides, every society has its own reservoir of knowledge. But neither the society nor its members were conscious about it. So, this potential power remained unused and the people were also totally ignorant about it. Tagore felt that the educated middle class was detached from this rural population although this population was the real basis of the Indian society and India would not be able to develop itself unless and until this section of the society was properly developed. It was only necessary to revive and reconstruct it.

So far, social thinking of Tagore has not been discussed very extensively as his contributions in other spheres. Besides his other activities, he was always engrossed with the idea of social development and never rested till he drew up a complete plan of rural reconstruction and gave it a practical trial initially at *Shelaidaha* and later at the neighbouring villages of *Bolepur.*

Rabindranath Tagore was not only a great poet rather he had got a deep feeling for rural reconstruction in India. He always tried to make people happy not only economically rather by his songs Dave's and *dharma* also. After successfully starting of Santiniketan at Bolepur in West Bengal he thought about another separate Centre for rural all-round development. It was Sriniketan. It visualized for self-supporting steps of rural people.

Starting with neighbouring villages, the institute has conducted its activities in many villages. These villages gripe under sub-centres. For the convenience of administration, the area has been divided into two zones:

1. Intensive area,
2. Extensive area.

The first comprises 26 villages which are under the direct guidance and supervision of Sriniketan. The activities of the institution may be broadly divided into nine spheres, namely:

1. Agriculture
2. Industry,
3. Village-welfare,
4. Co-operation,
5. Health and sanitation,
6. Education,
7. Social organisation,
8. Economic research, and
9. Soil erosion

Approach of Rural Reconstruction: Tagore's View

In the early nineties of the nineteenth century, a new phase began in Tagore's life. It fell to his lot to manage the paternal estate on behalf of the Tagore family. For a good many years he discharged all his duties and fulfilled all his responsibilities as a *Zamindar* with a devotion and skill and, of course, with the impress of a practical-minded man. His life amply proves that he did not dwell exclusively in the realm of ideas. He was a man of action as well. In the work which he started first at *Shelaidaha* and *Potisar* and later at *Sriniketan,* there was a silent protest against the indifference of his countrymen to the actual problems of the country (Sen, 1943: 111). As a *Zamindar* he had firsthand knowledge of the hardship and helplessness of the country people.

Politics found only a minor place in Tagore's social philosophy. That was the phase of political agitation, the ultimate objective of which was to bring political independence of India. Tagore, almost from the very beginning, was a critic of agitation politics and *he probably for the first time tried to divert the course of agitation politics towards a constructive one. In his constructive programme, the greatest stress was laid on the work of rural uplift.* His thoughts on rural problems give us an integral concept of rural reconstruction as well as about the methods on which he would rely for its realization (Sen, 1943). Accordingly, his plan was divided into two parts. The **first part** laid down certain basic ideals, principles and postulates of rural reconstruction while the **second part** was composed of actual schemes of social welfare and community development. *The Government of India while initiating its own plans of community development in 1952 had acknowledged Rabindranath Tagore as the forerunner of almost all its schemes* (Dasgupta, 1962: 8).

First Phase of Rural Reconstruction, i.e. East Bengal Experiment

Tagore came into direct contact with the rural Bengal after he took the charge of their *Zamindari* estate at East Bengal according to his father's order. That incident can be described as a landmark in his life for it was during that period the idea of rural reconstruction came to his mind. Being disillusioned by the role of the political leaders, he made up his mind to assume the responsibility himself. He was then about thirty years of age. His estate included mainly three districts. *Birahimpur* — headquarter *Shelaidaha, Kaligram* — headquarter *Potisar* and *Sahajadpur* where the headquarter was named after the district. That was the beginning of his rural reconstruction programme. But even from that very moment, he had a holistic vision and he was very sincere, honest and determined to achieve his goal even in the formative phase. His programme included health, education, cottage industries, agriculture, fisheries, weaving etc. An *all-round development of a village was his ultimate objective which to his mind was necessary for making a self-sufficient and self-confident society.*

The concept of *rural bank* occupies a very significant place in Tagore's Rural Reconstruction Programme. The only way, as he thought, to rescue the villagers was to lend money at a rate of lower interest. With this objective, Tagore established *Patisar Bank* in 1905 although it was not registered yet. The main capital was accumulated by borrowing from some of his friends and some rich persons of the locality. This was possible for when Tagore won the Nobel Prize in 1913 he deposited the money which was more than the lakh, in this bank. The poor peasants could take a loan from this fund and the *Santiniketan* school later *Visva-Bharati* received the interest money as long as the bank was there. Thus, the money-lenders were forced to wipe up their business from that area. This bank existed for nearly a period of thirty years. The borrowers failed to pay back the loans. So, the prize money got dissolved in that bank after the Law of Rural Indebtedness was passed. *Visva-Bharati* could never get back the money (Tagore, 1395 B.S., pp. 216- 217).

The institution of Sriniketan was not an isolated experiment, but an integral part of Tagore's total educational and reconstruction work. At the same time, Sriniketan was certainly a product of his restlessness to do something for poverty-stricken rural India. He purchased the Surul Kuthibari at the cost of Rs. 10,000 in 1912 to implement his plan. But, it still took one decade to start his programme due to two reasons: lack of fund and the absence of a leader. In 1921 Tagore met in ***America Leonard K. Elmhirst,*** a young agriculture graduate who was very impressed by Tagore's rural reconstruction idea and expressed his willingness to join the programme. Tagore decided to entrust the task to Elmhirst who had been acquainted with the conditions of Indian villages on some earlier occasions. Towards the end of 1921, Elmhirst came to *Santiniketan* and started work from *Surul Kuthibari* as a citadel of rural regeneration on February 6, 1922, after one year of *Visva Bharati* being formally established as a University of the unique type in 1921 (Mukhopadhyay, 1995: 4).

The strategy of *Sriniketan* Experiment proves the sincerity and thoughtfulness of Tagore about the total scheme. He could very correctly realize that the first step was not to abruptly jump in the villages, but to go slow in order to fully realize the nature and extent of the major problems of the village people and to gain their confidence through some very urgent welfare works for them. Unless and until the social workers would acquire the faith of the villagers, no amount of endeavour to improve their condition and quality of life through their own efforts would bear any fruit (Mukhopadhyay, 1995: 5). Tagore and Elmhirst started giving shape to a complete scheme of rural reconstruction. From the very beginning, the Institute of *Sriniketan* was organized under a *Democratic Karma Samity* (working committee), on which the representatives of total workers and many eminent men of the time came to serve. The most dedicated one in this venture was Kalimohan Ghosh. That was the beginning of *Sriniketan* (Dasgupta, 1962: 17).

In this process, *health received the first priority* in the social welfare action which intended to carry out the anti-malaria schemes from preventive and curative angles. The village people were trained for cleaning the bushes and jungles, and feeling the pools of stagnant water with earth to prevent mosquitoes from breeding and as a curative measure, distribution of medicine for malarial fever among the villagers through door to door supply and dispensary at *Sriniketan* and in some villages organized by the *Sriniketan* team of functionaries. The next set of work undertaken by the village people with the active assistance of the team included road repairing, the building of culverts and opening and repairing of drains for easy flow of water within the villages and crop fields. How the *Sriniketan* team earned the confidence of the villagers was illustrated by Tagore himself by mentioning one incident? One night fire broke out in the village of *Mahidapur* – one mile away from *Sriniketan* and on getting this news the *Sriniketan* team immediately rushed to the spot of fire and extinguished it with the help of the villagers. When these social workers could win the trust and confidence of the villagers, the next step was to undertake various development works. Since most of the rural populations were farmers, various measures were adopted to augment the rate of agricultural production, through introducing improved technology like the application of good seeds and manures, the arrangement of proper irrigation, offering cheap credit facility from cooperative credit societies and remunerative marketing of their produce. Elmhirst established a small laboratory to carry out experiments for the improvement of the rate of production in the particular soil types and climatic conditions of the villages. Improved variety of seeds of various crops and vegetables and horticulture plants were procured and distributed after imparting the application of improved methods of cultivation to the villages. The lessons of new farm technology were imparted not only to the farmers around *Santiniketan—Sriniketan* Campus of *Visva-Bharati,* but also to the farmers from different districts of Bengal and even other nearby provinces (Mukhopadhyay, 1995: 5-6). A complete plan of rural reconstruction experiments with seeds, manures, rotation of crops, cattle and poultry farming was drawn up by 1928. Appraisal of the village needs was estimated by methods of rural survey in 1923. A well developed cooperative society was charged with the responsibilities of promoting programmes of health, education, agriculture and rural industries. The society maintained a grain bank, played as an arbitrator in local disputes and carried on educational propaganda through many attractive methods (Dasgupta, 1962: 17). Tagore was very conscious about environmental protection and his rural reconstruction programme was eco-friendly. He loved nature and could feel the worth of it. So, he was keen to frame up the programme of development in consonance with nature.

Tagore's idea of rural reconstruction inspired Pannalal Dasgupta (1908 – 1999) who, in association with Jayprakash Narayan founded the Tagore Society for Rural Development, whose activities are now spread over states like West Bengal, Bihar, Orissa and Madhya Pradesh (Dasgupta, Pannalal, 1985). It is interesting to look at that site of rural reconstruction today. *Palli Bhavna*, a Quarterly News Bulletin of Rural Extension Centre, *Visva-Bharati, Sriniketan*, gives us an account of the present activities of the Rural Extension Centre, an organ operating under the Institute of Rural Development, which are now being carried on the rural reconstruction programme of Tagore. Tagore tried to make his *Sriniketan* experiment a complete one. So, he was conscious about including every aspect of 'reconstruction' in his programme. The organizations of *Siksha Satra, Lok Siksha Samsad, Siksha Charcha* and *Brati Balaka* prove his holistic concept in this context. He sought to unite the ideals of the old with the Western scientific genius.

Rural Industries

Tagore felt it necessary to revitalize the decadent cottage industries and to train the local artisans and village youth, so, that they could make use of the new innovations. With this idea, he set up *Shilpa*

Bhavana at *Santiniketan.* He did not only concentrate on making the villages self-sufficient, but also tried to encourage the villagers to make objects of beauty and utility for the luxury demands of the distant markets, so, that wealth could flow into the village treasury. So, a cottage industries training programme was undertaken by his initiative. He was also not against the application of power and introduction of a machine for increasing efficiency of production. It was his endeavour to build up a balanced industrial economy (Dasgupta, Sugata, pp. 47, 49).

Institute of Rural Reconstruction

The Institute of Rural Reconstruction started operating through two broad divisions of work. Its headquarter was situated at *Sriniketan.* It maintained a number of demonstration and service units concerning agriculture, animal husbandry, cottage industries, health, education and village organization. Each of these sections also organized a replica of its service units at the village level through the initiative of the people of the area and led by the village workers of the institute. The centre thus maintained a demonstration farm, a Dairy and poultry unit, an outdoor clinic, a department of cottage industries, a village school, and a number of other institutions at *Sriniketan.* The organization manifested itself in three different types of activities namely research, extension and education. The Institute also defined, in its turn, new education by its firsthand knowledge about the village problems. This was possible by a well defined administrative network by which distant villages were connected with the headquarters in the matter of needs and services to and from the village community (Dasgupta, Sugata, pp. 47, 49).

Rural Library

The rural library was an essential part of the rural reconstruction programme of Tagore. The utility of the library has been always recognized by Tagore. So, from the very beginning, there was a central library for learning and research and another local library to serve the local people and to grow interest in reading and learning among them. The most unique feature of this library system was the introduction of a circulating library in 1925. It was actually a mobile library where one village worker used to give door to door service by carrying books in a bag. Initially, it was done by walking, although later cycle was being used for this purpose (Nandi, 2007: 42).

Rural Library Services are one of the important services of Rural Extension Centre through which *literacy movement* are carried out in the villages. Apart from literacy activities, another objective of this programme is to develop the rural libraries as information and cultural centres in villages. This programme in rural areas has been carried out through a network of a number of rural libraries with an active financial support from Raja Rammohun Roy Library Foundation (RRRLF), Kolkata.

Tagore's idea of Rural Reconstruction Programme was, no doubt, a path-breaking one, although, it created much debate and criticism from every corner of the contemporary society. But, Tagore was firm, for he had a very strong logic behind his concept and fortunately he could find out his proper associates in his unique venture. He was sincere, honest and thoughtful but a bit utopian. *Yet, Tagore's model may be accepted as a micro-model to be followed all over the society of India, but the difficulty is to find out a proper leader upon whom the success of such a project depends exclusively. Such a programme, if implemented even partially, would benefit the society.* Any person, going to activate this type of programme should consult the scheme of Tagore as the pioneering one which throws light in the field of alternative/other Development with the emphasis on Human Development. Actually, Tagore tried to perceive and analyse the problem from a holistic perspective. Here, the renowned poet proves himself to be a successful social thinker as well as an activist in this sphere.

Conclusion

In India, Sriniketan Experiment in the beginning of this century was considered to be the first attempt in rural development. Sri Rabindranath Tagore, a visionary and a poet had brought a sea change in the environment surrounding Sriniektan in West Bengal. The programme aimed at socio-economic as well as moral rehabilitation of rural community. As part of the rural development programme, monkeys and malaria were eradicated in the first phase. Later on, a new strategy of agriculture, new breeds of cows, poultry and village crafts were introduced. Doors of education were opened to village children, adults. In addition, villagers were educated in the use of new agricultural implements by way of demonstrations. The experiment was quite successful in a small area and in a few villages. The level of economy looked up and the standard of living of people improved. New awakening and confidence arose among the villagers. The experiment, however, could not be carried out for want of continued professional guidance and trained personnel. Over and above, the government machinery tried to work in a mechanical routine.

In spite of innumerable handicaps, Tagore's ideas and influence inspired and penetrated every corner of Sriniketan. He constantly urged that "our practical achievements, our clean milk, our fresh eggs, our flourishing co-operatives, were all useful means, but still only means towards the achievement of much greater end." He urged to draw up all resources, in music, song, drama and dance at Sriniketan, so as to enrich lives and to increase delight in every kind of artistic expression, until the cultivators could produce richness and a wealth of cultural life and rejuvenation of these ancient art forms that still survived, but so tenuously around the village.

References

Bandopadhyay, A. (2007). *'Santi-Sri Avenue' in 'Paschimbanga', Special Rabindra Sankhya.* Kolkata: Government of West Bengal.

Dasgupta, S. (1962). *A Poet and a Plan.* Calcutta: Thacker Spink & Co. Private Ltd.

Mukhopadhyay, A. (1995). Tagore's Sriniketan Experiment – Past and Present: An Assessment. *Indian Association of Social Science Institution (IASSI).*

Nandi, S.G. (2007). *'Rabindranath Porikolpito Grampunorgathan O Gramin Library Byabastha' in Srishti—Special Issue.* Sriniketan: Palli Samprasaran Kendra, Visva-Bharati.

Rabindranath Tagore on Rural Reconstruction. (1943). Retrieved September 20, 2012, From: http://203.200.22.249:8080/jspui/bitstream/123456789/1008/1/Rabindranath%20Tagore%20Rural%20Reconstruction.pdf

Sen, A. (2004). Tagore and his India. In *Nobel Laureates In Search Of Identity and Integrity: Voices of Different Cultures* (pp. 177-212).

Sen, S. (1943). *Rabindranath Tagore on Rural Reconstruction.* Visva-Bharati, Calcutta.

Tagore, R. (1908). *Chithipatra*, Volume-XIII, No. 50. Kolkata: Visva-Bharati.

——(1962). *Swadeshi Samaj*.
——*Pitrismriti*. Kolkata: Jijnasa Publications Pvt. Ltd.
——*'Swadeshi Samaj: Sanbidhan' in Rabindra Rachanabali Centenary Volume XII*. Kolkata: Government of West Bengal.
Visva-Bharati. (2009). *Visva-Bharati Annual Report, 2008-2009*. Visva-Bharati.

4

Influence of Gandhian Philosophy in Social Work Profession

Sunil Prasad[1] and *Arul Actovin C.*

Introduction

> "The best way to find you is to lose yourself in the service of others"
> —*Mahatma Gandhi*

Social work is a practice-based profession and an academic discipline that promotes social change and development, social cohesion, and the empowerment and liberation of people. Principles of social justice, human rights, collective responsibility and respect for diversities are central to social work. Underpinned by theories of social work, social sciences, humanities and indigenous knowledge, social work engages people and structures to address life challenges and enhance well-being (IFSW).

Social work's commitment is to excavate World's most pressing social challenges to bring equality, justice for people from different caste, class, ethnicity, nationality, gender, age etc. through eliminating social discrimination and marginalization. It emphasizes on adopting an interdisciplinary approach to address the social issues with inherent respect for diversity and indigeneity. Principles of Gandhian Philosophy and Social work profession go hand-in-hand and are extremely compatible with each other. Gandhi's tremendous emphasis on the principle of truth and non-violence are innately linked with the principle of social justice and Human Rights which are the heart and soul of Social work profession. Hence, it is surprising that social work profession and its literature have given scant attention to this consistency. The development of the ethical theory building of social work profession, itself was a derivative of Gandhi's principle and values (Tom & Heather, 2000)

Mahatma Gandhi is considered one of the greatest leaders of the world but he was not made in a day. It took several events in his life which impacted his thought process and lifestyle and which was known for its commonness and simplicity. His ideology to date plays a vital role in influencing the social policies of the country and the social work profession. Every great leader's life bears a testimony and in order to understand his ideology, perception, approach towards his life and the leader's personality as a whole the authors have tried to throw light in the atmosphere and culture where Mahatma Gandhi was brought up and his contribution towards Social Work Profession.

He grew up, and was influenced by stories of Raja Chandra and Shravana which was based on the themes of truth. So, from this kind of other stories and personal experiences he learned that truth and love are two supreme values for human beings.

Gandhi played an important role when he was in Africa in fighting for the rights of the Indian Immigrants and against the inconsiderate rules and law of the government. Gandhi's exposure to racism, injustice against the Indians in Africa brought about the sense of social justice within him and through advocacy, he was able to unite all the Indian immigrants there and fight against the oppressor. He also set up the Tolstoy Farm which helped him to remove the social barrier among people and where every individual participated and making them feel that no work is small or beneath any racial identity.

After returning from Africa in 1915-16, Gandhi started the tour of India in order to understand the social issues of India. This tour gave Gandhi firsthand experience about the ground realities of the ground and showed the colonial practice which was existing and its impact on the social and economic life of the Indians. During this tour, Gandhi felt the need to challenge the social evils which were widespread prevalent in the country and to challenge the oppressor colonial power that was exploiting the Indians and keeping them void of their rights.

Gandhi had an amalgamation of both as a practical reformer and a reformer which brought about a massive change among the masses. After this incident, Gandhi gave a new dimension to every sphere of Indian social, political, education field. He considered all human beings as a living reality and everyone was born equal and hence everyone had the right to life and with freedom.

In the Indian context, the Gandhian value system has assisted the government policies and after its Independence and till date plays a vital role. His efforts reflect the rights like freedom of expression, the prohibition against discrimination on the grounds of religion, caste, or race, political participation, progress towards the welfare of the society, as he tried to explain with the concept of '*Sarvodaya*' meaning the well-being of all in all phase of life. He also raised the issue of discrimination against the lower caste underprivileged such as *Harijans*, women, destitute and laid emphasis on constructive programmes which deals with all aspects of individual and community life. He as a social worker did advocacy for social reforms and promoted mass programmers and tried to bring about change at the mass level. Its ideology was based on dignity and worth of an Individual which is one of the principles of social work profession (Khairnar, 2013).

His concept of *Sarvodaya* laid emphasis on the value system of *Lokniti* which allowed people to implement the self-rule to bring about equality and justice in the society. Gandhi's activities are focusing on the individual Self-development and use of non-violence action. He also lays emphasis on material simplicity. Gandhi focused and believed in the spiritual values like truth, non-violence, non-discrimination, social justice, the self-reliance which would bring about positive change in the society.

The professional social worker envisages a society which is free from any types of conflicts, without any discrimination where equality prevails, poverty is eradicated, no disparities of income among the individual and where full of opportunities are there. Gandhi too wanted to bring about the same kind of social order which keep the parallel thinking of that of the professional social worker and that could be brought about by the means of constructive measures given by him. Gandhi's concepts of "*aparigraha*", "*daridranarayana*", "trusteeship" decentralization, the dignity of labour, bread labour, *Antyodaya*, and *Sarvodaya* are some of the areas for social work practice (Raju, 2012). Hence, Gandhi and Social Work profession have a connection which aims at common goals and objectives and achieved through different means and approach to a present-day situation.

A Happy Union of Gandhi's Vision and Social Work Profession

Gandhi envisaged a society which was free from violence and strived for everyone's development with special emphasis on the betterment of the most downtrodden in society. His personal commitment to '*Satyagraha*' and '*ahimsa*' was coupled with his never-ending efforts to also propagate these values in societies and communities (*Mind of Mahatma Gandhi*).

In the present times, where uniform codes of equality and justice are being accepted and inculcated across the international community, instances of violations against Humanity, discrimination, violence against some communities are also at surge. At the heart of every social problem is a conflict of interests, power dynamics resulting in different kinds of violence. Gandhi's principles of '*ahimsa*', and '*antyodaya*' becomes all the more important in present times (Raju, 2012). The development of social welfare programmes in Independent India was highly inspired by Gandhi's influence for the betterment of the whole society and especially the poor people who are at the bottom of any development and growth. Majumdar, 1964 says that it was for Gandhi's effort and influence that social work profession in India developed at the first place and Gandhi in his day to day conduct used case work and group work to help out people out of their miseries (Chaturvedi, 1965). Gandhi preached and practised social justice and service to others which fits skillfully with the social work theory. He also emphasized the principle of social action for fighting violence and inequalities in society. Dr. Bishnu Mohan Dash in his article has mentioned that "The significant contributions and developmental models propounded by the great Indian thinkers particularly Swami Dayananda Saraswati, Swami Vivekananda, Dr. Bhim Rao Ambedkar, Mahatma Gandhi, Jyotiba Phule, Nanaji Deshmukh, Rabindranath Tagore, Narayan Guru, Anna Hazare, Baba Amte and others should be given sufficient emphasis, which is highly relevant in the reconstruction of Indian Society". He also said, in this critical period, social work academicians should come out of their *status quo* and look forward to study the traditional Indian roots of social work, initiatives of social reformers and philanthropists, models of rural reconstruction experiments and Indian spiritual ideals and values (Dash, 2018).

For Weaker Section of the Society

Even though Gandhi was not a social worker in a firm consideration, but his ideology and philosophy help the society and the nation in reconstruction of the society based on the principle of non-violence, social justice, welfare of the marginalized and weaker section of the society which he termed as '*Antyodaya*', the welfare of all the weaker sections of the society. His concept of '*Sarvodaya*' has its relation to Social work profession which states that development of all. Gandhi always believed that with the help of the Principles of Cooperation and collective work positive changes can be brought in a society. The weaker section of the society are the ones who are always the worst affected in any calamities and the catastrophic situation like famines, war, floods, colonialism and are most exposed to human injustice, economic exploitation, discrimination, and the biased and dominating caste system in our country. Gandhi wanted to empower this weaker section of the society through '*Sarvodaya*' through '*Antyodaya*'. The weaker section has been exploited for centuries and hence Gandhi felt the need of them getting justice in terms of social, economic and political rights by means of non-violence and solely freedom. He also fought against the untouchable and communalism and wanted to end these social evils.

In the Context of Women Empowerment

In the context of women's empowerment, he was also one of the propagators who fought for the women rights as he considered them to be one of the most long-neglected segment of the society and the most vulnerable in spite of having constitution providing several equal rights for them and other privileges. Gandhi had dedicated all his service to the poor and he felt that it would be incomplete without serving the women and he considered that women are the pillar of the society and India could not progress until the women of this country do their duty. Gandhi wanted the enlightened women of India to seek relentlessly the repeal of all legal disqualifications and removal of social discrimination against women in India. He considered legislation to remove the inequalities of women as essential. But at the same time, he did not favour women competing with men in all vocations. He advocated selective education for women, not with any sense of women being inferior to men, but he did believe that they were not identical and that their fields of work were different.

The woman is described as a man's better half. As long as she has not the same rights in law as the man, as long as the birth of a girl does not receive the same welcome as that of a boy, so long we should know that India is suffering from partial paralysis. Suppression of woman is a denial of *Ahimsa*. Every village worker will, therefore, regard every woman as his mother, sister or daughter, as the case may be, and look at her with respect. Only such a worker will command the confidence of the village people (Kher, 1976).

In the Context of Development

Gandhi considered development is a process of empowering people and he strived for movements for poverty alleviation and empowerment of women which is another important domain of the social work profession. Gandhi gave a new paradigm of development in an Indigenous context which would help the local and native Indians progress and to preserve our culture too in the colonial era. His concept of 'Trusteeship' implies that the property belongs to everyone and the owner should own only if they are the socially responsible trustee. This focused on decentralization of power and cooperation among the people themselves.

Individuals and Community Development

Gandhian approach towards rural community was based on village *swaraj* and *swadeshi* movement. The basic principle of village *swaraj* as outlined by Gandhi are trusteeship, *swadeshi*, full employment, bread labour, self-sufficiency, decentralization, equality, *Nai Talim* etc. Thus, the idea of an ideal village of Gandhian dream was a comprehensive one, encompassing the economic, social, political and educational dimensions. Therefore, in Gandhian plan of rural reconstruction, the ancient republican village without any kind of exploitation served as a model unit (Bora, 1994). Gandhi aimed at the attainment of village *swaraj* and said in 1942,

> "My idea of village *swaraj* is that it is a complete republic, independent of its neighbours for its own vital wants and get inter-dependent for many others in which dependence is a necessity. Thus, every villager's first concern will be to grow its own food crop and cotton for its cloth. It could have a reserve for his cattle, recreation and playground for adults

> and children. Then if there is more land available, it will grow useful money crops, thus excluding *Ganja*, tobacco, opium and the like. The village will be main a village theatre, school and public hall. It will have its own water works ensuring clean water supply (Pyarelal, 1977)."

In Social work methods, Gandhi's rural reconstruction 18 point programme had a significant role in community organization method as well as this programme mainly focusing on the development of the village as well as individuals. To him, the individual was as important, if not more, than the society, as he firmly believed that the happiness of the individual moulded an integral part of the happiness of the society. So, for him, social welfare meant the conscious submission of the individual and a voluntary contribution of one's possession to the society, which consisted of *all,* not a majority and, in return, the social system, built upon the principles of non-violence and democracy, was to give a complete guarantee for the maximum development of the individual's personality (Srinivasan, 2018).

The Gandhian concept takes a total perspective and focuses on the development of the moral and spiritual aspects with truth and non-violence as its base; with all the other aspects, such as physical, mental and economic, to enhance the individual's social sense, thereby creating a society of healthy individuals. "One important aspect of Gandhi's social thought was his tendency not only to bridge the gap between individual and social ethics, but also to regard social reality as a counterpart of man's inner reality". Social work principle 'Individuality' also giving more importance to the individuals as well as what they are in.

In the Context of Economic Upliftment

Gandhi's thought on economic reform and development is not as rigid as people think of him. Moreover, his economic thoughts were basically social thoughts (Kumar, 1995).

Gandhi always had a sustainable and fitting approach in his intervention for economic upliftment of the rural economy and the weaker section of the society. He had a constructive thinking which would help the rural economy grow. Gandhi started the movement of *Swadeshi* which was solely focused on eliminating the colonial made products and promoting the *Khadi* and Indian made goods. It will help the revival of *Khadi* industry and cottage Industries in India and provide employment to many people and a source of income. He believed in the self-sufficient village and empowered people and laid emphasis on the consumption of local products, which would safe guard the local producers. He also never separated ethics from economics. He believed that any economic policy, no matter how good it was, if harmful for the moral well-being of the people and society, should be unacceptable for good. He largely opposed the industrial corporations which distance themselves from people who were unable and least interested in catering to the spiritual and social development needs of the rural population.

Political Autonomy and Self-Reliance

Gandhi was in favour of the high level of localization and decentralization of power. He wanted Panchayati Raj system as a governing unit of administration at every village level and hence at micro-level, power is distributed and people participate in the election process. Gandhi was in favour of *Swaraj* which mean self-rule and he considered that we are capable of ruling ourselves. He encouraged the formation of social organizations which were more close to individuals and society, understood the local needs of the society and employed its own expertise to solve the issues. Gandhi's teaching of *Swadeshi* sought its legitimacy from people's ethical responsibility from its local environment and people.

Non-Cooperation Movement

In the year 1921, Gandhi gave a call for Non-Cooperation with the British Government and demanded with the youths, lawyers, and other Indian servicemen to boycott all British Government services and to burn all the foreign made clothes and declared All India Level social reconstruction programmers and promoted *Khadi* made clothes. During this period Gandhi laid down 18 constructive items which have its relevance in Social Work domain in the contemporary era. Among the 18 constructive items the main constructive items having relevance with social work field are:

1. Communal Harmony among Hindus and Muslims for a better society.
2. Removal of Untouchability for a just society where every

individual is treated equal and no discrimination exists.

3. Promotion of Village Industry for livelihood and self-reliance.
4. Promotion of education to make people aware.
5. Respect women.
6. Promotion of health and hygiene for a better and healthy environment.
7. Demand for economic equality and decentralized economic production where every individual has to right to work and earn.
8. Removal of social evils through education and awareness (Raju, 2012).

Social Movements

In Social work profession, Social Action method is an indirect method as well as achieving the goals with mass participation. In the Indian context, significant influences of Gandhian movements like *Ahimsa*, Non-cooperation movement and etc. in using social action method of the social work profession. One of the leading analyst and participant in social movements in India, Sanjay Sangvi, identified the major agendas of them as "Movements of landless, unorganized labour in rural and urban areas, *Adivasis*, *Dalits*, displaced people, peasants, urban poor, small entrepreneurs and unemployed youth took up the issues of livelihood, opportunities, dignity and development." Most well-known movements in the country are Chipko movement, Save Silent Valley, Narmada Bachao Andolan, Koel Karo, Chhattisgarh Mukti Morcha, and Jhola Aandolan. These movements largely distanced themselves from political parties or tried to cut across the ideologies of the political parties. Yet many of them rooted themselves or drew from ideologies of the Mahatma Gandhi, various shades environmentalisms or gender politics, or socialism (Rathi, 2018).

Mass movements can be a solution to solve many problems in the society. Just as Mahatma Gandhi led the freedom struggle, there is a need to launch a mass movement for the development of better Society and a stronger nation.

Conclusion

Gandhi played an important role in social reform and prepared an intellectual climate for the growth of social work professional in India. His inherent belief that poor people are more close to God and Truth motivated him to fight for the poor people against poverty, which is also considered the root of many social problems. His vision for harmonic society with the help of non-violence as a tool for bringing about the social change has its connection with Social Work Profession. As a social worker we work for making a better society where everyone gets justice. As a social worker, Gandhi too laid emphasis on resistance against violence and discrimination and marginalization of any section of the society. Even though Gandhi was criticized for his non-modern thoughts, but in the context of Social work his ideology is very influential and can be put into practice in the field. Gandhi's practice was quite common if seen in the context of the domain like gender issues, racial issues, social justice, for empowering the people, for poverty alleviation and human growth which is also one of major driving forces and guiding principles for many government schemes in our country.

Professional social work got influenced by Gandhian thoughts, but remained distinct and indifferent due to various reasons. Gandhism could not provide an indigenous touch to imported social work. Gandhian thoughts have been imbibed by Indian society and government; we can see this impact in the Indian Constitution, particularly on the directive on principles of state policy and fundamental rights. Social worker's concern for socially deprived people, the idea of intimate family ties, the concept of nutrition and health care for everyone, fight for social justice, decentralization of power, efforts to minimize the gap between rich and poor and the concept of communal harmony look like an echo of Gandhian thoughts. Gandhian thoughts do not want to promote parasites in the society and believe in self-help and mutual help and not in charity. As well as Gandhi believed purity in the form of achievement with a proper process like social work profession (Kumar, 1995).

The professional social worker can enrich themselves from Gandhian Ideology and thought as it is a storehouse of wide knowledge based on ground realities and issues and ethical concepts which would help the social worker to define the ends and means of any practice. Even in today's context, the Gandhian idea can solve many issues in the Indian society. Gandhi as that of Social Work Profession was always opposed to any kind of discrimination and exploitation and the path of '*Ahmisa*' or non-violence to be used to tackle any issues in the society. Both Gandhi Ideology and Social Work Profession look forward to social transformation which is progressive and for the betterment of any society. According to Paulo Freire, the need of conscientization helps the society to be aware and Gandhi and Social Worker too lay emphasis on making the people conscious as it is one of the greatest weapons to bring about social change. And "the Gandhian and social work approaches believe in teamwork. Help seekers may or may not be a team, but helper are usually working with a team. It may be a team of various types of helpers or various organizations and service agencies. Liaison with them is very important. Social workers and Gandhian constructive workers take extra care that they should have a team behind them" (Kumar, 1995).

Social work Profession has its own professional code of ethics which includes moral principles like Principles of Non-Judgement, principles of Confidentiality, Principles of Individualization and other more. The Gandhian thought also enriches the social work ethical standards with many of his principles like *ahimsa*, truthfulness, *Sarvodaya*, *Swadeshi*, Self-Reliance, Self-Sufficiency, Material Simplicity, and other which adhere to the sole purpose of welfare of the society.

Hence, Gandhi's Ideology has a deep influence and connection with Social Work Profession and will guide the new generation's social worker to achieve the similar aim for the welfare and betterment of society where there is harmony, social justice, economic equality, empowerment of the weaker section of the society.

References

Bora, P.M. (1994, February). Gandhian Model of Rural Development. *Khadi Gramodyoga: Journal of Rural Economy, 40*(5): 482.

Desai, C. (n.d.). *Gandhi's Concept of Social Welfare*. Retrieved from: http://www.gandhi-manibhavan.org/activities/essay_socialwelfare.htm

Dash, B.M. (2018). Revamp Social work education, *The Pioneer*, March, 14, 2018.

Gandhi, M.K. (1947). *India of My Dream* (16th ed.). Ahmedabad, India: Navajivan Publishing House.

H.R. Chaturvedi. (1965). Gandhi, Social Worker. *The Economic Weekly*, 1166.

Khairnar, Y.H. (2013). Mahatma Gandhi and Professional Social. *Indian Journal of Research.*

Kher, V. (1976). *Social Service Work and Reform, Volume II.* Ahmedabad: Navjivan Publishing House.

Kumar, H. (1995). *Theories in Social Work Practice.* New Delhi: Friends Publications (India).

M. Lakshmipathi Raju, B.S. (2012). Ethical Values of Social Work Profession and Gandhism. *International Journal of Research in Social Sciences.*

Prabhu, R.K., and Rao, U.R. (1996). *The Mind of Mahatma Gandhi.* Jitendra T. Desai.

Pyarelal. (1977). *Mahatma Gandhi on Human Settlements.* Ahmedabad: Navajivan Publishing House.

R. Srinivasan, U.T. (2018, May 7). *Gandhi Website.* Retrieved May 7, 2018, from Mahatma Gandhi's Writings, Philosophy, Audio, Video and Photography: https://www.mkgandhi.org/articles/social_work.htm

Raju, M.L., and Raju, B.N. (2012). Ethical Values of Social Work Profession and Gandhism. *International Journal of Research in Social Sciences,* 202-210.

Rathi, D.S. (2018, May 11). *Mahatma Gandhi and Today's Mass Movement.* Retrieved May 11, 2018, from Mahatma Gandhi's writing, philosophy, audio, video and photograph: https://www.mkgandhi.org/articles/mass_movement.html

Walz, T., and Header, R. (2000, May 1). *Gandhian Principles in Social Work Practice: Ethics Revisited.* Retrieved from: http://www.biomedsearch.com/article/Gandhian-Principles-in-Social-Work/62161018.html

5

India's Tryst with Social Democracy and Justice

Iconization of Ambedkar and Gandhi

Biplove Kumar

Introduction

> "Constitutional morality is not a natural sentiment. It has to be cultivated". —*Dr. Bhimrao Ramji Ambedkar*

India is known for its Democracy. With the promulgation of India's Constitution—on January 26th, 1950 laws of '*Manu' was* replaced by the laws of *Mahar* (emphasis added). The creation of India as a Democratic and Republican nation was indeed an audacious step; because of its many social schisms. It, in fact, became the first country in the non-Western world to choose a resolutely Democratic Constitution. Both political and social revolutions became the conscience of Indian Constitution. Apart from the argumentative tradition that was initiated with *'Objectives Resolution'* and reflected in *'Constituent Assembly Debates (CAD)'* from December 1946 to December 1949; the whole phenomenon represented insight, intellect, passion and competing ideas as to what will be the *"Idea of India"*. (Sen, 2005)

In general, democracy was and is expected to be synonymous with good governance and political rights. But the benefits or more precisely to say experiences, from the failure and success of existing democracies as well as the legacies of *'social reform movements'* in colonial India; made the Indian lawmakers realise that their path should be a different one. It valued its liberty and resented inequality and dominance (resulting particularly from imperialism). The history presented the alternative and this rationality was reflected among Indian intelligentsia.

The whole spirit was ignited with Nehru's first major speech in Constituent Assembly on 13th December, 1946, when he moved Objectives Resolution. It was perhaps the initiation of India's *"tryst with future"*. It proclaimed India as an 'Independent Sovereign Republic', guaranteeing its citizens 'justice, social, economic and political; equality of status; of opportunity, and before the law; freedom of thought, expression, belief, faith, worship, vocation, association and action, subject to law and public morality – all this while assuring that "adequate safeguards shall be provided for minorities, backward and tribal areas, depressed and other backward classes." (Guha, 2007). It was an extraordinary speech which not only provided the base and direction for India's future but also reflected the several legacies that went in parallel with India's struggle for Independence. The shared experiences and historical encounter between India and the Western world, in fact, created the whole idea of India. It gave primacy to social equality and justice as a cardinal principle of governance.

The opening pages of the Indian Constitution envisaged a nation where equality, liberty and fraternity would be supreme. Drawn mostly from historical experience and cultural traditions of West, these ideas reflected a vision for liberal democracy and a modern society that were to ensure a dignified existence to each and every individual and endow them with certain fundamental rights *vis-à-vis* the state and fellow citizens. They contradicted very fundamentally the spirit of inequalities that persisted in the society. Caste system with its horrendous form of 'vertical hierarchy' based on purity and pollution; was among the most tragic inequalities that persisted in Indian society. Casteism and its annihilation, in fact, became a serious concern for the leaders – who thought it has no place in modern democratic India. In his well-known book '*The Discovery of India*', Pandit Jawaharlal Nehru, India's first Prime Minister noted this concern:

> "In the context of society today, the caste system and much that goes with it are wholly incompatible, reactionary, restrictive, and barriers to progress. There can be no equality in status and opportunity within its framework, nor there can

be a political democracy. Between these two conceptions conflict is inherent and only one of them can survive. (Nehru, 2004)."

No political concept is more used and misused, than that of democracy. Many meanings are attached to the word democracy. If there is one true meaning then it is indeed, as Plato might have said, 'stored up in heaven'. India not only adopted the *'Westminster style'* of Parliamentary Democracy and hugely took inspiration from Euro-American models; but it also contributed its own genuine and syncretic ideas to it. Granville Austin writes "India's original contribution to constitution making lies in its immense capacity of accommodation, the ability to reconcile, to harmonize, and to make work without changing their content apparently incompatible concepts" (Guha, 2007). One such apparently incompatible concept (which still is being debated in contemporary India) is those of 'legal equality' that defines all are equal under the rule of law and of compensatory or positive discrimination (more precisely reservations) that puts: the notion of liberal equality under strain.

Notwithstanding of constitutional benefits and social engineering projects; any perusal of Indian society generates a common standpoint, that the anathema of casteism has blocked the roads for an egalitarian society. From Belchi to Khairlanji to Una; episodes of social injustice and exclusion on the basis of caste still dominates contemporary India. Early leaders of contemporary India was fully aware of the fact that addressing this issue was central to building a cohesive nation, capable of fulfilling the needs and aspirations of a modern society. The Republican Constitution of India formally, through various Articles (14 to 17), have abolished discrimination on the basis of caste. However, the canker of casteism with its vulgar phenomenon of untouchability still exists. The atrocities that gyrate around casteism and its magnitude show the failure of state and constitutional protection towards the oppressed people.

With economic and political advances, the tools of domination and suppression have changed. The whole project of social reform was put on hold before independence, in the wake of the political one. Still, in independent India, the whole idea of social reform is dominated by political discourse. Intermediate castes whose political and economic clout has increased over the years since independence have joined the class of oppressors. The democratisation of Indian politics has shown the phenomenon of *'sectional elevation'* (Lohia,

1964). This sectional elevation has changed some relationships within the caste system, but had left the basis of caste unaltered. Caste consciousness that showed unconditional affinity to fellow caste members have not only defeated moral affinity, but have also strengthened casteism.

The spirit of Political democracy with an eye on vote bank politics has certainly become an anathema for social and economic democracies. It has become the character of post-colonial politics that only acts for strengthening itself for political gains. But the question arises here that is a democracy only about just institutions and power politics or it is beyond that?

Pre-independent India witnessed several social reformers who tried to eradicate the monster of caste and untouchability. But the discourse and the 'hermeneutic engagement' between Gandhi and Ambedkar are regarded as the most prominent one. In all historical fairness, it was after the holistic debate between Gandhi and Ambedkar that the whole idea of oppressed caste and their upliftment gained momentum. The whole trajectory from *the Round Table Conference to the Poona Pact* not only witnessed the holistic clash between Gandhi and Ambedkar; but also created space for the social reform agenda along with the political one. The twain never met in their own life even if their tracks were complementary to each other with a united aim of equality and social justice.

Independent India's caste discourse has changed the whole dynamics and the meaning of Gandhi's and Ambedkar's framework of justice and equality. In the era of iconization and populism, the threat to their ideas are prominent and needs a serious detour. Iconization of Ambedkar and Gandhi has not only betrayed the whole idea of social justice and equality, but also the very idea of democracy or *swaraj*. Fluidity among masses, the idea of oneness, self-purification, self-respect *et al.* depends on the *behavioural pattern* and is beyond the politico-legal question. These all are the ingredients of social relationship that defines the ideal democratic society; without any barriers of social anathema. In the era of populism — one can be selective in their argument in order to divide masses. But as a whole, it sets the agenda for social justice and equality. It shows where we have failed and it also shows where we have to try to get to. It sums up for the transformative mission that is of casteless egalitarian society. The whole idea that twain should meet needs a serious detour.

Democracy and Post-colonial Caste Discourse: Iconization of Ambedkar and Gandhi

The whole idea of India represented the social sensibilities and responsibilities among our forefathers; right after India's Independence. These were reflected in the *Constituent Assembly Debates (CAD)* in a pronounced manner. H.J. Khandekar's (an untouchable member from Berar) opined during CAD that *"State law is one thing, social practice is another"*. It certainly reflected the concerns related to the future of oppressed people in Republican Democracy of India (Khandekar, 1949). Ram Manohar Lohia put it in another way: Social democracy and equality are still a distant dream for oppressed classes in developing India. Canker of casteism still dominates the social fabric of Indian society. Caste is the most overwhelming factor in Indian life. Those who deny it in principle also accept it in practice. (Lohia, 1964). Empirical studies also quite clearly depict this regressive feature of the Indian subcontinent. The latest socio-economic caste census data, released in July 2015; reveals that 1,80,657 households are still engaged in the degrading work of Manual Scavenging (Venkat, 2015). Manual Scavenging is a practice or rather a menial job that was assigned to untouchables (outcastes on the basis of pollution versus purity principles), under the domain of caste oppression. The Employment of Manual Scavengers and Construction of *Dry Latrines (Prohibition) Act, 1993* defines 'manual scavenger' as "a person engaged in or employed for manually carrying human excreta". The employment of manual scavengers is prohibited as a criminal offence.

The recently enacted Prohibition of Employment as Manual Scavengers and their Rehabilitation Act, 2013 gives a detailed definition of 'manual scavenger' as:

> "a person engaged or employed, at the commencement of this Act or at any time thereafter, by an individual or local authority or an agency or a contractor, for manually cleaning, carrying, disposing of, or otherwise handling in any manner, human excreta in an insanitary latrine or in an open drain or pit into which the human excreta from the unsanitary latrines is disposed of, or on a railway track or in such other spaces or premises, as the Central Government of a State Government may notify, before the excreta fully decompose in such manner as may be prescribed..." (The Wire: 28/

072016; *https://thewire.in/54596/what-is-manual-scavenging/*)

Social Democracy or Social Justice in India is referred to the entire gamut of affirmative actions aimed at redressing caste inequalities. But Policies and Politics of Social Justice have reached a dead end in contemporary India (Yadav, 2012). Flashpoints of obnoxious violence from Belchi to Khairlanji to Una; depicts the failure Republican Constitution of India.

Several laws have been passed during the course of 65 years, but the idea of a casteless and egalitarian society is yet to bè realised. The *Dalits* or untouchables (also known as scheduled caste), have been the victims of the caste system and victimization still remains a challenge. The question arises why and what went wrong, that still such exclusion and victimization prevails; in spite of the constitutional provisions.

Caste is a unique way of social stratification that divided the people on the basis of purity and pollution. This particular stratification is very complex in nature. It was because of its complexity that eminent Scholar G.S. Ghurye pointed out that:

> "Any attempt to define caste system is bound to fail."
> (Ghurye, 2000)

Briefly, the whole idea of caste is often defined in the context of hegemony created by the upper caste (mainly *Brahmins*), in order to dominate the lower caste. Brahminical hegemony connected the whole idea of stratification to religion as well as to texts (*Dharmashastras, Bhagvad Gita, Manusmriti etc.*) and traditions; in order to establish the authority of casteism. It was also attached to the whole idea of *Karma* (one's deeds) and *Dharma* (one's duty). It took centuries for the caste system grow into the prominent idea of social demarcation based on a "hierarchy" whose placement is related to theoretical degrees of purity. By the twentieth century, caste had acquired a real meaning in the lives of most if not all Indians, nevertheless, the concept of pollution barrier and the Brahminical ideal of purity were familiar to more people in the subcontinent than had been the case of past centuries (Bayly, 2011). *Varna* (order, class, and kind) and *Jati* (birth group) are regarded as the two corporate of the caste system. The *Varna* consists of a broad four-fold division of the Hindu society: *Brahmins*, *Kshatriyas*, *Vaishyas* and *Shudras*. The concept of *Varna* also involves several factions of divisions under its umbrella of four corporates. It is divided into thousand endogamous groups which are known as *Jatis*. The term *Jati* has often been used for the communities of thousand or sometimes millions of people with whom one may identify with and more specifically for such purposes as marriage.

Broadly, the basis of caste division in Hindu society is related to the four *Varnas*, collectively referred as "*Savarnas*" (those who fall under fourfold division) and some people, who stand outside the *Savarna* groups are known as "*Avarnas*". Members of *Avarna* group are the people known as *Panchama* or Outcastes (untouchables or *Dalits*). Chamars, Mahars, Malas, Raegars, Dushadhs, Bhangis, Doms, Dheds and many more — they belong to the larger group called untouchables. (Lelyveld, 2011). These were the people who do not have any caste or *Varna*; they were and are in a contemporary stage known as untouchables or *Dalits* (broken people). The structural divisions among these castes were identified in terms of purity *versus* pollution. The "*Tindal*" or higher castes were all-time pure in relation to the lower castes and the *Avarnas*. In theory civilized caste Hindus should regard it as wrong and unnatural to share food or other intimate social contacts with those who are radically unlike them in the caste system (Bayly, 2011). These divisions were being certified by the idea of kinship. Individual's life, mainly one's occupational and social status, was determined by the caste in which an individual was born.

Post-Independence trajectories related to India's politics have undergone significant changes; altering somewhat the rules of engagement between politics and society (Manor, 2016). With the Economic and political advances, the tools of domination and suppression have changed. Democracy, in other words, is related to the government with numbers. The whole project of social reform is dominated by political advancements and power discourse. These new phenomena have created the whole idea of 'sectional elevation' of one caste or group; who with their number tries to acquire economic and political privileges. Sectional Elevation certainly changes some relationships within the caste system, but it leaves the basis of caste unaltered. The undeniable fact persists in contemporary discourse is that; politicians calculate their prospects on caste lines and leaders are too chosen on this basis (Gupta, 2000). Politics has caught up with the oppressed class people in a big way because it is seen as the means to secure state power. The inherent contradictions among lower castes and segmentation of hierarchies have created a new class of oppressors. Despite the motion set in by the state and political parties, the *Dalits* had to contend with a new kind of oppressive structure, what could be described as *"Neo-Brahminism"* phenomenon (Ananth; 2014). Anand Teltumbde a leading social activist, in his writing, has clearly targeted this neo-Brahminism phenomenon among *Dalits*. He aptly opines:

> "...even the current pseudo-intellectual trends like *Dalit* capitalism, *Dalit* bourgeois, etc can also be seen as mere aping the models of larger societies". (Teltumbde, 2011).

Rammanohar Lohia was one of the genuine thinkers who perhaps understood the future repercussions that will be created by the new political discourse of independent India. He wrote:

> "It is futile to talk of revolutionary politics unaccompanied by efforts for social change and conscious effort to bridge the gulf between *Dvijya* leadership and the *Dalits*" (Lohia, 1964).

This view also allowed Lohia to create a unitary front or alliance with Ambedkar (popular leader of *Dalits*) in order to get rid of casteism and its branches (for example women segregations). But the sudden death of Ambedkar ceased that opportunity.

Casteism became stronger with the *Jati* – clusters, often banded together to maximise their numerical strength in the hope of gaining advantages in the public sphere (Manor, 2016). Caste became the heated controversy that ran parallel to the politics from 1970s to 1990s. The rise of regional parties and the utilisation of caste as platform became common. With the birth of *Dalit Panthers* to the process *Mandalisation*; caste was everywhere as the unit of social action. Far from disappearing with the democracy, the modernization of caste continued to determine influence in and on Indian society. The rising self-consciousness escalated caste conflicts. *Dalits* were usually on receiving ends (Guha, 2013). The whole idea of social justice was fragmented between the caste rivalries, now mostly represented by OBC-*Dalit* conflicts. M.N. Srinivas defined this peculiar phenomenon by noting down the fact that Sanskritization not always meant that a lower caste should ape the *Brahmans*; on contrary, it also meant fitting into the roles of another upper caste domain.

Casteism grew and sectional elevation based on *Jati*–clusters phenomenon provided "debility" to the nation's agenda of social justice. Political parties based on caste disintegrated masses. Gandhi's or to say Lohia's views for future became reality in the churning decades. Lohia once wrote:

> "...ever and ever again the revolt of downgraded caste has been misused to upgrade one or another caste rather than to destroy entire edifice of caste" (Lohia, 1964).

The whole discourse of several political parties based on caste (RJD, SP, DMK, BSP *et al.*) depicts the phenomenon of sectional elevation and divisive agendas to gain momentum; rather destroy the monster of casteism. The politicisation of caste as Rajani Kothari views – has deepened its roots and has betrayed the idea of Phule, Gandhi, Ambedkar, Lohia *et. al.*

While the process of social reformation was taken up by several reformers during the course of independence; the discourse of Gandhi and Ambedkar proved to be a holistic one. The rise of backward classes and regional parties not only iconised Ambedkar, but their political consolidation began with Ambedkar (Ananth, 2014). But the irony of ironies was that to understand the nature of Babasaheb's political career one has to place it along with Gandhiji; for the apparent divergence between the two will highlight the unique problems of the former. The era of iconisation boosted the politics and provided caste blocks to form the caste-based oriented parties. On one hand, ruling classes needed some means to reconsolidate the independent masses and on the other masses were disillusioned by their leaders, nostalgically needed an icon to lean upon. These two processes resonated into the creation of Ambedkar icons, sourced from the persona of the historical Ambedkar sans complexity and profundity in latter, so as to have mass appeal (Teltumbde, 2010). Ambedkar's name reappeared in the Indian political discourse in 1980s (Jaffrelot, 2016; Ananth, 2013; Guha, 2010). From BSP to BJP, Ambedkar became greatest social reformer ever to fight against the social inequalities.

Time and again, the discourse of Gandhi-Ambedkar was interrogated to provide lifeline political manoeuvres. Ambedkar became the *Dalit* God; although he considered himself as idol breaker and against idol worship. It is clear that with all politics, flags and statues that, *Dalits* have placed Ambedkar top of the world (Omvedt, 2002). A similar trend was adopted by Congress after Independence in the context of Gandhi. As Ambedkar became the symbol of the Political Mobilization of the lower caste (Jafferlot, 2016); the campaign to malign Gandhi also started. *Social Democracy* of Ambedkar and *Swaraj* of Gandhi was negated and was duly dominated by the cult of divisive politics and political propaganda. Several parties accumulated Ambedkar and feared that their defence of Gandhi would erode their vote banks. Their new mantle of Prophethood conceals the inner core of power politics and hunger (Limaye, 1995).

To mould history is an anti-intellectual strategy which leads to the denial of history. Partial views were utilised in the context of Gandhi and Ambedkar, which allowed the passionate forces to act. This whole phenomenon according to Dr. D.R. Nagraj represented the 'Seductive *Charm*' of history (Nagraj, 2010). Discourse from *Round Table Conference* to the *Poona Pact* became the final layout of Gandhi's and Ambedkar's personality assessment. This assessment ignored the evolving spaces of both the leaders and narrowed down their visions. We can no more hold *Gandhi's defence of Varna system* in his early stages against him than we can hold Dr. Ambedkar's opposition to the *adult franchise and representation for Adivasis and so-called Criminal tribes* in the period from 1928 to 1945 against him. (Limaye, 1995).

The twain never met in their lifetime, but, their vision did. Both worked as a catalyst for each other. The importance of their discourse is that they both strived for an egalitarian society. Iconisation and politicisation have utilised Gandhi and Ambedkar for self-benefits. The impasse that exists in the whole idea of social justice reflects the disservice and betrayal which contemporary politics have awarded to them. Whenever the question of *Dalits* and Caste comes, the debate of Gandhi and Ambedkar still tend to find important episodes. History pitted Gandhi and Ambedkar as adversaries. Their public exchanges were marked by acrimony (Palshikar, 2015). But, it is hard to negate that they were complementary to each other at a fundamental level.

The trajectory of Gandhi evolved over time. But Gandhi since his inception as a social reformer stressed the idea of *self-purification* (Nagraj, 2010). For Gandhi, it is not the untouchables practising untouchability or caste system; it is the *Savarna* group, hence they have to purify their minds and hearts. Gandhi wanted behavioural redemption to clean caste (Bayly, 2003). But, the whole epistemology and discourse of Gandhi is today a topic of moot among historians. His initial stand on *Varna* and caste has bestowed on him a number of critics. It is true that Gandhi revisited traditions but he tried to make them the bearers of interdependence, responsibility and freedom (Rodrigues, 2011). His own writings reflected that approach, on *Varna* he wrote:

> "The law of *Varna* is the antithesis of competition which it kills" (CWMG, 1998).

Gandhi never hesitated to change his stand if he is not satisfied with traditions. Gandhi knew how to risk his popularity (Lohia, 1964). It was the evolving progressive perception of Gandhi which allowed him to declare that *"caste has to go"* (Mukherjee, 1993). The personality of Gandhi was enigmatic and the tragedy with Gandhi was that his colleagues in national movement either did not understood his concern with caste and untouchability or even actively deplored it:

> "One can point finger upon Gandhi and term his evolution as vacillations. But he himself opined that–" (Mukherjee, 1993).

The contemporary discourse criticises Gandhi as if the abolition of the caste system as a whole – lock, stock and Barrel – was quite possible ready at hand, and Gandhi alone stood on the way (Ray, 1996). To negate Gandhi's work as a political stunt is a naïve thought. He was the one who vouched for Ambedkar's Ministry India's first interim cabinet. The roots and branches of casteism still exist and have grown tremendously with political development. Gandhi's vision of self-purification needs a detour because he reminded the leaders of future repercussions of what can happen; if caste and untouchability are not erased from the minds and hearts of wrongdoers.

Ambedkar was a radical leader and his whole idea of emancipation gyrates around the idea of self-respect (Nagraj, 2010). Moral and political framework, which Ambedkar perceived was derived from the European enlightenment paradigm (Rodrigues, 2011; Lelyveld, 2011; Guha, 2010). The radicalisation that manifested in Ambedkar placed *Dalit* struggle on the forefront of nationalist agenda. The political clashes and bonhomie between him and Gandhi changed the whole discourse of social reform. The initial political phase of

Ambedkar was inspired by Gandhi and "*Mahad Satyagraha*" was an example of it (Omvedt, 2004). But the whole approach of Congress and Gandhi frustrated him. He realised that Gandhi was moving slow (Jaffrelot, 2016). Ambedkar became the visible leader of *Dalits* and tried to carve out the political arena for them. "*We want to become the ruling community*" was the viewpoint of Ambedkar (Patankar, 1979).

Gandhi and Ambedkar differed in their understanding of modernity, in assessing traditions and in proposing the options for India and the world. Social actions based on modernity became an essential tool for Ambedkar. Liberty, equality and fraternity to all the oppressed classes was the dream of Ambedkar. The contemporary discourse which carries the legacy of Ambedkar has limited his ideas to the political power and ionisation. It is true that Ambedkar had considered political action as one of the untouchables' instruments of emancipation (Jaffrelot, 2016). But one cannot nullify the fact he also wrote and opined that:

> "Political democracy cannot succeed where there is no social and economic democracy." (Rodrigues, 2002).

Dr. Ambedkar and Gandhi thought through different paradigms and spoke about different frameworks (Palshikar, 2015). Three interrelated and overlapping issues constituted the core of their exchanges – the issue of representation of the depressed classes; removal of untouchability; and the case of caste question. If looked rationally, beyond their acrimonious discourse and varied trajectories; the concern for oppressed masses and their emancipation was their final agenda.

Notwithstanding their legacies, Ambedkarites and Gandhites dominate the present discourse. The Ambedkarites ideology of political power and divisive agendas has negated the work of Ambedkar; they are not at all concerned about the annihilation of caste. Anand Teltumbde opines if Ambedkarite ideology is of the annihilation of castes, there are a number of Ambedkarites who proclaim to the contrary and still claim to be Ambedkarites (Teltumbde, 2012). On the contrary, the travesty with Gandhites is that they never supported his idea of self-purification in past and presently they have reduced his cult only to a political reformer, not a social one; in fear of vote bank politics.

Any attempt to find a syncretise ground between the two leaders for future prospects either becomes a naïve phenomenon or a ***"Spontaneous Gandhian Argument"***. In spite of interrogating their ideas in a holistic manner, the whole issue of casteism thrives upon the fake and half-baked ideas of them; produced in front of masses. These divisive discourses have created stagnation and fragmentation, which in turn have created subversion in the politics and policies of social justice (Yadav, 2012). If politics is limited to elections; the policies for social justice are just related to reservations.

The apprehensions of Ambedkar about political democracy before social and economic were reflected in his writings. *Social and economic democracies are the tissues and the fibre of political democracy*; he wrote (Rodrigues, 2002). This was similar to the worries of Mahatma Gandhi's inclusive society and *Swaraj*. Both the leaders firmly believed that democracy should thrive upon social fluidity and engagement. The roots of Democracy as Ambedkar opined in his last days, are to be searched in social relationships. Both Gandhi and Ambedkar must have been aware of the reality that caste could not be destroyed with only one weapon. They both, therefore, kept exploring multiple strategies and approaches to the issue of social change (Palshikar, 2015). Gandhi and Ambedkar both worked as a catalyst for each other. It was not only Gandhi who evolved with time; Ambedkar's personality also witnessed several Ambedkars at given space and time.

Conclusion

Nobel laureate Amartya Sen, who also happens to be one of the great thinkers of our times on Justice; have departed from John Rawls "*Theory of Justice*". This departure gyrates around the whole idea of ***"Niti and Nyaya"***, which he took from classical Indian philosophy. *Niti* which deals with Institutions and principles of justice should be tested through the actual social realization of those institutions. This latter phenomenon is related to *Nyaya* and comprises the core of Sen's ***"Idea of Justice"*** (Sen, 2010). "*Sarvodaya* through *Antyodaya*" or *Swaraj* was the core principle of Gandhi's idea of justice, which can be defined as synonym of Ambedkar's Social endosmosis and to the Sen's idea of *Nyaya*.

Contemporary India today lacks the fluidity or free mobility among individuals without any social stratification. Ambedkar had defined this whole concept as "***Social Endosmosis***" in his writings. Ambedkar firmly believed that the endosmosis project is blocked because society is divided into privileged and subject class. He through his constitutional and political project wanted that endosmosis to be programmed for Indian society. Gandhi respected the sheer radicalism of Ambedkar and supported his ideas. But Gandhi firmly believed that without the Self-Purification any such kind of endosmosis is impossible. His Views on Article 17 of the Indian Constitution projects his deep understanding of Indian society. He appreciated the revolutionary step but also showed its limitations; that untouchability has to be purged out from the hearts and minds of the people (*CWMG*, 1998).

An impasse exists in the whole aspect of social justice as well as with the policies and politics attached to it. It is the need of the hour that contemporary political framework should turn back and look onto the path tracked. Gandhi-Ambedkar's discourse has not only provided the hope for social justice in past, but, it also defines the upliftment that Indian social movement has made till now. The intellectual energies of both should be utilised for comprehending and fighting against the on-going struggle. It should not be narrowed down for creating differences among the masses and dividing them into two separate blocs.

Founding fathers of India knew that the political democracy shall become the reality with the Constitution of India. But, the journey towards socio-economic democracies had, in fact, has to start with its promulgation. The crisis of inequalities was/is still defined the realities of new the nation. On 25th November, 1949, the day before the constituent assembly wound up its work Dr. Bhimrao Ramji Ambedkar (The architect of India's Constitution) reminded the whole nation that mere political democracy was not the "only" idea that their leaders fought for and urge Indians not to feel content with it only. He gave three warnings to the new nation and the third was perhaps the most prominent one; in a moving speech he opined:

> India had got rid of the alien rule, but it was still riven by inequality and hierarchy. Thus, once country formally became a republic on 26 January, 1950, it was going to enter a life of new contradictions. In Politics, we will have equality and in social and economic life, we will have inequality. In Politics, we will be recognizing the principle of one man one vote

> and one vote one value. In our social and economic life we shall, by reason of our social and economic structure, continue to deny the principle of one man one value. How long shall we continue to live this life of contradictions? How long shall we continue to deny equality in our social and economic life? If we continue to deny it for long, we will do so only by putting our Political democracy in peril (*Collected Works of Dr. B.R. Ambedkar*, 2014).

Politicisation of caste and iconization of leaders represents a kind of paradoxes. India's success in building and consolidating a vibrant democracy remains unequalled in the political world. But, ironically, it had betrayed the very idea of social justice and equality enshrined in its constitution. India's "*Tryst with Caste Inequalities and Injustice*" continues.

References

Ambedkar, Dr. Babasaheb (2014). *Writings and Speeches of Dr. Babasaheb Ambedkar (17 Volumes)*: Ministry of Social Justice and Empowerment, Government of India. Retrieved from: http://www.mea.gov.in/books-writings-of-ambedkar.htm

Anand, S. (ed). (2013). *Annihilation of Caste: The Annotated critical edition B.R. Ambedkar*. New Delhi: Navyana Publishing Pvt. Ltd.

Ananth, Krishna V. (2014). *Politics in the Times of Churning: A Journalist Perception*. Madurai: Daya Publications.

Bayly, Susan. (2011). *Caste, Society and Politics in India: From the Eighteenth Century to the Modern Age*. New Delhi: Cambridge University Press.

Constitution Assembly Debates (CAD). 1946 – 1950. Retrieved from: http://parliamentofindia.nic.in/ls/debates/debates.htme

Crisis of Ambedkarites and Future Challenges By Anand Teltumbde. (n.d.). Retrieved from: https://www.countercurrents.org/teltumbde220411.html

Gandhi, Mahatma. (1998). *Collected Works of Mahatma Gandhi (CWMG: 98 Volumes)*. Retrieved from: http://www.gandhiserve.org/e/cwmg/cwmg.htme

Gandhi, R. (2015). Independence and Social Justice. *Economic & Political Weekly*, *50*(15): 35.

Ghurye, G.S., *Caste and Race In India*, New Delhi: Sage Publications India Pvt. Ltd.

Guha, Ramchandra. (2001). *An Anthropologist Among Marxists and other Essays*. New Delhi: Permanent Black.

Guha, Ramchandra. (2013). *Gandhi before Gandhi*. New Delhi: Penguin Books.

Gupta, Dipankar. (2000). *Interrogating Caste: Understanding Hierarchy and Difference in India Society.* New Delhi: Penguin Random House.

Jaffrelot, Christophe. (2016). *Analysing and Fighting Caste: Dr. Ambedkar and Untouchability*. New Delhi: Permanent Black.

Kothari, Rajani. (2016). *Caste in Indian Politics*. New Delhi: Orient Black Swan.

Lelyveld, Joseph. (2011). *Great Soul: Mahatma Gandhi and His Struggle with India*. New Delhi: Harper & Collins Publishers India.

Limaye, Madhu. (1995). *Manu, Gandhi and Ambedkar and Other Essays*. New Delhi: Gyan Publishing House.

Lohia, Rammanohar. (1964). *The Caste System*. Hyderabad: Navahind Prakashan.

Momin, A.R. (2005). *The Legacy of Ghurye: A Centennial Festschrift*. New Delhi: Popular Prakashan.

Mukherjee, Rudrangshu (ed.).(1993). *The Penguin Gandhi Reader*. Haryana: Penguin Books.

Nagraj, D.R. (2010). *The Flaming Feet and Other Essays: The Dalit Movement in India*. New Delhi: Permanent Black.

Nehru, J. (2004). *The Discovery of India*. Gurgaon: Penguin Books.

Omvedt, Gail (1993). *Dalits and the Democratic Revolution: Dr. Ambedkar and the Dalit Movement in Colonial India*. New Delhi: Sage Publications.

Omvedt, Gail. (2004). *Ambedkar: Towards an Enlightened India*. Haryana: Penguin Books.

Palshikar, S. (1996). Gandhi-Ambedkar Interface. When Shall the Twain Meet? *Economic and Political Weekly*, 2070-2072.

Palshikar, Suhas. (2014). Ambedkar and Gandhi: Limits of Divergence and Possibilities of Conversation. Unpublished work.

Patankar, B., and Omvedt, G. (1979). The Dalit liberation movement in colonial period. *Economic and Political Weekly*, 409-424.

Rodrigues, V. (2011). Reading Texts and Traditions: The Ambedkar-Gandhi Debate. *Economic and Political Weekly*, 56-66.

Rodrigues, Valerian. (2008). *The Essential Writings of B.R. Ambedkar.* New Delhi: Oxford University Press.

Sen, Amartya. (2005). *The Argumentive Indian: Writings on Indian Culture, History and Identity.* New Delhi: Penguin Books.

Sen, Amartya. (2010). *The Idea of Justice*. New Delhi: Penguin Books.

Srinivas, M.N. (1957). Caste in Modern India. *The Journal of Asian Studies*, *16*(4): 529-548.

Staff, T.W. (2016, July 28). *What Is Manual Scavenging*? Retrieved from: https://thewire.in/rights/what-is-manual-scavenging

Teltumbde, A. (2015). *In Thy Name, Ambedkar*.

Teltumbde, A. Ambedkarites against Ambedkar, *Economic and Political Weekly*, 3 May, 2013, www.epw.in/journal/2013/19/margin-speak-columns/ambedkarites-against-ambedkar.html.

Tharoor, S. (2016): *An Era of Darkness: The British Empire in India*, New Delhi: Aleph Book Company.

Venkat, V. (2016, April 06). *Manual Scavenging Still a Reality*. Retrieved from: https://www.thehindu.com/news/national/manual-scavenging-still-a-reality-socioeconomic-caste-census/article7400578.ece

Yadav, Y. (n.d.). *Rethinking Social Justice*. Retrieved from: http://www.india-seminar.com/2009/601/601_yogendra_yadav.html

6

Revisiting Phule and Ambedkar Approaches of Social Justice and its Relevance in Contemporary Social Work Practice

Shashi Rani

Introduction

Social work practice is based on values of social justice, human worth and dignity, the importance of human relationship, integrity, competence (NASW, Code of Ethics, 2017). In this context, it is worth to trace the history of Indian social transformation and approaches used by different social reformers. Mahatma Joyti Rao Phule and Dr. B.R. Ambedkar were among the first thinkers who made efforts to draw attention to the genesis of caste, its impact on contemporary Indian society. They not only emphasized the protection of human rights, dignity, inclusiveness and social justice but also in the contemporary context, they challenged the hegemony of religion and structural arrangement. They advocated for the protection of human dignity and rights for marginalized communities. The social work profession also advocates for human dignity and rights of marginalised. The global definition of social work profession defines, "Social work is a practice-based profession and an academic discipline that promotes social change and development, social cohesion, and the empowerment and liberation of people. Principles of social justice, human rights, collective responsibility and respect for diversities are central to social work. Underpinned by theories of social work, social sciences, humanities and indigenous knowledge, social work engages people and structures to address life challenges and enhance well-being (IFSW, 2014). This definition has a very broad meaning to promote the well-being of the local community through the concert and continuous engagement. It emphasizes that in practice for change and liberation of the people while fostering the values of social justice and human rights. Thus, it becomes important to train the social workers to explore the indigenous methods of social transformation by addressing the issue of structural inequalities.

Indian society is known for its religious and cultural diversity. This will not be an exaggeration if we define the Indian society as a complex mix of the rigid structure with liberal dreams. This complexity needs to address by the social work academia by generating knowledge on historical structural rigidity and efforts to made by social activist to bring change in the social and political domain. Among this rigid structural arrangement, religion and caste are important matters to discuss in the context of Indian society. The caste question today is no longer simply an academic matter, a subject for empirical enquiry and analysis. We must begin our engagement with caste today by recognizing these complicated intellectual landscapes in which contemporary discourses on the subject are being carried out (Jodhka, 2015).

Mahatma Joyti Rao Phule and Dr. B.R. Ambedkar were among the first thinkers of marginalized communities who made efforts to draw attention to the genesis of caste, structural inequalities and its impact on contemporary Indian society. They fought against the deliberate attempt of creation of social inequalities through popular Hindu religious beliefs. Mahatma Jyoti Rao Phule and Dr. B.R. Ambedkar adopted the approach which was based on principles of protection of human rights, dignity, inclusiveness and social justice. They challenged the hegemony of religion and structural arrangement. They advocated for the protection of human dignity and rights for marginalized communities. In this context, the chapter is focusing on the philosophical groundings and approaches adopted by these change agents and activists to address the issue of caste discrimination and marginalization of certain communities. Further, an attempt is made to locate the issue of caste in contemporary times and challenges it is posing in modern societies.

The social work academia must recognize the efforts of the social thinkers and change agents who were influenced by their lived experiences and engaged themselves in protecting Human rights values and dignity of the individual. Thus, the focus is on to revisit Mahatma Joyoti Rao Phule and Dr. B.R. Ambedkar approaches of Social Justice and its relevance in contemporary Social Work Practice.

To revisit their approach it is quite important to discuss the process of marginalization of some communities and their social exclusion in India. Broadly marginalization refers to structures and processes in which individuals and entire communities of people are systematically blocked from rights, opportunities and resources (e.g. housing, employment, healthcare, civic engagement, democratic participation) that are normally available to members of society and which are key to social integration. Marginalization appears in our everyday life it is real and constructed. We cannot achieve a state of social justice without addressing the issue of marginalization. There can be a different approach and ways to deal with the issue of marginalization. The people who are deprived/marginalized are outside the existing systems of protection and integration. This limits their opportunities and means for survival. When it excludes the communities for centuries, it becomes the matter of debate and protest. Human history provides evidence and therefore the process of marginalisation and purpose of dominant power to operate this is important to discuss. As Oommen rightly described that:

> Human history can be viewed through different lenses—history of class struggle, of creating marginals, of excluding people from mainstream. On the other hand, it could also be seen as gradual inclusion of erstwhile marginals into mainstream. Exclusion is nothing new in human history; it is a normal social fact in the Durkheimian sense of the term in that one cannot visualise a society entirely exempt from social exclusion. But one must recognise the nature and types of exclusion to evolve a strategy of inclusion, which can be formulated and implemented so that avoidable exclusions can be eliminated and the intensity of inevitable ones be reduced. Even in the much acclaimed direct democracy of ancient Greek city-states, the slaves were completely excluded, the plebeians grudgingly included, and only the patricians fully included in the decision-making processes. Ancient India's patricians were caste-Hindus consisting of

> Brahmans, Kshatriyas, and Vaishyas; the plebian's were today's Backward Classes, the Shudras above the pollution line. the untouchables of those days were worse than slaves, totally excluded from all aspects of public life (Oommen, 2014).

The Issue of Caste in Contemporary Times and Challenges in Modern Societies

India is largest Democracy and second most populated nation (17.5% share of world population) and the largest concentration of Hindus in the world. According to 2011 census is not available in public domain on religious segregation of population, but according to 2001 census, 80.5 per cent population are Hindu in India (IHDS, 2015). Hindu religion has the very distinct feature of the caste-based division of Hindu population. There are numerous Castes and around 3000 castes are in existence in India. The issue of caste has a problem in its order which is based on hierarchy and thus restricting the social mobility of the Hindu society. It divided society into four *varnas*, 'Brahmin', 'Kshatriya', 'Vaishyas' and 'Shudra', and untouchables as '*Avarnas*'. Historically, the social, economic and political rights were as per the strict social hierarchical order and nobody was allowed to change or challenge this order. It has a various adverse effect especially on those who were at lower hierarchy 'Shudras and Untouchables' and were forced to serve other and to consider it as their duty and not to challenge it (Pannikkar, 1933). They were assigned lower level jobs and social status and future generations were also supposed to follow that order. IHDS (2015) published the paper and revealed that untouchables (*Dalits*) still perform menial jobs that are traditionally considered polluting and assigned to them. The untouchability was abolished constitutionally, but it continues in private social interaction and in public sector jobs. The Indian railways employ 3,00,000 manual scavengers on a contractual basis. SKA also studied the problem of manual scavenging and profiled 6,709 manual scavengers. Further IHDS (2015) study found that 30 per cent of household in rural areas reported practising Untouchability and 20 per cent in urban areas. Among Religious groups 35 per cent Jains practising Untouchability, followed by 30 per cent Hindus, 23 per cent Sikhs, 18 per cent Muslims, 5 per cent Christians, 5 per cent Tribals and 1 per cent Buddhist. The study found that education plays important role in having a negative inclination of practising Untouchability.

The problem of caste in Hindu society lies in the arrangement of its social order, which dictates terms and conditions of religious practices, social mobility, economic activities and accumulation of political power. It is evident that this hierarchical order is not serving any good to people who are at lower in the hierarchy and social status rather it is violating their basic human rights of survival with dignity and freedom. As critically analysed by Dr. B.R. Ambedkar in his writings on Hindu Social Order:

> "The Hindus are only people in the world whose social order—the relation of man to man is concerted by religion and made sacred, eternal and inviolate. The Hindus are the only people in the world whose economic order —the relation of workman to workman, is consecrated by religion and made sacred, eternal and inviolate".
>
> (*Dr. Ambedkar Writings and Speeches*, Department of Education, Government of Maharashtra, 1987, volume III, pp. 95-129).

Dr. B.R. Ambedkar strongly put forward his views on caste and wrote in Annihilation of Caste (1936),

> "Caste is no doubt primarily the breath of the Hindus. But the Hindus have fouled the air all over and everybody is infected, Sikh, Muslim and Christian. You, therefore deserve the support of all those who are suffering from this infection, Sikh, Muslim, and Christian. Yours is more difficult than the other national cause, namely *Swaraj*. In the fight for *Swaraj*, you fight with the whole nation on your side. In this, you have to fight against the whole nation and that too, your own. But it is more important than *Swaraj*. There is no use having *Swaraj* if you cannot defend it. More important than the question of defending *Swaraj* is the question of defending the Hindus under *Swaraj*, in my opinion only when Hindus society becomes a casteless society that it can hope to have strength enough to defend itself. Without such internal

> strength, *Swaraj* for Hindus may turn out to be only a step towards slavery."

It is worth to relate his speech to the contemporary sociological assessment of caste issue in India. Even in Independent India this caste system affecting many generations over the period of time due to its religious sanction and unchangeable nature. Indian Constitution adopted by Independent India laid down the Fundamental Rights to every citizen of India. In its Article 17 Indian Constitution abolished the practice of Untouchability in any form. India also formed the legislations to deal with the problem of atrocities against Scheduled Castes and Scheduled Tribes (SC/ST) people. These are Untouchability Offence Act, 1955, Protection of Civil Rights Act of 1976 and Scheduled Caste, Scheduled Tribe Prevention of Atrocities Act, 1989. The aim to enact these legislations was to prevent and provide legal remedies in case of caste-based atrocities or violence. Though the Indian Government after the independence officially abolished the practice of Untouchability in social life, it is not able to remove that heinous practice from the Indian society. The reason lies in the existence of religion based caste hierarchy in society, especially in Hindu Religion. This problem of caste not only affecting the people of lower caste, but also pushing India into backwardness due to inability to deal with social and economic development issues. As prominent sociologist studied the caste issue in India and found that "*The available literature from different regions of India shows that though the older structures of social and economic life have been declining, prejudice against the untouchables has not gone away, and in some regions it remains quite strong*" (*Navsarjan* and RFK Centre, 2009; Shah *et al.* 2006) in (Jodhka, 2015).

The country is witnessing the result of this structural inequality in form of caste-based crime and atrocities in Independent India. If we look at the last 16 years data of National Crime Record Bureau (NCRB) since 2001 to 2016 it shows that atrocities cases in 2001- 34 per cent, 2004 - 23.4 per cent, 2006 - 23 per cent, 2008 - 31 per cent, 2010 - 38.4 per cent, 2012 - 19 per cent, 2014 - 17 per cent, 2016 - 16 per cent. This is clearly indicating the existence of caste-based hierarchy and dominance of upper caste on lower caste in independent India. There are several cases and incidence of atrocities happene in India which grabbed the national media attention. Further, if we analysed the caste issue from social, economic and political development and social exclusion viewpoint we need to be careful in adopting the approach to look at the issue of caste problem. Generalisation of social problems with caste issue will not be able to serve the objective to create an inclusive society in Independent India. The various academicians indulged in explaining the concept of social exclusion from a development viewpoint and in this context Professor Amartya Sen's observation are important to mention. Amartya Sen (2000) conceptualised the social exclusion and listed out the parameters to assess the exclusion of certain marginalised communities. The parameters he discussed are livelihood insecurity, chronic unemployment, inadequate consumption levels and nutrients, and had poor housing and education. Further, he suggested that "an individual's capacity to relate to others and participate in community life can also result in social exclusion. Thus, it is evident that a wide range of practices is believed to be resulting in social exclusion, leaving very few in the category of included". Buvinic and Mazza (2005) conceptualised the social exclusion as "the denial of equal accesses to opportunities imposed by certain groups of society upon other". About this explanation Oommen (2014) stated that "If one follows the conceptualisation of Sen and Buvinic and Mazza, the vast majority of humans remain socially excluded" further he added that groups such as tribes, lower caste are victims of social construction by dominant groups. Thus, we need social morphology of the socially excluded in order to pursue a meaningful policy of social inclusion. The Social Work Professionals committed to create inclusive society and removal of discrimination of all forms, it is quite important to understand and conceptualise the caste issue from logical framework and approach adopted by Mahatma Jyoti Rao Phule and Dr. B.R. Ambedkar whose work is very well recognised internationally for emancipation and empowerment of the socially excluded community.

In India, this institutionalized structural inequalities in the form of caste division in Hindu religion and marginalization of a lower caste was first strongly challenged by Mahatma Jyoti Rao Phule and Dr. B.R. Ambedkar. They brought awareness among the illiterate masses of India and worked on many social issues and problems. They worked for removal of untouchability and structural inequality, removal of irrational beliefs and blind following of Hindu religion, they advocated for social democracy, social mobility, protection of human rights through social action and policy, legal remedies against discrimination, the constitutional protection against violation of rights and so on.

Social Movement and Campaigns Led by Jyoti Rao Phule

The first formal debate on eradication of caste system was initiated by Mahatma Jyoti Rao Phule (11 April, 1827 to 28 November, 1890). Mahatma Jyoti Rao Phule who was born on 11th April, 1827 in Satara district belonged to *Mali* community. He studied in English convent school during his schooling. He learned about social issues and need of social reforms in India. Though he was educated and learned person he experienced caste-based discrimination in social life and this led to raise questions against the legitimacy of the caste system and to work for *shudras* (untouchables) who were deprived of all their rights as human beings under the caste system (Sirswal, 2013).

He challenged the oppressive practices based on popular religious ideas. His efforts were focused on education and social change to remove structural inequalities and caste hierarchies. He emphasized rational thinking over blind worship of imaginary ideals/God. His efforts were made to ensure State responsibility and government duty in British period to educate all through proper allocation on budget. He led many movements and campaign. These were based on Right to Education, Women Empowerment, Removal of Untouchability, Peasant Rights and the problem of Corruption, Protection of Child Rights etc.

On 1st January, 1848, India's first school for girls was started at Bhide's Wada in Pune by Mahatma Jyoti Rao Phule and his wife Savitribai Phule. Savitribai Phule started Mahila Seva Mandal in 1852, which worked for raising women's consciousness about their human rights, the dignity of life and other social issues. She went on to organise a successful barbers strike in Mumbai and Pune against the prevailing practice of shaving of widows' heads. On 28 January, 1853, first ever infanticide prohibition home of India was started by Savitribai Phule. In 1863, first ever orphanage home was started by Mahatma Joyti Rao Phule and Savitribai Phule, hence gave protection to pregnant widows. On 28 January, 1866, Vishnushastri, inspired by Phule's movement opened an institution to promote widow remarriage. The institution (a society) was known as *Punar Vivahtojak Mandal* (remarriage association). On 16th November, 1852, Phule family was honoured by the British government for their works in the field of education and Savtribai was declared as the best teacher.

Mahatma Jyoti Rao Phule's famous work "*Gulamgiri*" came into the public domain in 1873. He highlighted the issue of corruption and exploitation of workers (untouchables). At a time when even the shadow of untouchables was considered impure when the people were unwilling to offer water to thirsty untouchables, Savitribai Phule and Mahatma Jyoti Rao Phule opened the well in their house for the use of untouchables. He challenged the popular religious beliefs through his writing. He brought out the struggle of marginalized communities due to caste-based hierarchies. He pointed out lower representation and lack of authority of lower caste in political and social domain due to illiteracy and imposition of caste through religion.

As we know Mahatma Jyoti Rao Phule struggled and fought as a social reformer and revolutionary activist, but remains under dark in the domain of social work curriculum and very little known even in academia. Mahatma Joyti Rao Phule and his wife Savitri Bai Phule addressed many social issues and problems throughout their life. They worked for the upliftment of marginalized communities through knowledge dissemination, awareness generation, advocacy and social action. Their contribution should be part of knowledge dissemination through social work curriculum. Mahatma Jyoti Rao Phule was a courageous mass leader who took on the forces of caste and patriarchy. It is unfortunate that this historical important figure fails to find any mention in the history of Social Work across India. His life and struggle deserve to be known to a wider group of learner and efforts should be made to disseminate his ideas to a larger body of Social Work Professionals.

Dr. B.R. Ambedkar's Philosophical Approach

Dr. Bhimrao Ramji Ambedkar was born on 14th April, 1891 in Mahu Cantt in Madhya Pradesh. He was the fourteenth child of his parents. The life of Dr. Bhimrao Ramji Ambedkar (14th April, 1981 to 6th December, 1956) was marked by struggles but he proved that every hurdle in life can be surmounted with talent and firm determination. The biggest barrier in his life was the caste system adopted by the Hindu society according to which the family he was born in was considered 'untouchable (Ambedkar Foundation, GOI, 2018).

Dr. B.R. Ambedkar adopted the approach of Social Justice and the attainment of individual rights through legal remedies. His writings are as relevant today as were at the time when these were penned. He firmly believed that our political democracy must stand on the base of social democracy which means a way of life which recognizes liberty, equality and fraternity as the principles of life. He educated people on constitutional rights, according to him if we want to maintain democracy not merely in form, but also in fact, we must hold fast to constitutional methods of achieving our social and economic objectives. He advocated for individual rights and that in our political, social and economic life, we must have the principle of one man, one vote, one value".

He emphasized on measuring the progress of a community by the degree of progress which women have achieved. He focussed on women issues; health, sanitation, education, work participation, maternity benefits. More particularly he advocated for women social and economic rights. He proposed Hindu Code Bill which intended mainly: (1) to abolish different marriage systems prevalent among Hindus and to establish monogamy as the only legal system; (2) Conferment of right to property and adoption on women; (3) restitution of conjugal rights and judicial separation; attempts to unify the Hindu Code in tune with progressive and modern thought. He opposed child marriages and *devdasi* system. He focused on labour issues, trade unions and labour welfare and social security.

Social Movement and Campaigns Led by Dr. B.R. Ambedkar

Dr. B.R. Ambedkar created awareness among poor, illiterate women and inspired them to fight against the unjust and social practices like child marriages and *devdasi* system. In the Kalram Temple entry *Satyagraha* at Nasik in 1930, five hundred women participated and many of them were arrested along with men and ill-treated in jails. The historic *Mahad Satyagrah* (1927) led by Dr. B.R. Ambedkar witnessed participation of three hundred women along with their male counterparts. The goal of *Mahad Stayagrah* was to protect rights of untouchables to access water equally from the public sources of water. In the same year burning of *Manusmriti* (Hindu religion first guiding book or Law of Manu) was one of radical action movement initiated by Dr. B.R. Ambedkar. The movement organized at different temples in Pune and Nasik in Maharashtra with the demand to access of untouchables in Hindu temple. The goal of these movements was to remove all old practices which divide society in the name of religion and caste and to reconstruct society on the basis of liberty, equality and fraternity.

He also used print media for circulation of information and awareness on social inequalities issues through periodicals namely '*Mooknayak*' (1920), '*Bahishkrit Bharat*' (1927), '*Samatha*' (1929) and '*Janata*' (1930). On 20th July, 1942, The All India Dalit Mahila Conference was organized and 25,000 women attended that conference. He also emphasized on to secure political rights for untouchables and placed his demand for having separate electoral for untouchables, which did not get approval from M.K. Gandhi. But in 1932 *Puna Pact* happened which guaranteed the reserved seats for untouchables to have equal political representation. He also formed Independent labour party to raise the awareness on social and political issues of marginalized and socially excluded communities of India. He utilized his experienced caste discrimination to emancipate and empower the religiously and socially excluded communities.

He was influenced by the writings of Karl Marx and Buddha philosophy. He advocated for social and political equality and to reconstruct the society on the principle of human rights protection and social inclusion. He advocated for fighting for rights by adopting legal remedies and non-violence approach. His ideology and philosophical views reflected in the Constitution of India. This guiding book for Independent India based on the philosophy of social justice and well-being through the adoption of principles of equality, liberty and fraternity. In order to maintain these principles Constitution of India secured "Fundamental Rights" for citizens of India and Responsibility of state ensured through "Directive Principles of State Policy".

In 1956, Dr. B.R. Ambedkar took an extreme radical call to convert his religion from Hindu to Buddhism. He was a mass leader who worked day night for the upliftment of the socially excluded community (untouchables) and conversion from Hindu religion to Buddhism was his one of bold steps to give a message to the nation about eradication of caste-based discrimination else people will find other religion in search of equality. He calls upon the Hindus to Annihilate of Caste which is a great hindrance to social solidarity and the demands to set up a new social order based on the ideals of equality, liberty and fraternity in order to create social democratic country under political democratic nation.

United Nations (UN) in 2017, recognised him as a symbol of knowledge and declared as a world leader. United States (US) parliament passed a Bill to celebrate 14th April in memory of Dr.

B.R. Ambedkar contribution to human society. Columbia University recognised his presence in the list of all scholars since its inception and it is a matter of proud for India that in 100 people list Dr. B.R. Ambedkar secured first ranking in this list. His ideas and approach to social justice are very well acknowledged at the global level by national and international scholars.

Way Forward

Social work and principle of social justice are inseparable, the guiding principles and philosophy are interlinked with each other. We need to mainstream the ideas of Mahatma Jyoti Rao Phule and Dr. B.R. Ambedkar in Social Work academia and areas of practice. As Social Work aimed to create change agents with knowledge of structural issues of our society, who can understand the local context with different perspectives, this is the time to address the structural inequality with rational assessment through quantitative and qualitative methods of exploration. India is a signatory to Sustainable Development Goal and became part of global social agenda to reduce all forms of Inequality. As Goal number 10 of Sustainable Development is "to reduce inequality within and among countries", Goal 16 of the Sustainable Development Goals is dedicated to the promotion of peaceful and inclusive societies for sustainable development, the provision of access to justice for all, and building effective, accountable institutions at all levels.

With this backdrop, it becomes important to trace the history of our indigenous practices and adopt the approaches that are suitable in the local context and appropriately address the issue of structural inequality and to create inclusive societies. In this context, Mahatma Jyoti Rao Phule and Dr. B.R. Ambedkar work are important to study and learn both of them focused on core issues of social inclusion and protection of human dignity by protecting human rights which is central to social work practice. Social workers/change agents must ensure that the empowering process must be continued by adopting legal methods. All forms of discrimination based on caste and gender need to challenged through legal measures. The social work profession must uphold its principles of Human Rights and Social Justice, as advocated by Mahatma Jyoti Rao Phule and Dr. B.R. Ambedkar we need to remind ourselves that the diversity must be enjoyed, but not at the condition of social division, which is based on birth hierarchies.

References

Ambedkar Foundation, GOI. (2018). Retrieved from: http://ambedkarfoundation.nic.in/html/profile-Drambedkar.pdf

Ambedkar, B.R. (2014). *Annihilation of Caste: The Annotated Critical Edition*. Verso Books.

Ambedkar, B.R., and Moon, V. (1987). *Dr. Babasaheb Ambedkar, Writings and Speeches* (Vol. 3). Education Department, Government of Maharashtra.

Ambedkar, B.R. *Who Were The Shudras*? Retrieved from: http://www.satnami.com/WHO%20WERE%20THESUDRAS.pdf

Basu, D.D. (1982). *Introduction to the Constitution of India*. Prentice-Hall of India.

International Federation of Social Workers. (n.d.). Retrieved from: https://www.ifsw.org/

Jodhka, S.S. (2017). *Caste in Contemporary India*. Routledge India.

National Crime Record Bureau (NCRB) Retrieved from: http//ncrb.gov.in/

Oommen, T.K. (2016). *Social Inclusion in independent India: Dimensions and Approaches*. Orient Black Swan.

Panikkar, K.M. (2004). *Caste and Democracy and Prospects of Democracy in India*. Critical Quest.

Sirswal, Desh Raj. (2013). Mahatma Jyotiba Phule: A Modern Indian Philosopher. *Darshan: International Referred Quarterly Research Journal for Philosophy and Yoga*. Year 1, pp. 28-36.

Slavery/*Gulamgiri* book by Mahatma Jyoti Rao Phule in Hindi and English (2017, April 11). Retrieved from https://drambedkarbooks.com/2015/04/06/slaverygulamgiri-book-by-mahatma-jotiba-phule-in-hindi-and-english/

Thorat, A., and Joshi, O. (2015). The continuing practice of untouchability in India: Patterns and mitigating influences. *India Human Development Study Working Paper, 3*.

Writings and Speeches of Babasaheb B.R. Ambedkar. (n.d.). Retrieved from: http://drambedkarwritings.gov.in/content/

7

Dr. B.R. Ambedkar's Model of Community Organization and Social Action

Amod Gurjar

Introduction

In July 1924, Ambedkar founded the "Bahishkrit Hitkarini Sabha", to fight the evil of untouchability.[1] Speaking on the occasion of the foundation of the Bahishkrit Hitakarini Sabha, the organisation which heralded his public life as the leader of the *Dalits*, Ambedkar declared that the motto of the organisation would be **"Educate, Agitate and Organise."**[2] As it was beginning of the organization process. Then after he insisted that to his *Dalit* people, "Educate to organize and to Struggle" for their own betterment using whatever educational facilities (Pandey & Singh, 2016). This was the basic ideology of Dr. B.R. Ambedker to drive *Dalit* movement in India. *Dalit* movement in India is one of the most successful and result oriented movement till the date. The movement which was initiated in July 1924 by initiating Bahishkrit Hitkaraini Sabha is still going on. This could be one of the longest social movements even in world. Even the death of Dr. B.R. Ambedkar could not stop it. The movement is still going on with different leaderships. This basically reflects the professional manner adopted by Dr. B.R. Ambedkar to drive *Dalit* Movement in India. His vision, methods and techniques for this movement can strongly linked with the Professional Social Work in India especially in concern with Community Organization and Social Action.

What is Community Organization?

Community organization covers a series of activities at the community level aimed at bringing about desired improvement in the social well being of individuals, groups and neighbourhoods.

It is being often used synonymous to community work, community development and community mobilization. It can represent both community-based organizations, operating as civil society non-profits, and also as a function of organizing within communities defined by geographical location, shared work space, and/or shared experience or concerns. Community organizing is a democratic instrument to create sustained social change. Community organization is a process by which a community identifies needs and takes action, and in doing so develops co-operative attitudes and practices (Murray G. Ross, 1967).[3]

Murray G. Ross in 1955 defined community organisation as a process by which community identifies its needs or objectives, orders (or ranks) these needs or objectives, develops the confidence and will to work at these needs or objectives, finds the resources (internal and/or external) to deal with these needs or objectives takes action in respect to them and in so doing extends and develops co-operative and collaborative attitudes and practices in the community.

What Is Social Action?

Social action as a method of social work can be defined as efforts to bring about change or prevent change in current social practices or situations, through education, propaganda, persuasion, or pressure on behalf of objectives believed by the actionists to be socially desirable. Generally, social action involves organised efforts to influence public opinion or official policy or executive action with the support of groups or individuals.[4]

Mary Richmand has defined social action as "Social action is mass betterment through propaganda and social legislation; a method of bringing about a change in the social environment of the clients."

"Mass betterment through propaganda and social legislation". This definition stresses on improving the condition of huge sections of population as an aim of social action with propaganda and social legislations as main strategies.[5]

Ambedkar's Model of Community Organization and Social Action

Ambedkar was very much influenced by Dewey's ideas on scientific method, experimental approach, democracy and pragmatism in the field of education. He insisted to his *Dalit* people, **Educate to Organize and to Struggle** for their own betterment using whatever educational facilities.[6] Education develops the thinking ability which broadens the vision of the human being. Through the education the awareness and conscious about suffering gets developed. Once the conscious is developed then it leads to the organization of the community to agitate. His simplest idea behind it was making aware exploited community that they are exploited and they will get up and revolt. The basic crux of this three point model is to develop the consciousness through the education.

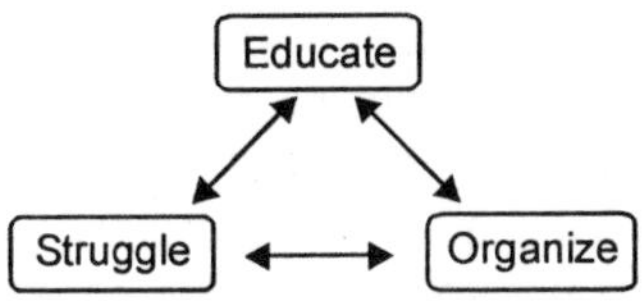

Fig. 7.1: Dr. B.R. Ambedkar's Model of Community Organization and Social Action.

What is Education?

Process of Education is that initial point where the thinking ability gets developed. Here the meaning of education is not limited to the formal type of education, but it is the education which makes you aware about the surrounding, your abilities, strengths, injustice, exploitation, oppression by developing conscious. Here, the education is the medium to liberate and enable the community and also helps to develop the decision making ability. Here the education also is medium of identifying available resources and optimum use of it.

In the Context of *Dalit* movement in India, Dr. B.R. Ambedkar focused complete *Dalit* community and educated them about their surrounding, abilities, strengths, injustice, exploitation, oppression and developed the consciousness among them, this basically was the main root of Ambedkar's *Dalit* Movement in India.

But when the education process starts it leads to mental agitation because humans are with set of knowledge and understanding, but when education stands in contradictory position then it leads with mental agitation. The word 'agitate' is not actually mean to agitate physically; it is a psychological process of revolution in its place. It does not mean to go out and start protesting violently on the streets, without getting educated. Here verbatim meaning of agitate need not to be taken in to the consideration. After getting educated, by understanding situation, the individual can start agitating mentally. Agitated mind, as Dr. Ambedkar presumed, would force educated people to form the problems. Many people, quite often, who profess Dr. B.R. Ambedkar, limit his slogan to these three points. But the actual message of Dr. Ambedkar lies in "have faith in your strength." (Pandey & Singh, 2016)

What is organization?

As education leads to the mental agitation and once the mental agitation is done then it becomes easy to organize community for a common mission. Once the community is organised for a common mission, it will help them to unite and struggle for their common goal as one force. This was even basic ideology adopted by Dr. B.R. Ambedkar in driving *Dalit* Movement in India. It was a key factor of achieving aim of *Dalit* movement in India.

What is Struggle?

Once the community is organised for a common mission, it will help them to unite and struggle for their common goal as one force. This struggle is with the power structure and the state. This we can also find in *Dalit* movement. The struggle has achieved basic rights and taken out entire community from the injustice, exploitation, oppression. This struggle was multidimensional in nature. It has covered social, religious, cultural, economic, and political aspects of life.

Can Dr. B.R. Ambedkar's Model consider as Model of Community Organization and Social Action?

For considering Dr. B.R. Ambedkar's Model there is need to match up this with the Definition of Community Organization and Social

Action. But before going to the main argument, there is need to understand the work done by Dr. B.R. Ambedkar.

Work done by Dr. B.R. Ambedkar

1920 : Started *Muknayak* Newspaper and spoke at a Depressed Classes conference in Mangaon in Kolhapur State.

1924 : Foundation of Bahishkrit Hitkarini Sabha.

1927 : Chavdar Talab Satyagrah, addressed a second Depressed Classes Conference in Mahad; he attacked the Laws of Manu and then a copy of this ancient text was publicly burned.

1929 : Dr. Ambedkar closed his second journal, "*Bahishkrit Bharat*" ("Excluded India"), which he had started in 1927, and replaced it with the "*Janata*" ("The People"), which was published until 1956, when it took on the name "*Prabuddha Bharata*" (after his conversion). Kalaram Mandir (Nasik) Satyagrah.

1930 : Participation in round table conference, Dr. Ambedkar presided over the Depressed Classes Congress at Nagpur.

1932 : The All-Indian Depressed Classes Conference, held at Kamtee near Nagpur on May 6th, backed Dr. Ambedkar's demand for separate electorates and the Poona Pact.

1935 : On October 13th, Dr. Ambedkar presided over the Yeola Conversion Conference, held in Yeola, in Nasik District. He advised the Depressed Classes to abandon all agitation for temple-entry privileges; instead, they should leave Hinduism entirely and embrace another religion. He vowed, "I solemnly assure you that I will not die as a Hindu."

1936 : Founded political party "The Independent Labour Party", The Maharaja of Travancore issued a proclamation allowing temple entry to the Depressed Classes, Conference of Maharaj Parishad.

1937 : Published second edition of *The Annihilation of Caste*

1938 : In January Congress adopted Gandhi's own term "*Harijans*" ("Children of God") as the official name for the "Scheduled Castes." In protest against a term that he considered condescending and meaningless, Dr.

Ambedkar and his party staged a walkout from the Bombay Legislative Assembly.

1942 : Founded political party "the All-India Scheduled Castes Federation".

1944 : Presided over the second meeting of the Scheduled Caste Federation, in Kanpur.

1945 : Addressed the Annual Conference of the All India Scheduled Caste Federation, held at Parel, Bombay (Now Mumbai).

1946 : Founded Siddharth College, in Bombay (Now Mumbai), and published "Who Were the Shudras? How They Came to Be the Fourth Varna in the Indo-Aryan Society".

1947 : Dr. Ambedkar accepted Nehru's invitation to become Minister of Law in the first Cabinet of Independent India. Appointed Chairman of the Drafting Committee for the New Constitution.

1948 : Published "The Untouchables: a Thesis on the Origin of Untouchability".

1949 : The Constituent Assembly adopted the Constitution, including Article 17, which formally abolished untouchability.

1951 : Introduced "Hindu Code Bill" in Parliament. Then resigned from the Cabinet and became the Leader of the Opposition.

1956 : Brought the manuscript of "*The Buddha and His Dhamma*", Conversion to Buddhism, Many thousands of *Mahars* and other *Dalits* accepted Buddhism along with him.[7]

By understanding all work done by Dr. B.R. Ambedkar, it can be strongly observed that the complete work was based educate, organise and struggle. Whereas, it also can be analysed that it was not only a community organization, but the social action too. In addition to this, it can be said firmly that his work was a well defined process, by which *Dalit* community identified their own needs or objectives and prioritised it, developed the confidence among the community, the will to work on needs and objectives has also been developed, internal and external resources were nicely identified and used, and to deal with these needs or objectives takes action in respect to them and develops co-operative and collaborative attitudes and practices in the community. All this points are mentioned in the definition of community organization given by Murray G. Ross.

This model also extends to the Social Action, a method of Social Work. The model has achieved mass betterment through propaganda and social legislation and brought about a change in the social environment of the *Dalit* community. This fulfils all the criteria mentioned in the definition of Social Action given by Mary Richmand.

Understanding all this discussion, it can be firmly said that Dr. B.R. Ambedkar's Model can be considered as Model of Community Organization and Social Action. It can also be said Dr. B.R. Ambedkar's trilogy Model of Community Organization and Social Action.

Key Argument

Social Work Education has completed more than eighty years in India. In the Indian society, there are numerous social problems. Hence, the methods related to working with communities and social action are more relevant than others.

Dr. B.R. Ambedkar Model of Community Organization and Social Action is well tested in Indian Context and had sound result to accept it as model in Social Work Education on the basis of analysis of *Dalit* movement in India and its result. The model also fulfils all the considerations, morals, values and principles of professional social work in India as well as at global level.

Most of the books in Social Work talks about various models of Community Organization and Social Action given by foreign or Western social activists or scientists. There are some models given by Indians too, but this model **Educate, Organise and Struggle** has not been recognised as Dr. B.R. Ambedkar's Model of community Organization and Social Action by the field of social work education in India. It is also missing in most of the syllabus of the Social Work course in India.

It is an appeal to the social work fraternity to accept it as model of community organization and social action as it is tested and result oriented in India. There is need to add this model in social work curriculum throughout country.

Notes

1. http://www.yourarticlelibrary.com/essay/role-of-ambedkar-in-upliftment-of-dalitas-in-india/40281 accessed on 14_02_2018
2. http://shodhganga.inflibnet.ac.in/bitstream/10603/28174/14/14_chapter%209.pdf accessed on 14_02_2018
3. https://en.wikipedia.org/wiki/Community_organization accessed on 20_02_2018
4. http://www.guide2socialwork.com/social-action/ accessed on 20_02_2018
5. https://www.slideshare.net/gaya3lavanya92/concept-of-social-action accessed on 20_02_2018
6. http://www.researchfront.in/20%20JAN-MARCH%202016/3.pdf accessed on 09_02_2018
7. http://www.columbia.edu/itc/mealac/pritchett/00ambedkar/timeline/1950s.html accessed on 12_03_2018

References

Kausalyayan, B.A. (2015) *Yadi Baba N Hote,* Delhi: Siddharth Books, ISBN: 978-81-909068-9-0

Murray G. Ross (1955). *Community Organization*. Harper & Row Publishers. New York.

Pandey, I. and Singh, O. (2016) "A Philosophical Approach of Dr. B.R. Ambedkar for the Empowerment of Dalit Through Education", *Satara: Research Front*, Volume 4, No. 1, Jan.- Mar., 201, ISSN: (Print) 2320-6446, (Online) 2320-8341 pp.13-18 Extracted from http://www.researchfront.in/20%20JAN-MARCH%202016/3.pdf on 20_02_2018

Cited Links

http://www.yourarticlelibrary.com/essay/role-of-ambedkar-in-upliftment-of-dalitas-in-india/40281 accessed on 14_02_2018

http://shodhganga.inflibnet.ac.in/bitstream/10603/28174/14/14_chapter%209.pdf accessed on 14_02_2018

https://en.wikipedia.org/wiki/Community_organization accessed on 20_02_2018 http://www.guide2socialwork.com/social-action/ accessed on 20_02_2018

https://www.slideshare.net/gaya3lavanya92/concept-of-social-action accessed on 20_02_2018

http://www.researchfront.in/20%20JAN-MARCH%202016/3.pdf accessed on 09_02_2018

http://www.columbia.edu/itc/mealac/pritchett/00ambedkar/timeline/1950s.html accessed on 12_03_2018

8

Dr. B.R. Ambedkar as a True Defender of Human Rights

Avtar Singh

Human Rights–Global Understanding

Human rights are natural rights of human beings. The Vienna Declaration (1993) states that all human rights begin with human dignity and the humans are the central subject of human rights and basic freedoms. In other words, humans themselves are the objects of human rights and are at the core of this basic freedom. To develop a human rights basis for social work requires that the concept of human rights and the problems and criticisms associated with it be carefully examined.

Defining Human Rights

Human rights *per se* refer to rights of individuals which are deemed necessary by virtue of their being the members of the human community. It is in bracketing these rights for effective practice that human rights took the form of a bunch of rights that spread to all—political, economic and social—areas. In 1987, United Nations defined human rights as those rights which are inherent in our nature and without which we cannot live as human beings. Human rights and fundamental freedoms allow us to fully develop and use our human qualities, our intelligence, our talents and our conscience and to satisfy our spiritual and other needs.

Human rights have priority over other claims of rights and need to be differentiated from other rights. For example, the right to food needs to be differentiated from the right to bear arms. Questions can be raised as to which and what kinds of rights are or claimed to be human rights. Recently, Jim Ife (2001) has proposed **five-fold criteria** to define what constitutes a human right or to make a claim on the basis of human rights:

- Realization of the claimed right is necessary for a person or group to be able to achieve their full humanity, in common with others.
- The claimed right is seen *either* as applying to all of humanity and is something that the person or group claiming the right wishes to apply to all people anywhere *or* as applying to people from specific disadvantaged or marginalised groups for whom realisation of that right is essential to their achieving their full human potential.
- There is substantial universal consensus on the legitimacy of the claimed right; it cannot be called a 'human right' unless there is widespread support for it across cultural and other divides.
- It is possible for the claimed right to be effectively realized for all legitimate claimants. This excludes rights to things that are in limited supply, for example, the right to housing with a panoramic view, the right to own a TV channel or the right to 'own' large tracts of land.
- The claimed right does not contradict other human rights. This would disallow as human rights the 'right' to bear arms, the 'right' to hold other people in slavery, 'right' to beat his wife and children, the 'right' to excessive profits resulting in poverty for other, and so on.

Thus, the class of human rights does not include all the rights that people might claim, and that a claim to human rights has to pass certain stringent tests as narrated above.

Key Concepts in Human Rights

When beginning to study human rights, a social worker needs to understand the basic concepts relating to those rights. Human rights are commonly referred to as universal, indivisible, inalienable, inabrogable and intergenerational. The concept of **universality** underpins human rights and implies that human rights apply to all human beings and every individual has a claim to the enjoyment of human rights, irrespective of his other attributes. The concept of **indivisibility** means that human rights come as a package. It refers to the necessity that governments and individuals recognize each human right and not to selectively promote some rights over others. One cannot pick and choose, accepting some and rejecting others as the denial of one human right can easily impact the enjoyment of other rights and directly or indirectly deny other human rights. **Inalienable** nature of human rights provides that they cannot be taken away from someone and remain all through the human lifespan. Human rights are also **inabrogable,** which means that one cannot voluntarily give up one's human rights or trade them for additional privileges. Human rights are not to be idly dispensed with. We may choose not to exercise all our rights all the time, but we still have those rights. The concept of **intergenerational** rights reflects the most recent and important changes that have taken place in human rights discourse in extending our understanding of human rights obligations beyond the present. It forces us to think historically, to locate our actions in their historical context, and to understand that the definition and realization of human rights are not static, but have an important historical dimension (Ife, 2001).

Ahead of the International Human Rights Day on December 10, the Working Group on Human Rights (WGHR) in India and the UN have expressed concerns over the "deteriorating" human rights conditions in the country, adding that all the marginalized groups were feeling insecure. While releasing the "Human Rights in India – Status Report 2012", WGHR convenor Miloon Kothari appealed to the Indian Government to fulfil its national and international human rights commitments in these areas. Expressing concern at the increased militarization, lawyer and activist Vrinda Grover highlighted that the last four years have seen a marked increase in the deployment of security forces and draconian laws by the Indian Government to deal with socio-economic uprisings and political dissent and also to push the State's development agenda (Ali, 2012).

Dalit and Human Rights Violation

There are different forms of human rights violation to marginalized section of society, especially on *Dalit* people, often seen civil and political rights leading to physical assault, verbal abuse, sexual violation and assault.

A total of 45,003 cases of total crimes committed against SCs (which include atrocities as well as non-atrocities cases) were registered in the country as compared to 47,064 cases registered in 2014, showing a decrease of 4.4 per cent in 2015 over 2014. It may be mentioned that during 2015, out of 45,003 cases of crime against SCs 38,564 cases under various sections of IPC along with the SC/ST (POA) Act [atrocities cases, i.e. where SC/ST (POA) Act applied], 6,009 cases under various sections of IPC wherein the SC/ST (POA) Act was not applied, 324 cases under other SLL crimes. The highest incidents of crime against SCs were reported from Uttar Pradesh (8,358 cases) followed by Rajasthan (6,998 cases), Bihar (6,438 cases) and Andhra Pradesh (4,415 cases), they accounted for 18.6 per cent, 15.5 per cent, 14.3 per cent and 9.8 per cent of total such crimes registered during 2015 respectively. During 2015, crimes rate of 22.3 per cent was reported under crimes committed on persons belonging to SCs.

A total of 10,914 cases of crimes committed on persons belonging to Scheduled Tribes (include atrocities as well as non-atrocities cases) were registered in the country during 2015 against 11,451 cases registered in 2014, indicating a decrease of 4.7 per cent during 2015 (NCRB, 2016).

Civil Rights

Untouchability is abolished and its practice in any form is forbidden under Article 17 of the constitution. Parliament set to work on a statue to spell out the practical details and application of the principles embodied in the fundamental right. The result was the Untouchability (Offence) Act of 1955. The Act was amended in November 1976 and named as "Protection of Civil Rights Act, 1955", it provides "penalties for preventing a person, on the ground of untouchability from entering a place of public working and offering a prayer or taking water from a sacred tank, well or spring. Enforcing any kind of social disabilities such as denying access to shop, restaurant, hotel, public hospital or educational institution or any place of public entertainment or denying the use of the road, river, well, tank, water tap, bathing *ghat*, cremation ground, etc. attract the provisions of this Act". A total of 106 cases under this Act were registered during 2015. Maximum cases under this Act were reported in Bihar (74 cases) followed by Karnataka (11 cases), Maharashtra (9 cases), Himachal Pradesh (3 cases) and Odisha and Delhi UT (2 cases each) during 2015 (NCRB, 2016).

Do we really care for our women? Still, Dalit women are subjected to a civil and sexual violation. A total of 62 cases were reported during the year 2013. Maharashtra has reported 21 cases under the protection of Civil Right Act, 1955 followed by Pondicherry (15 cases), and Andhra Pradesh (6 cases) during the year 2013. These four States together have accounted for 85.5 per cent of total cases reported in the country. As per CPI reports, every 18 minutes a crime is committed against a *Dalit*. Every day 3 *Dalit* women are raped, 2 *Dalits* are murdered and 2 *Dalits* houses are burnt in India, 11 *Dalits* are beaten. Every week 13 *Dalits* are murdered, 5 *Dalits* homes or possession are burnt, and 6 *Dalits* are kidnapped or abducted.[1]

The number of cases of atrocities involving murder, dacoity, robbery, arson, rape works out of 1,73,088 from 2009 to 2013. A total of 38,564 cases of atrocities against SCs [in which SC/ST (POA) Act applied] were registered in the country during 2015. The highest incidents of atrocities against SCs were reported from Uttar Pradesh (8,357 cases) followed by Bihar (6,293 cases), Rajasthan (5,911 cases) and Madhya Pradesh (3,546 cases). Majority of victims under atrocities against SCs were also reported from Uttar Pradesh (8,459 persons) followed by Bihar (6,552 persons), Rajasthan (5,979 persons) and Madhya Pradesh (3,693 persons) (NCRB, 2016).

Sexual Violation

A total of 3,27,394 cases of crime against women (both under various sections of IPC and SLL) were reported in the country during the year 2015 as compared to 3,37,922 in the year 2014, thus showing a decline of 3.1 per cent during the year 2015. These crimes have continuously increased during 2011-2014 with 2,28,650 cases in 2011, which further increased to 2,44,270 cases 2012 and 3,09,546 cases in 2013, to 3,37,922 cases in 2014. It declined to 3,27,394 in 2015 (NCRB, 2016). Although we do not have a break-up of PCR and IPC cases separately for *Dalit* men and women, the Scheduled Case and

Scheduled Tribe Commissioner's report, however, provides information on sexual violence against *Dalit* women. Sexual Suffer; in the case of *Dalit* women, it is far more intense and widespread. Because of lower social attitude towards *Dalit* women and their economic dependence, they become victims of the high caste sexual violence, on a scale far greater than that of the non-*Dalit* women. A total of 2,073 cases of rape of women belonging to Scheduled Caste were reported in the country during the year 2013 as compared to 1,576 cases in the year 2012, throwing an increase of 31.5 per cent. Madhya Pradesh has reported 397 cases accounting for 19.1 per cent of the total 2,073 cases reported in the country followed by Uttar Pradesh 18.9 per cent (391 out of 2,073 cases). (NCRB, 2013).

In December 2012, the High Commissioner for Human Rights Navi Pillay condemned the escalation of violence and of rapes against *Dalit* women, a well-known problem neglected at the National level, until it has become an emergency after an alarming number of sexual violence occurred, and have been globally widespread. The High Commissioner hoped for fundamental changes in wake of India rape tragedy, and for "at the National level, the transformation in systems that discriminate against women to a culture that respects the dignity of women in law and practice."[2]

In January 2013, the European Parliament adopted a resolution on violence against women in India, which includes several references to caste discrimination and the situation of *Dalit* women. The resolution expresses "deep concern about the widespread violence committed against *Dalit* women and girls in India, including sexual violence committed by men of dominant castes."[3]

Victims of Social and Religious Practices like *Devadasi* and *Joginis*

Under this social and religious system, the unfortunate village girls are married to a village god by their parents. These girls are then sexually exploited by the upper caste landlords and rich men of the village who have initiated the process of "Divine marriage". This socially "Sanctioned" prostitution has been prevalent in large areas of Telangana, which adjoin Karnataka where the similar practice of *Devadasi* exists. The *Devadasi* system also exists in parts of western Maharashtra (Kolhapur, Solapur and Dharwad).

The system of *Jogins* is worse than that of *Devadasi*, who are dedicated to a god and look after a temple. Unlike a *Devadasi* who lives in a temple, a *jogin* lives in a *jhuggi*, with her parents, where the landlord visits her. They take no responsibility of the option, but to become *Joginis*. These girls cannot marry again, cannot step out of their village and are no better than bonded labourers. This sanctioned prostitution has been in existence for a long time (Thorat, 2001).

Human Rights Violations in Political and Educational Fields

Besides, the sexual exploitation, *Dalits* also suffer from political, economic and the educational rights also. Unfortunately, enough studies are not available on the Human Rights violation of *Dalit* women in these areas. Nevertheless, the limited evidence indicates that the *Dalits* suffer from discrimination and unequal treatment in the field of economic activities and in education. There is evidence that *Dalits* do not find jobs inside the houses of high castes. They are rarely employed as a maidservant due to the practice of untouchability. Similarly, quite a few studies point out the practice of discrimination in the schools. In the area of politics, women do not enjoy full freedom. Thus, they are deprived of their political rights.

However, research on the subject categorically brings forth shocking statistics, 37 per cent of *Dalit* living below poverty in India. More than half (54%) of their children are undernourished in India. 83 per 1000 children born in *Dalit* community are probabilities of dying before the first birthday. 45 per cent of *Dalit* do not read and write in India. *Dalit* women burden double discriminations (gender and caste) in India. Only 27 per cent of *Dalit* women give institutional delivery in India. About one-third of *Dalit* households do not have basic facilities. Public health workers refuse to visit *Dalit* women homes in 33 per cent of villages. *Dalits* are prevented from entering a police station in 27.6 per cent of villages. *Dalit* children had to sit separately while eating in 37.8 per cent of Govt. schools. *Dalits* do not get mail delivered to their homes in 23.5 per cent of villages. *Dalits* are denied access to water sources in 48.4 per cent of the village because of segregation and untouchability practice. Half of India's *Dalit* children are undernourished, 21 per cent are severally underweight and 12 per cent die before their 5th birthday. Literacy rates for *Dalit* women are as low as 37.8 per cent in Rural India.[4]

Ambedkar's Movement for Human Rights

During the last decade of the 19th century, many Indian leaders born among the lower castes like Narayan Guru (1854-1928), Jyoti Rao Phule (1827-1890), and Ramaswamy Naicker (1879-1973) launched massive struggles for the dignity of *Dalits* throughout India. Ambedkar was the most towering figure among these *Dalit* leaders. In 1917, he joined the Baroda State Service after returning from his studies in the USA and the United Kingdom, as part of the terms of his scholarship agreement. He worked in the city of Baroda, the place of the ruling family of Gaikwad, which financed his studies abroad. He worked as a Secretary in the Defence Office of the Maharaja of Baroda State.

However, despite his foreign education, he had to endure insults while at work due to his low caste origin. He was a victim of the cruel *Dalit* discrimination. He suffered the ignominy of having document files hurled by peons at his face. He suffered the humiliating experience of not being served drinking water during official functions. At the officer's club, he had to sit in a corner and keep his distance from the other members belonging to higher castes. He also had difficulties in finding a rented house, as he was not allotted government bungalow. He stayed in an inn owned by Parsis (members of Zoroastrian religion).

Dr. Ambedkar was fully familiar with the pitiable situation of women in the Hindu society, he made a multidimensional contribution to the empowerment of women in India by advocating girls' education, removal of social attitudes treating women during menstrual period as untouchables, right of women of act as priests, maternity benefits for working women during the period of pregnancy and the right to separation, divorce maintenance, adoption and succession (Pawar & Moon, 2008).

Gender equality, gender mainstreaming, networking, leadership, financial freedoms are the essential aspects of women empowerment. Dr. Ambedkar realized this at his time and included in the process of social reforms. Dr. Ambedkar started involving women in the struggle, for the eradication of caste systems and upliftment of the underprivileged sections. He realized that this could not be achieved without liberating the women themselves. He motivated women and addressed them to participate in the struggle against caste prejudices. During the Mahad Tank Struggle, women marched in the procession along with men. He encouraged women to organize themselves. Impressed by the large gathering of women at women's conference held at Nagpur on 20th July, 1942, he told women to be progressive and abolish traditionalism, ritualism and customary habits, which were detrimental to their progress (Dhanvijay, Vaishali, 2012).

He also launched numerous movements. One of the memorable struggles of the *Dalits* was the *Vaikkom Satyagraha* in Travancore in Maharashtra which asserted the right of the *Dalits* to worship in Hindu temples without hindrance. Another very significant movement was Mahad March to assert the rights of *Dalits* to take water from public watering places. Ambedkar organized the *Dalit* rally to assert their legal right to take water from the Chowdar tank. The Chowdar tank of Mahad was made a public tank in 1869. In 1923, the Bombay Legislative Council passed a resolution to the effect that the *Dalits* be allowed to use all public watering places. Another temple entry movement took place at the Kalaram temple at Nasik in Maharashtra State. On 13 October, 1935, at a conference convened on the issue, Ambedkar recounted the experience of the depressed classes and the immense sacrifices made by them to secure minimum human rights under the aegis of Hinduism.

The demand for safeguards and protection of Scheduled Castes (earlier called Depressed Class) has a long history dating to Montague-Chelmsford Reform of 1919 during the British Raj period. Ambedkar had been closely involved in the struggle to give Scheduled Caste people solid statutory safeguard. He was a delegate at the Round Table Conference in London, where he asked for separate electorate for the *Dalits*. It is not a surprise that subsequently Ambedkar saw to it that the welfare of the Scheduled Caste people was guaranteed in the 1949 Constitution of India in the form of reservation in legislative, employment and educational fields.

Ambedkar fought for the rights of workers and peasants. In the late 1920s and especially in the 1930s when he had formed his Independent Labour Party, he took up the cause of tenants (from both the *Dalit Mahars* and the caste Hindu *Kunbis*) in the Konkan region of Maharashtra. With the support of radicals then in the Congress Socialist Party, the Independent Labour Party organized a huge march of 20,000 peasants to Mumbai in 1938, the largest pre-independence peasant mobilization in the region. In the same year, Ambedkar joined with the Communists to organize a strike of Mumbai textile workers in protest against a bill about to be introduced by the British

Government to curve labour strikes. Ambedkar took the lead in condemning the Bill in the assembly and argued that the right to strike was simply another name for the right to freedom of assembly.

Ambedkar was a great champion of the *Dalit* cause because he succeeded in turning the depressed class movement into a revolutionary movement throughout India. Today India has witnessed the oppressed classes walking on the streets of cities and villages with confidence and poise; of course, many despicable acts of discrimination and violence against the *Dalits* still occur. Yet the juggernaut of equality is rolling on remorselessly and forcefully. He adopted various means to safeguard *Dalit* rights. Ambedkar launched a movement against *Dalit* discrimination by creating public opinion through his writings in several periodicals such as *Mook Nayak, Bahishkrit Bharat*, and *Equality Janta*, which he started for the protection of *Dalit* rights.

Ambedkar on Rights of Minorities

Minorities are groups held together by ties of common descent, language, or religious faith or feelings. On the consciousness of difference, the minorities base certain political claims, either equality with the majority, or for special treatment based upon the recognition of these differences, or for autonomy.

Dr. Ambedkar was very particular on the issue of the rights of minorities. He felt minorities needed special provisions for their protection, representation, growth, education and development. He felt that the minorities should have reservations in public employment as well as in the legislature in proportion to their population. In his documents submitted to the Constituent Assembly, he had raised the issue of setting up a Commission for Minorities. The Commission shall be submitting an annual report to the Parliament regarding the development status of the minorities, the levels of economic development, plan special schemes for their welfare etc. and the status of the Commissioner shall be similar to the Attorney General. Though these suggestions were not considered when the Constitution was finally adopted, the Union Government had created the National Commission for Minorities in the year 1993 *vide* The National Commission for Minorities Act, 1992.

The Relevance of Dr. Ambedkar Ideology for Social Work

Dr. Ambedkar has left a permanent impression both on our Constitution and on social life. He was a great patriot. The life history of Dr. Ambedkar epitomized the relentless struggle of the downtrodden community in our country against social ostracism and economic oppression. He created a mission to fight for their human rights. Dr. Ambedkar was a saviour of an individual from bondage, slavery and inhumanity. He said the society has tyranny, authority and denial of liberty, equality and justice. Dr. Ambedkar was an emancipator. The main aim of his life was to try to lead the depressed classes towards a higher social, political and economic status and to free from Dark Age. Dr. Ambedkar ideology, i.e. equality and equity should provide all people without any discrimination. All new babies should bear, live and survive in Indian society without any fear and discrimination, Dr. Ambedkar philosophy should imbibe in all personality, particularly in social work academician and students.

Dr. Ambedkar said, my final words of advice to you is "*Educate, Agitate, Organize*" have faith in yourself. With justice on our side, I do not see how we can lose our battle. The battle to me is a matter of joy. The battle is in the fullest sense spiritual. There is nothing material or social in it. For ours is a battle not for wealth or for power. It is a battle for freedom. It is a battle for reclamations of the human personality.

Similarity between Professional Social Work and Dr. Ambedkar Approach

There are about more than 350 schools in India as per the sources gathered from experts of social work from across the country (Rambabu, 2012). In the process of imparting social work training, 'Ambedkarism' lays foundations for identifying, understanding, analysing and prioritizing issues in India. Ambedkarism is of great relevance to Indian society even today in achieving social justice, in establishing equality and freedom and true democracy. It is imperative to recognize and incorporate the valuable contributions of people and institutions in Social Work practices. The philosophers and academicians in the social work discipline should adopt Ambedkarism as a guiding force in building a native knowledge base and prioritizing the Social Work goals.

In social work, the main objective of social work is to enhance the working capacity of Individual and make then self-reliant. Dr. Ambedkar had aroused and awakened them against social injustice and installed them in the spirit of self-reform, self-emancipation, self-reliance, self-respect, and self-confidence. Dr. Ambedkar tried to free their minds from inhibition and inferiority complex.

In social work, there are six methods, three primary and other three secondary methods, i.e. Social case work, Social group work, Community organization, Social Action, Social welfare administration and social work research. Dr. Ambedkar has used *Satyagrahas* to seek the human rights for downtrodden people and asserts human rights. He advocated three traits: educate, organize and agitate. Indeed the first principle will provide rational thought, the second principle will give mental/physical strength and the third principle will lead to fight for human rights, be it, men or women. In social work also, we used different principles, skills and techniques to achieve our desired goal. (Mohan, 2013). In 1927 Ambedkar started *Satyagrah* at Mahad, a place in Kolaba district of present Maharashtra to secure to the untouchables the right to access to the Chhavdar Tank. He also started *Satyagrah* at Kalaram Temple, Nasik to secure the right to enter into the temple by untouchable, in 1930. In 1937, he formed the Independent Labour Party. This party was committed to education, industrialization and social equality.

Social work profession has borrowed the knowledge from the different disciplines like, sociology, psychology, economics, political science, social medicine, public administration, human resource management etc. to strengthen the knowledge base. Dr. B.R. Ambedkar also equipped himself with in-depth knowledge of political science, law, sociology, social anthropology, religions, economics and philosophy.

Conclusion

Ambedkar is India's foremost human rights activist during the 20th century. He is an emancipator, scholar, extraordinary social reformer and a true champion of human rights. It can be said that he is one of the highly regarded Indians whose emancipation and empowering role for oppressed groups that cut against the gender divide has inspired subaltern groups all over the world. All should try to take inspiration from Dr. B.R. Ambedkar's life and work for the creation of a just and gender-neutral world.

The proposition that all individuals who inhabit planet Earth share inherent privileges and rights has great attraction. Human rights cover domestic, as well as international circumstances. A human rights perspective upholds both individual rights and collective rights and are universal and inalienable and have spatial (e.g. across communities or nations) and temporal (intergeneration rights) dimensions as well. Human rights starting formally with Universal Declaration of Human Rights are not static, but have evolved over the period of time in waves with varying currents or what is called as the three generation of human rights. The nature of each generation of rights reflects the influence of specific philosophy or ideology and hence the dominance and scope of particular for disciplines/professions.

The United Nations Declarations, Covenants and Conventions provide the basic framework and guidelines to the State Governments who are the signatory to these documents or have ratified these. The State Governments in further pursuance of these documents have upheld and enforced these and also formulated their own policies and designed a related legal mechanism to ensure effective implementation of human rights. Social work professionals who uphold humanitarian values and are guided by principles of human rights and justice need to understand the legal, spatial and temporal matrix of human rights as enshrined in international documents and committed by State Governments, for smooth practice and promotion of human rights. They should also note that taking action to support human rights many times means negotiating risks, either with respect to the client system or in relation to themselves, and the outcome of these negotiations cannot be guaranteed. However, they are only to be cautious of rather than being bamboozled with the risk factor. Nevertheless, the social work professionals should also be proud of the fact that a human rights orientation is a reflection of social workers' commitment to empowerment perspective.

Notes

1. Report by CPI, Crime against Dalit in India, *Red Star*, January 2013. http://www.cpiml.in>Home>Red Star January 2013 (accessed on 04/06/2015)
2. High Commissioner for Human Rights Navi Pillay, December 2012

Declaration. http://www.ohchr.org/SP/NewsEvents/Pages/Display News.aspx?NewsID=12910&LangID=E

3. European Parliament resolution of 13 December 2012 on caste discrimination in India (2012/2909(RSP)
4. Report by CPI, Crime against Dalit in India, *Red Star*, January 2013. http://www.cpiml.in>Home>Red Star January 2013 (accessed on 04/06/2015)

References

Abinaya, R. (2006). Why is Domestic Violence a Human Rights Concern? *EPW*, 12(3).

Ali, M. (2012, December 07). All marginalized groups are insecure. Retrieved July 29, 2018, from: https://www.thehindu.com/todays-paper/tp-national/all-marginalized-groups-are-insecure/article4177094.ece

All India Dalit Mahila Adhikar Manch (2013). Preliminary Report: National Tribunal on Violence against Dalit Women. New Delhi: AIDMAM.

Andharia, J., and Batliwala, S. (2007). *The Dalit Women's Movement in India: Dalit Mahila Samiti*. Toronto, Canada: Association of Women's Rights in Development.

Bakshi, P.M., and Kashyap, S.C. (2012). *The Constitution of India*. Universal Law Publishing.

Barry, N.P. (1995). *Introduction to Modern Political Theory*. London: MacMillian.

Baxi, U. (2007). The Future of Human Rights. Oxford University Press.

Bhargava, R., and Acharya, A. (2008). *Political Theory: An Introduction*. Delhi: Pearson.

Botcha, R. (2012). Problems and Challenges for Social Work Education in India: Some Recommendations. *International Journal of Multidisciplinary Educational Research*, 1(3).

Bunch, C. and S. Frost. (1997). *Women's Human Rights: An Introduction*. Unpublished manuscript.

Casting Rape: 101 Cases of Sexual Violence Against Dalit Women After Damini that Failed to Generate Mainstream Outrage. (2013, September 08). Retrieved July 29, 2018, from: https://indiaresists.com/after-damini-101-brutal-atrocities-heinous-crime-against-dalit-women-india/

Devi, L. (1998). *Crime Atrocities and Violence Against Women and Related Laws and Justice* (Vol. 5). New Delhi: Anmol Publications Pvt. Ltd.

Devi, U.K., *International Instruments for Women's Rights*. Social Welfare.

Dominelli, L. (2004). *Social Work: Theory and Practice for a Changing Profession*. Polity Press (Indian Reprint 2005).

Fathima, B. (2001). *Women in Law—An Indian Panorama*. New Delhi: Rawat Publications.

Freeman, M. (2002). *Human Rights: An Interdisciplinary Approach*. Cambridge: Polity Press (Indian Reprint, 2003).

Gurnam, S. (2002). Human Rights for Human Resource Development. *Contemporary Social Work*, 12, 109-117.

Hazra, A. (2013). *India's Social Sector and Millennium Development Goals—Issues, Challenges and Policy Measures*. New Delhi: Rawat Publications.

Human Rights Watch. (2007). *A Report on 'Caste Discrimination' Against Dalits or so-called Untouchables in India*. New York: Human Right Watch.

Ife, J. (2001). *Human Rights and Social Work: Towards Rights-based Practice*. Cambridge: Cambridge University Press.

International Federation of Social Workers; and International Association of Schools of Social Work. (2004). *Ethics in Social Work, Statement of Principles*. Bern: IFSW & IASSW.

Jaytilak, G.R. (2004). *Human Rights for the Twenty-first Century*. Delhi: IIPA.

Kohli, A.S. (Ed.). (2004). *Human Rights and Social Work: Issues, Challenges and Response*. New Delhi: Kanishka Publishers.

Kumar, M.S. (2005). Gender-Based Violence: A Negation of Human Rights. *Legal News & Views*, 19 (6), 4-7.

Kurian, J. (2012). Women Laws and Justice for Women. *Legal News and Views*. 26(4): 10-12.

Mangubhai, J.P., and Lee, J.G. (2012). *Dalit Women Speak Out: Caste, Class and Gender Violence in India*. New Delhi: Zubaan.

Mittal, M. (2010). *Dalit Women in India: Survival and Current Dilemmas*. New Delhi: Arise Publication and Distribution.

Mohan, S.B. (n.d.). Life and Philosophy of Dr. B.R. Ambedkar's for Mankind. *Paripex—Indian Journal of Research*, 3(5).

Morsink, J. (1999). *The Universal Declaration of Human Right: Origins, Drafting and Intent*. Philadelphia: University of Pennsylvania Press.

National Commission for Scheduled Castes and Scheduled Tribes. (1990). Atrocities against Scheduled Castes and Scheduled Tribes. New Delhi: Government of India.

NCRB. *Crime in India—2013 Compendium*. New Delhi: NCRB.

NCW. (1996). Women of weaker sections: Socio-economic development of Scheduled Caste women. New Delhi: National Commission for Women.

Pawar, U., and Moon, M. (2008). *We Also Made History—Women in the Ambedkarite Movement*. New Delhi: Zuban, an Imprint of Kali for Women.

Priya. (2013). *Addressing Violence Against Women—Insights Based on Field Experiences in Haryana*. New Delhi: PRIYA.

Raval, D. (2013). Women Empowerment and Gender Justice, *Legal New and View*, 2(6): 15-16.

Reichert, E. (1998): Women's rights are human rights: A Platform for action. *International Social Work,* 15(3): 177-85.

Reichert, E. (2003). *Social Work and Human Rights—A Foundation for Policy and Practice*. Jaipur & New Delhi: Rawat Publications.

Sidel, R. (1996). *Keeping Women and Children Last: America's War on the Poor*. New York: Penguin Book.

Singh, A.K. (2011). *Crimes against Dalit Women*. Delhi: DPS Publishing House.

Thorat, V. (2001). *Dalit Women and Human Rights: Some Neglected Issues*. New Delhi: Gyan Publishing House.

United Nations (1948). *Universal Declaration of Human Rights*. New York: United Nations.

United Nations. General Assembly. (1979). *Convention on the Elimination of all Forms of Discrimination against Women*. UN.

SECTION II
Indigenous Models in Social Work

9

Swami Vivekananda's Model of Human Development as an Effective Means of Happiness

Puneet Kumar Ojha

Introduction

An extraordinary commitment of Swami Vivekananda for the humankind was the completeness of his vision. He was outstandingly widespread who went to bat for humankind as a rule without refinement of race or nationality, belief or culture, sex or age. Swami Vivekananda's contemporary social and religious reformers taught the people about metaphysics, but Vivekananda's theory was different. He said, "An empty stomach is no good for religion" (Yadav and Kumar, 2018, p.1). He saw the heavenly self of man and viewed the human frame as the genuine image of the Divinity. In the expressions of Swami Satprakashnanda, "In Vivekananda the widespread soul has discovered a cherishing, dynamic and comprehensive articulation which is once in a while to be discovered somewhere else." Vivekananda in his idea of instruction owes much to the Vedantic perspective of indication or unfoldment driving towards satisfaction. To him, the whole brain science of instruction in India depends on *Yoga* and *Advaita*. On the off chance that *Advaita* is the guideline, religion is the medium and *Yoga* the best possible way. What Vivekananda goes for is training for life rather than instruction for calling. An instruction that has such a restricted goal and an absolutely utilitarian point is certain to taunt itself. Then again, training forever should be essentially expansive and extensive, in character. It is a persistent long-lasting procedure unless one stops at a specific point and stagnates there. Perfect training does not mean simple social affair of data. Vivekananda characterized training as "the appearance of the flawlessness as of now in man." And he characterized religion as "the sign of the Divinity as of now in man." So, in a definitive examination, genuine instruction and genuine religion are relatively compatible terms. Banarjee and Meeta (2015) reveals that "Vivekananda's concept of potential diversity gives a new concept of universal humanity. It divinizes human relationships and makes life meaningful and worth living. Instruction without religion may deliver scholarly mammoths. In any case, they might just swing out to the mammoth beasts, however, obviously, exceptionally educated. Training with genuine religion additionally can make scholarly goliaths however, they will never end up being devils. The repeating note in Vivekananda's arrangement for the recovery of India is to evacuate destitution, joblessness and numbness and begin instructing the majority so their lost uniqueness can be reestablished. Through along these lines he was constantly worried about the general advancement of individuals. Today very tuned in to the thoughts of Vivekananda we see all through India various instructive undertakings, which go for the improvement of the person in an evolving society. While underwriting the essential destinations of Vivekananda's thoughts of man-production training, the purpose of accentuation given by these instructive endeavours lays on social solidarity and step up of financial condition. However, accidentally they do make a stamped take off from the goals of training lectured by Swami Vivekananda in as much as he needed all instruction to be put on the fundamental establishment of a deep sense of being. That is the living picture of Vivekananda idea of mass instruction. To recover the centre of masculinity and to revive the well-established otherworldly fire were similar to his profound targets and between the two, he saw an inescapable connection. Swami Ji said once that genuine training prompts the self-change and self-change prompts the joy. Swami Ji additionally relates the idea of human identity advancement to satisfaction. Swami Vivekananda has propounded five measurements of human identity advancement that he considers to be the viable methods for satisfaction. They are as per the following:

1. Physical Self

2. Vitality Self
3. Scholarly Self
4. Mental Self
5. Joyful or Ecstatic Self

Physical Self—As the name infers it is the best possible support and development of the physical body. A solid personality in a sound body is simply the rule of the physical. Weight training and appropriate exercise support one's physical quality as well as the ethical quality. Swami Vivekananda's announcement, "It is smarter to play football than to peruse Gita" demonstrates how emphatically he felt about one's physical self.

Vitality Self—Along with the physical self, the vitality self is the one without which nothing can manage for long. The basic demonstration of breathing shows this kind of vitality. All around directed orderly breathing conveys comfort to the psyche and lifts vitality. Sentiments of narrow-mindedness, fretfulness, outrage, and tension can be adequately controlled by the vitality self.

Scholarly Self—A man has been supplied with the endowment of astuteness. This blessing ought to be appropriately developed and sustained. Perusing great books and writing that stands the trial of time strengthens the brain. The scholarly self is invigorated by the perusing of books on rationality, moral science, and memoirs. As Swami Vivekananda says, "Fill the brain with high contemplations, most noteworthy standards, put them day and night before you, and out of that will come extraordinary work."

Mental Self—A solid mental self is required for the propping up of the identity. The psyche by nature is anxious. It meanders all over and makes us stray from our goal. Full control over the brain is an unquestionable requirement for everyone. For this, the tranquillity of psyche and fixation are essential, and ought to be developed.

Joyful or Ecstatic Self—The happy self, frequently called *Anandamaya Kosha*, is a definitive objective of humanity. To take care of the business identity one needs to achieve this phase where just rapture or *Ananda* wins. He who has achieved this stage can confront the world with a grin. Neither delights nor distress of any sort remains in his direction.

The previously mentioned models of human advancement propounded by Swami Vivekananda is a through which one can accomplish satisfaction adequately. When an individual can accomplish that most extreme joy, he will overcome the cycle of disappointment or achievement. Disappointment or achievement, bundles or brickbats do not divert him from carrying on his work. This prompts his definitive achievement when he gets supplied with a higher vision. As per the Swamiji, at whatever point we accomplish a higher vision, the lower vision vanishes of itself.

Through these standards, Swami Vivekananda basically centres to the way that the human body is the way to play out our obligations and duties. Unless and until the point that our body is not solid, we are not ready to play out our obligations and duties successfully and effectively. Basically, we can state that it is difficult to envision about the joy without a solid body and brain. That is the reason Swami Ji said that "It is smarter to play football than to peruse Gita". The perfect of joy, what brings man more joy, is of more noteworthy utility to him than these higher things which do not enhance his material conditions or bring him such extraordinary satisfaction. Everyone of the sciences is for this one end, to convey bliss to humankind; and that which brings the bigger measure of satisfaction, a man takes and surrenders what brings a lesser measure of joy. We have perceived how satisfaction is either in the body, or in the brain, or in the *Ātman*. With creatures, and in the most minimal individuals who are particularly similar to creatures, joy is all in the body. No man can eat with an indistinguishable joy from a starving pooch or a wolf, so in the puppy and the wolf, the satisfaction is totally in the body. In men we locate a higher plane of bliss that of thought; and in the *Jnani* there is simply the most elevated plane of joy in the Self, the *Ātman*. So to the scholar, this information of the Self is of the most astounding utility since it gives him the most noteworthy bliss conceivable. Sense-satisfactions or physical things cannot be of the most noteworthy utility to him since he does not discover in them a similar joy that he finds in learning itself, and all things considered, information is the one objective and is extremely the most elevated joy that we know. All who work in numbness are, in a manner of speaking, the draft creatures of the Devas. The word Deva is here utilized as a part of the feeling of an astute man. Everyone of the general population that work and drudge and work like machines does not generally appreciate life, however, it is the savvy man who appreciates. A rich man purchases a photo at a cost of a hundred thousand dollars maybe, however, the man comprehends workmanship that appreciates it; and if the rich man is without learning of craftsmanship, it is futile to him, he is just the proprietor. Everywhere throughout the world, it is the insightful man who appreciates the satisfaction of the world. The unmindful man never appreciates; he needs to work for others unwittingly. Man thinks absurdly that he can make himself upbeat, and following quite a while of battle discovers finally that genuine happiness comprises in slaughtering self-centredness and that nobody can make him glad with the exception of himself.

Nobody is extremely upbeat here. In the event that a man is well off and have a bounty to eat, his processing is out of request, and he cannot eat. On the off chance that a man's absorption is great, and he has the processing of a cormorant, he has nothing to put into his mouth. In the event that he is rich, he has no kids. On the off chance that he be eager and poor, he has an entire regiment of kids, and does not know what to do with them? Why is it so? Since satisfaction and wretchedness are the front-side and switch of a similar coin; he who takes joy must take hopelessness moreover. We as a whole have this silly thought we can have satisfaction without wretchedness, and it has taken such ownership of us that we have no power over the faculties.

Swami Vivekananda had delightfully explained the nexus of joy and distress through this specific illustration. He talked about a story as in some oil processes in India, bullocks are utilized that go all around to crush the oil-seed. There is a burden on the bullock's neck. They have a bit of wood jutting from the burden, and on that is secured a wisp of straw. The bullock is blindfolded such that it can just look forward, thus it extends its neck to get at the straw; and in doing as such, it pushes the bit of wood out somewhat further; and it makes another endeavour with a similar outcome, but then another, etc. It never gets the straw, however, goes all around in the expectation of getting it, and in this manner granulates out the oil. Similarly, we as a whole are conceived slaves of nature, cash and riches, spouses and kids, are continually pursuing a wisp of straw, an unimportant figment, and experiencing an incalculable round of lives without acquiring what we look for. The immense dream is love, we are for the most part going to be glad and never meet with hopelessness, however, the more we go towards satisfaction and the more it leaves from us. What brings man more bliss, is of more noteworthy utility to him than these higher things which do not enhance his material conditions or bring him such extraordinary joy. Everyone of the sciences is for this one end, to convey bliss to mankind; and that which brings the bigger measure of satisfaction, a man takes and surrenders what brings a lesser measure of joy. We have perceived how bliss is either in the body or in the brain, or in the *Âtman*. With creatures, and in the most reduced of people, who are particularly similar to creatures, bliss is all in the body. No man can eat with an indistinguishable joy from a starving pooch, or a wolf; in this way, in the canine and the wolf, the bliss is altogether in the body. In men, we locate a higher plane of bliss, that of thought, and in the *Jnani* there is simply the most astounding plane of satisfaction in the Self, the *Ātman*. So to the logician, this learning of the Self is of the most noteworthy utility since it gives him the most noteworthy joy conceivable. Sense satisfaction or physical things cannot be of the most noteworthy utility to him since he does not discover in them a similar delight that he finds in the information itself, and all things considered, learning is the one objective, and is extremely the most astounding bliss we know.

The *Advaita* is the main framework which gives unto man finish ownership of himself, takes off all reliance and its related superstitions, in this way influencing us to overcome to endure, overcome to do, and over the long haul achieve Absolute Freedom. Can any changeless satisfaction be given to the world? In the sea, we cannot raise a wave without causing an empty elsewhere. The entirety of the great things on the planet has been the same all through in its connection to man's need and ravenousness. It cannot be expanded or diminished. Take the historical backdrop of the human race as we probably are aware today. Do we not locate similar agonies and a similar satisfaction, similar joys and torments, similar contrasts in position? Are not some rich, some poor, some high, some low, some sound, and some unfortunate? This was the same with the Egyptians, the Greeks and the Romans in antiquated circumstances as it is with the Americans today. So far as the history is the known, it has dependably been the same; yet in the meantime, we locate that, running alongside all these hopeless contrasts of delight and torment, there has at any point been the battle to mitigate them. Each time of history has brought forth a large number of people who have endeavoured to smooth the section of life for others. Also, how far have they succeeded? We can just play at driving the ball starting with one place then onto the next. We take away torment from the physical plane, and it goes to the psychological one. It resembles that photo in Dante's hellfire where the grumpy persons were given a mass of gold to move up a slope. Each time they moved it up a bit, it again moved down. Everyone of our discussions about the thousand years is exceptionally pleasant as school-young men's stories, however, they are no superior to that. All countries that fantasy of the thousand years additionally surmises that, of all people groups on the planet, they will have the best of it then for themselves. This is the magnificently unselfish thought of the thousand years.

We cannot add satisfaction to this world; comparably we cannot add torment to it either. The entirety of the energies of delight and agony showed here on earth will be the same all through. We simply push it from this side to the opposite side, and from that side to this, however, it will continue as before, in light of the fact that to remain so is its exceptional nature. This recurring pattern, this rising and falling, is on the planet's extremely nature; it would be as consistent to hold generally as to state that we may have existed without death.

Philosophy demands that there is a delight which is supreme, which never shows signs of change. That satisfaction cannot be the delights and joys we have in this life, but then *Vedanta* demonstrates that everything that is happy in this life is yet a molecule of that genuine euphoria since that is the main happiness there is. Each minute we are getting a charge out of the outright happiness, however, concealed, misjudged exaggerated. Wherever there is any gift, ecstasy, or euphoria, even the delight of the cheat in taking, it is that Absolute joy turning out, just it has moved toward becoming darkened, jumbled up, in a manner of speaking, with a wide range of incidental conditions, and misconstrued. After each bliss comes wretchedness; they might be far separated or close. The further developed the spirit; the all the more rapidly completes one take after the other. What we need is neither bliss nor wretchedness. The two influences us to overlook our actual nature; both are chains, one iron, and one gold; behind both is the *Ātman*, who knows neither bliss nor hopelessness.

Happiness presents itself before man, wearing the crown of distress on its head. He who invites it should likewise welcome distress. Then alone would death be able to stop when I am unified with life, at that point alone would misery be able to stop when I am unified with joy itself, at that point alone would error be able to stop when I am unified with information itself. The tragedies of the world cannot be cured by physical help as it were. Until the point that man's inclination changes, these physical needs will emerge, and agonies will dependably be felt, and no measure of physical help will cure them totally. The main arrangement of this issue is to make humanity unadulterated. Obliviousness is the mother of all the shrewd and all the wretchedness we see. Give men a chance to have light, given them a chance to be unadulterated and profoundly solid and instructed, at that point alone will hopelessness stop on the planet, not previously.

So long as there is want no genuine bliss to come. It is just the thoughtful, witness-like investigation of articles that conveys to us genuine satisfaction and bliss.

The creature has its satisfaction in the faculties, the man in his astuteness, and the God in the other terrestrial examination. It is just to the spirit that has achieved this thoughtful express that the world truly winds up excellent. To him who wants nothing, and does not blend himself up with them, the complex changes of nature are one display of excellence and sublimity.

To understand the complex changes of nature one ought to have learned and that extreme information is just conceivable through instruction. Swami Vivekananda has particularly accentuated the significance of training since he realized that instruction is the foundation of the general advancement of person also for improvement of a country. He additionally said that for him information without anyone else is not training unless joined by the essential human qualities that are good and other terrestrial qualities. Actually, science and innovation have demolished physical separation amongst man and man yet the issue of obliterating the psychological and passionate separation amongst man and man remains yet to be illuminated. His instructive point prompts the improvement of aggregate human identity, to connect a bay amongst man and man as one unending self.

By the meaning of religion as the indication of heavenly nature as of now in man, Vivekananda has not propounded any new idea. He has just communicated in the cutting edge phrase what all schools of Vedanta have from the start held, to be specific, that the spirit or *Ātman* is a necessary piece of *Brahman* or is indistinguishable with *Brahman*. The fundamental issue during the time spent self-appearance is the evacuation of impediments as childishness and resulting indecencies. For this expulsion of obstructions, for showing one's potential holiness, *Yoga* is vital. By training Vivekananda does not mean formal tutoring alone. This is clear when he says, "if training were indistinguishable with data, the libraries will be the best sages on the planet and reference books the *rishis*." In his view, instruction separated from life and restricted to the four dividers of the classroom winds up manufactured and loses its esteem.

A kid's training ought not to be kept to schools. To realize the aims of education, Swamiji suggested a curriculum as 'what are western science coupled with vedanta, Brahmacharya the guiding motto and also shraddha and faith in one's self. Yet the root is the religion' (Mandal, 2017, p. 23). It must understand the entire reality where he can create himself completely in a regular environment. Vivekananda called his instruction for India 'man-production'. He needed to make man for he envisioned a reality that the majority of India had not accomplished the full grandness of human instinct. He buckled down for man-production instruction and man-production religion that were intended to make an example of magnificence in the general public and additionally in singular individuals. Stressing the requirement for other terrestrial training for current India Vivekananda has endorsed contemplation as an educational module in the investigation. Fixation and reflection are the central techniques for acknowledging the truth, experienced by sages of the old India. The past is our establishment, the present is our material, the future our point and summit. Each must have its due and commonplace in a national arrangement of training.

About contemplation, Vivekananda commented, "Before we can control the mind we should consider it. We need to grab this precarious personality and drag it from its meandering and fix it on one thought; again and again, this must be finished. It is the real man, the personality of the man that runs through us. Our actions are but effects. Actions must come when the man is there; the effect is bound to follow the cause. The ideal of all education, all training, should be this man making. But, instead of that, we are always trying to polish up the outside.

What use polishing up the outside when there is no inside? The end and aim of all training are to make the man grow. The man who influences, who throws his magic, as it were, upon his fellow-beings, is a dynamo of power, and when that man is ready, he can do anything and everything he likes: that personality put upon anything will make it work. Now, we see that though this is a fact, no physical laws that we know of will explain this. How can we explain it with chemical and physical knowledge? How much of oxygen, hydrogen, carbon—how many molecules in different positions, and how many cells, etc., can explain this mysterious personality? And we still see, it is a fact, and not only that, it is the real man; and it is that man that influences, moves his fellow-beings and passes out, and his intellect and books and works are but traces left behind.

Think of this and compare the great teachers of religion with the great philosophers. The philosophers scarcely influenced anybody's inner man, and yet they wrote the most marvellous books. The religious teachers, on the other hand, moved countries in their lifetime. The difference was made by personality. In the philosopher it is a faint personality that influences; in the great Prophets, it is tremendous. In the former we touch the intellect, in the latter, we touch life. In the one case, it is simply a chemical process, putting certain chemical ingredients together which may gradually combine and under proper circumstances bring out a flash of light or may fail.

In the other, it is like a torch that goes around quickly, lighting others. The science of Yoga claims that it has discovered the laws which develop this personality, and by proper attention to those laws and methods, each one can grow and strengthen his personality. This is one of the great practical things and this is the secret of all education. This has a universal application. In the life of the householder, in the life of the poor, the rich, the man of business, and the spiritual man, in everyone's life, it is a great thing, the strengthening of this personality. There are laws, which are behind the physical laws, as we know. That is to say, there are no such realities as a physical world, a mental world, a spiritual world. Whatever is, is one. Let us say, it is a sort of tapering existence, the thickest part is here, it tapers and becomes finer and finer; the finest is what we call Spirit; the grossest, the body. And just as it is here, in the microcosm, it is exactly the same in the macrocosm.

This universe of ours is exactly like that; it is the gross external thickness, and it tapers into something finer and finer until it becomes God. We also know that the greatest power is lodged in the fine, not in the coarse. We see a man take up a huge weight, we see his muscles swell, and all over his body we see signs of exertion, and we think the muscles are powerful things. But, it is the thin thread-like things, the nerves, which bring power to the muscles; the moment one of these threads is cut off from reaching the muscles, they are not able to work at all. These tiny nerves bring the power from something finer still-thought, and so on. So, it is the fine that is really the seat of power. Of course, we can see the movements in the gross; but when fine movements take place, we cannot see them. When a gross thing moves, we catch it, and thus we naturally identify movement with things which are gross. But all the power is really in the fine. We do not see any movement in the fine, perhaps because the movement is so intense that we cannot perceive it.

But if by any science, any investigation, we are helped to get hold of these finer forces which are the cause of the expression; the expression itself will be under control. There is a little bubble coming from the bottom of a lake; we do not see it coming all the time, we see it only when it bursts on the surface; so, we can perceive thoughts only after they develop a great deal, or after they become actions.

We constantly complain that we have no control over our actions, our thoughts. But how can we have it? If we can get control over the fine movements, if we can get hold of thought at the root, before it has become thought, before it has become active, then it would be possible for us to control the whole. Now, if there is a method by which we can analyse, investigate, understand and finally grapple with those finer powers, the finer causes, then alone is it possible to have control over ourselves, and the man who has control over his own mind assuredly will have control over every other mind. That is why purity and morality have been always the object of religion; a pure, moral man has control of himself. He who knows one lump of clay has known all the day in the universe. He who knows and controls his own mind knows the secret of every mind and has power over every mind.

Every man in his childhood runs through the stages through which his race has come up; only the race took thousands of years to do it, while the child takes a few years. The child is first the old savage man—and he crushes a butterfly under his feet. The child is at first like the primitive ancestors of his race. As he grows, he passes through different stages until he reaches the development of his race. Only he does it swiftly and quickly. Now, take whole of humanity as a race, or take the whole of the animal creation, man and the lower animals, as one whole. There is an end towards which the whole is moving. Let us call it perfection. Instead of waiting and being reborn over and over again for ages until the whole human race has attained to that perfection, they, as it were, rush through them in a few short years of their life. And we know that we can hasten these processes if we are true to ourselves. If a number of men, without any culture, be left to live upon an island and are given barely enough food, clothing and shelter, they will gradually go on and on, evolving higher and higher stages of civilization. We also know that this growth can be hastened by additional means. Even this hastening of the growth must be under laws.

Suppose we can investigate these laws and understand their secrets and apply them to our own needs; it shows that we grow. We hasten our growth, we hasten our development, and we become perfect, even in this life. This is the higher part of our life, and the science of the study of mind and its powers has this perfection as its real end. The utility of this science is to bring out the perfect man, and not let him wait and wait for ages, just a play-thing in the hands of the physical world, like a log of drift-wood carried from wave to wave and tossing about in the ocean. This science wants us to be strong, to take the work in our hand, instead of leaving it in the hands of nature, and get beyond this little life, this leads to the achievement of happiness.

Swamiji further said that achievement of happiness is possible through bliss. One of the best ways of obtaining bliss is to love and serve others. The scriptures say: "that which is limitless is bliss; there is no happiness in the little, in the limited. A person marries and becomes two. His bliss increases. He begets children and his family expands. His bliss further increases. It is a common experience that a single, isolated and alienated is never happy. By service, we identify with others. It breaks our egoistic limitations and makes us expand. We find ourselves among our own people everywhere. To make others our own through love, service and help, is the method taught by the Holy mother to attain peace, happiness and bliss. The day we would actually realize that no one is a stranger, and all are our own, that day we shall be the happiest. He is the happiest person who actually feels that none is a stranger, none is an enemy and that all are his own. In this way one can feel the essence of that supernatural power, i.e. God. By the vitality of will, we ought to get hold of the mind and impact it to stop and consider the amazing quality of God."

Thus both concentration and reflection are required in finishing mind with the objective that it very well may be created into a fit instrument for getting data. Preparing should help each man in taking up his own ideal and endeavour to accomplish it. According to Vivekananda, "there are four general sorts of men—the goal, the eager, the captivated and the worker." So, in the preparation of these unmistakable sorts of men differing methods are to be taken after. Vivekananda recognized long earlier that guideline should be liberal and tried and true in the national lines. Direction should fuse both conventionalist and creative edges and accomplish change in the overall population by giving us dynamic musings and new estimations of life. One of the basic measures to be underlined in the socialist case of society is that individual fulfilment will come, not through self-important and limited loyalties to an individual or get-together intrigue yet through the commitment of all to the more broad loyalties of national change. The direction introduces day India has been wrongly masterminded and heedlessly executed. The bleeding edge instructors have ignored the real longing of man to comprehend his best self. This is much against the acknowledged objectives of the Indian just system and thus, every effort should be made to reinsulate the honest to goodness soul of Indian culture in the minds of the all-inclusive community.

Swami Vivekananda's message in this setting is particularly basic particularly in light of its propriety to deal with the jumbled issues of the nation. In case we can change our informative course of action on national lines as exhibited by Vivekananda by then and from that point onward, independent from anyone else, we ought to have the ability to build up a structure which will be truly man-generation and character-building. In addition, this is vital for the recuperation of India, and additionally for the recovery of the whole world. At the point when Vivekananda says, "Yet preparing still cannot be on the planet, and human advancement-improvement has begun no place yet." Modern community foundations solely rely upon science, its achievements have furthermore wound up being most of the way and compelled. The blend of the energies of science and most significant feeling of being in the life of man will convey totally organized individuals, and thus, help to propel an aggregate human advancement for which the world is delaying.

Swamiji additionally said that human advancement is outlandish without the most elevated truth and for that purpose; we need to think about the substance of the soul. Give us a chance to revere the soul in soul, remaining on the soul. Give the establishment a chance to be a soul; the centre, soul; the zenith, soul. Stand thou in the soul; that is the objective. We know we cannot achieve it yet. It does not mind. Try not to lose hope, however, do not drag the perfect down. The critical thing is: how significantly less you think about the body, of yourself as an issue, as dead, dull, insentient issue, the amount more we think about our self as sparkling eternal being. The more we consider ourselves sparkling interminable soul, the more excited we will be to be totally free of issue, body, and faculties. This is the extraordinary want to be free.

Thus, one can understand the genuine reason for mankind. A conclusive explanation behind Swami Vivekananda for the mankind is to exhibit the certified and practical strategies for bliss and most of his exercises conceivably it is about Duty, Education, Faith, Ethics, Salvation, *Ātman* or Spirituality all prompts achieve none other than delight. The lines given underneath that is made by Swami Vivekananda is extraordinary among different cases to describe the *bona fide* fulfilment.

When I Asked God for Strength
He Gave Me Difficult Situations to Face
When I approached God for knowledge
He Gave Me Puzzles to Solve.
When I Asked God for Happiness
He Showed Me Some Unhappy People
When I Asked God for Wealth
He Showed Me How to Work Hard
When I Asked God for Favours
He Showed Me Opportunities to Work Hard
When I Asked God for Peace
He Showed Me How to Help Others
God Gave Me Nothing I Wanted
He Gave Me Everything I Needed.

References

Banerjee, Arindam Kanta & Meeta, Madhu (2015). Educational philosophy of Swami Vivekananda. Retrieved from *International Journal of Educational Research and Development* Vol. 4(3), (p.030-035), Available online at http://www.academeresearchjournals.org/journal/ijerd ISSN 2327-316X ©2015 Academe Research Journals

Development of Personality. (1962). The Complete Works of Swami Vivekananda. (p. 25-30) Advaita Ashrama.

Divine beings: Sayings of Swami Vivekananda-Happiness, Retrieved from http://hindu-sanathana-dharma.blogspot.com/2008/06/colloquialisms of-Swami-Vivekananda-happiness.html

GODS: Sayings of Swami Vivekananda- Happiness, Happiness, Retrieved from http://hindu-sanathana-dharma.blogspot.com/2008/06/colloquialisms of-Swami-Vivekananda-happiness.html

Happiness, Teachings of Swami Vivekananda (1962). The Complete Works of Swami Vivekananda, (pp. 103-108). Advaita Ashrama, Kolkata.

Islam, Merina, Sirswal & Deshraj (2013). Philosophy of Swami Vivekananda. Retrieved from https://www.researchgate.net/profile/Desh_Raj_Sirswal/publication/272477405. The Complete Works of Swami Vivekananda., Vol. VI (p. 448).

Jayakrishna, .K. _Philosophy.pdf.

Mandal, Samar Kumar (2017). Reflection and Relevance of Teaching and Philosophy of Swami Vivekananda in the present Educational System. *ECONSPEAK: A Journal of Advances in Management, IT & Social Sciences* Vol. 7, (p. 23). Retrieved from https://www.academia.edu/33472948/.

Personality Development and Swami Vivekananda. Retrieved from http://www.psychologydiscussion.net/identity improvement 2/identity advancement and-Swami-Vivekanand/1175

Relevance of Swami Vivekananda's Ideas in the Present Context.docx. Retrieved from http://s3-ap-southeast-1.amazonaws.com/ijmer/pdf/volume4/volume4-issue10(3)-2015.pdf

Retrieved from http://www.psychologydiscussion.net/personality-development-2/personality-development-and-swami-vivekananda/1175

Search for Everlasting Bliss (1962). The Complete Works of Swami Vivekananda. Retrieved from Chhandogya Upanishad, 7.23.1, (p.80). Advaita Ashrama

The logic of Swami Vivekananda. Retrieved from (https://www.researchgate.net/production/272477405

Vivekananda's Contribution to the Present Age (1978). Retrieved from writings of Swami Satprakashnanda, (p. 135). Vedanta Society of Louis, Kolkata & USA

Yadav, Ishwar & Kumar, Mukesh (2018). Nationalism and Swami Vivekananda, *Journal of Advances and Scholarly Researches in Allied Education*, Vol.15. (p. 186-188). Retrieved from http://www.ignited.in/I/a/57749

10

Rethinking and Redesigning Fieldwork in Social Work

A Quality Perspective

Y.S. Siddegowda

Modelling into Social Work Professional Culture

Fieldwork practice subsidizes to the socialization of students into the skill sets of the profession. Fieldwork is an Opportunity to perceive and model from practice professionals and expose the students to subtle, unspoken social mores of the profession and the practice culture. Professional modelling contributes to the development of relevant professional values and attitudes and the skills of working in the fields of their choices.

Fieldwork practice is a vital component of social work education. It consists of accumulating knowledge in different situations. It is a dynamic process of observing, amassing, implementing creative and innovative ideas. Positive Fieldwork supervision, based on principles of learning is vital to the integration of theory and practice during the Fieldwork experience. Social work grew out of humanitarian and democratic ideals, and its values are based on respect for the equality, worth, and dignity of all people. Development or social work is a form of professional service to the people, comprising a composite of knowledge, skills, attempting at assisting them, as individuals, groups or communities for attending satisfying relationship and standards of life in accordance with particular needs, wishes and capacities and in harmony with that community. The social work profession promotes social change, problem-solving in human relationships and the empowerment and liberation of people to enhance well-being. Utilizing theories of human behaviour and social systems, social work intervenes at the points where people interact with their environments. Principles of human rights and social justice are fundamental to social work. Fieldwork practice in social work is a comprehensive, student-friendly guide for those beginning their social work field experience. The Chapter examines the most important questions, concerns and problems students encounter in their field practicums and provides them with essential information for completing the field experiences successfully and an attempt to rethink and redesign Fieldwork in social work to bring a qualitative change. The role of Fieldwork as an integral part of the training for professional social workers has to be recognized by all concerned, so, that the best effort is made by the student, the school and the agency to provide such learning opportunities to the student, which will have a carryover effect in his professional career Fieldwork.

The Gap between Social Work Theory and Practice

Combination of Theory into practice is a central goal for all professions, the question of how to bridge the gap between theory and practice and between the classroom and the Fieldwork practice is one which has preoccupied social work education since its very beginnings.

Social work education has always accentuated the reputation of Fieldwork experience within the curricula for fixing students to practice, the purpose being to contextualize classroom learning. Fieldwork practice is the mechanism for diffusing theoretical knowledge into the practical work. On the other hand, what social work students do during their Fieldwork practice is a crucial issue for a quality social work education.

Social work education goals to make students for social work practice, which is not certainly reflected in the experiences of social work students. This dislocation between the goals of social work and its preparation is reflected in the words of a few social work educators. Studies that have examined students' views on the application of social work theory to field practice reveal that students have observed the conflict between curricula and agency.

Targeted goal of Fieldwork is to empower students to apply the theories and skills they have learned in the classroom to field practice and to use their practical experiences to enhance classroom learning. However, there is often a lack of connection between theories learned in the classroom and field experiences.

Challenges on Integrating Theory into Practice: Theories for Social Work or Social Work Theories

Social work course is under such confusion that we have Theories for Social Work or Social Work Theories. The Syllabus we have designed is guaranteeing the clarity of Theories for Social work or Social Work Theories? And the same thing is also carried to field practice. So, while designing the curricula, schools of social work should also focus to develop the curricula guiding the students to Fieldwork practice.

Fieldwork practice is conventionally combined into social work education, the competence of agency settings to provide quality education in the field is a challenge. Because many organizations are operating under economic restraint, Paraprofessionals are employed and they are training social work students and the staff is experienced with stress and overload. This is the situation in which social work students undertake the Fieldwork placements and it is essential that they should be equipped to manage learning and the practical challenges in working within existing human development settings.

Key Players or Stakeholders in Social Work Fieldwork Practice

We have four key players in Fieldwork of social work practice. Each side of the learning is squared that is University, social work educators, Fieldwork supervisors and students play the game in contributing the professional social worker. The affiliated University and Social work educators are at the top of the curricula designing and conveying the curricula to the students. So, these two players will set the quality and benchmarks for Fieldwork. They should focus on simplifying the process of implementation, learning and Evaluation. They teach interposition in the fields and play a major role in progressing theory. They convey competency, skills and attitudes, teaching and learning styles in the classroom and as well as concurrent fieldwork. University and social work educators are expected to straight and screen student Fieldwork training. They motivate the learning process in coordination with an agency based supervisors in developing students study habits and the desired outcome of the Fieldwork. Agency supervisors are trusted with the responsibility of developing students' Fieldwork competence.

Agency supervision assists the students to develop practical skills as well as integrating theory into practice. Agency supervisors also act as a guide and also as evaluators, instructing theory and skills and evaluating students' improvement together, social work educators and field supervisor's rate and evaluate students' professional development.

Fieldwork Learning Strategies

We may classify social work practice at three levels. These include: (i) micro-level, (ii) meso-level, and (iii) macro-level. There are different ideologies that predominantly guide social work practice at each level. Also, at different levels, there are different methods of social work practice that take primacy in the field. However, the predominance of a particular ideological position or a method of social work practice does not imply that other ideological positions or methods of social work practice are of no use at that level.

Micro-level social work practice is individualistic in orientation and therapeutic in nature. At this level, the social worker deals with individuals or groups, comprising of individuals, facing similar problems. But, at the same time, individualistic practice highlights causative economic, political, and social factors that give rise to problems at the micro-level.

At the meso-level, social work practice is focused on a larger collective, namely, community. Predominantly, the social worker applies community organization (a method of social work practice) to address the concerns raised by people in the community. While engaging in community work, the social worker also develops knowledge about the rights of people and deliberates on the macro-interventions to realize these rights. Thus, at this level, the practice is either therapeutic or critical in nature or both.

At the macro-level, social work practice is predominantly, critical in nature and involves the application of social action and social work research as methods of social work practice. The social worker is engaged in a political process of organizing people to alter the oppressive structures in the society. The aim is to bring about a social change by empowering people.

The Fieldwork training process is called Fieldwork practicum in Social Work. It comprises of different parts. Broadly, these include: orientation programme, concurrent Fieldwork placements, rural camps, study tours, inter-agency meets, and block placement. The most prominent and continuous of all the components is the concurrent Fieldwork placement. The students are placed in two different, institutional (voluntary/agency organization) and non-institutional (community) settings during the two years of the master's programme. The Fieldwork placements are continuously supervised by an educator who also plays the role of a Fieldwork supervisor in Social Work. Fieldwork supervision includes two important components, namely, (i) individual conference, and (ii) group conference. Individual conferences facilitate developing a one to one relationship between the Fieldwork supervisor and the supervisee/student. It helps the students to express the learning and the challenges faced by them in the field. Consequently, it helps in integrating classroom learning with fiel d practice and *viceversa*.

Challenges Experienced by Social Work Students during their Fieldwork Training

Criteria Used in the Choice of Fieldwork Agencies

Fieldwork will occur in a setting that reinforces the students, "Identification with the objectives, values, and ethics of the profession nurtures the combination of empirical and practice-based information and promotes the professional competency development".

But in many situations, students were told to identify the Fieldwork agencies of their choices and social work schools will have a set of agencies which are routinely placed at their convenience without the professional requirement. But the real spirit of Fieldwork practicum should be based on the philosophy, values and ethics of social work. This type of Fieldwork placements will help the students to get nurtured with the professional requirements.

Quality of Agency Supervision

Though the use of qualified and experienced supervisors is quite critical in any professional training in some situation, we have more of supervision by non-social work background. This is not surprising that there is an acute shortage of suitable Fieldwork agencies and agency supervision. Also problematic is that most of the agency supervisors did not have a programme showing how the teaching and learning are to happen. It was indicating that social work schools did not provide them with any guidelines and as a result, they just ended up improvising. An agency supervisor indicates that there was just an understanding with the student, that in a Fieldwork day she/he would spend time doing administrative work at the office and visit to community carrying out assessment visits.

Support Given to Agency Supervisors

Agency supervisors are partners in the learning process of social work with the responsibility to manage the transition from the classroom to the field and this requires support and continuous dialogue between the training institution, the agency supervisor and the agency. It is probably in recognition of this fact that the IASSW and IFSW spell out the need for training institutions to provide Fieldwork manuals and orientation to agency supervisors. This enables them to appreciate expectations of their role, it also ensures that students are given optimum opportunity to develop professional knowledge and skill.

Fieldwork Education: University Perspectives

University holding the responsibility of designing the course pattern and curricula works for the quality of social work education. But the present practice mentions that university may design the course but it will be diluted at the level of implementation. So, the university should further work some strict guidelines to enhance the quality in Fieldwork. The focus may be given to the following criterias:

- Designing the Fieldwork curriculum for all the semesters rather giving guidelines.
- Criteria to be followed in the choice of Fieldwork agencies.
- Fieldwork course materials.
- Fieldwork formats.
- Supervision during Fieldwork placements.
- The knowledge base of agency supervisors.
- Students' Attitude and Attributes.
- Evaluation parameters of 360 degrees.

- Development of a strong agency, university/department and student partnership.
- Exploring the use of non-traditional models of field instruction.
- Training of agency supervisors.

Fieldwork Practice: Student Perspectives

Many of the social work schools in India have kept the students in the dark about the process of Fieldwork practice. They are not clear with the requirement of Fieldwork so a student will have a different perspective on Fieldwork. And also the schools of social work should reduce the communication gap in the learning process during Fieldwork practice. So, students are in the need of clear communication about Fieldwork practice in the form of Fieldwork course materials and Fieldwork formats. So, schools can develop the Fieldwork course materials and formats on the following requirement:

Course Materials

- Fieldwork Manual.
- Fieldwork Checklist.
- Social Work Ethics, Guiding values and Principles to be followed in the Fieldwork.
- Do's and Don'ts in Fieldwork.
- Fieldwork Diary.
- Guidelines for a Home visit and Interview.
- Counselling guidelines.
- The responsibility of Faculty Supervisor/Agency Supervisors and Students.
- Fieldwork Curriculum.

Formats for Fieldwork

- Fieldwork placement forms.
- Information forms.
- Assessment forms.
- The format for Home Visit.
- Case work format.
- Group Work Formats.

- Group activity formats.
- Interview Formats.
- Observation Report formats.
- Orientation Visit.
- Counselling format.
- Guidelines for writing Fieldwork reports.
- Contract forms.
- Letters of introduction for students.
- Individual and Group conference report format.
- Case study format.
- Tour/exposure/camp/block placement/survey report formats.
- Evaluation Formats

Fieldwork Practice: Agency Perspectives

Social work professional in Fieldwork education remains to indicate training for Fieldwork supervisors, particularly in learning theories, as a major gap. Although agency supervisors try to expect transfer practice knowledge and skills to the new role of Fieldwork supervisor, the responsibility also requires a new set of knowledge and skills, like how to structure supervision, provide feedback, establish learning objectives, and how to help the students to develop a professional identity. Schools or Departments of social work expect new Fieldwork supervisors an orientation that addresses such areas as learning contracts, evaluations, the schools' and/or departments' curriculum, and the transition from practitioner to educator.

Attitude and Attributes of Students and Social Work Schools

Agency supervisor also expects a learning attitude and professional attributes from social work students and social work schools. Many are lacking with this, so, the agency expects the students to be trimmed with professional attitudes and attributes before we send them to the Fieldwork practice. And many of the schools do not have a proper beginning for Fieldwork, which lacks the students to develop the professional attitudes and attributes.

Learning Areas for Social Work Students during Fieldwork Practice

Professional courses are entrusted by society to ensure that students have mastered the knowledge and skills necessary for ethical and effective practice. In meeting this requirement, courses identify the components of professional performance that are associated with the effective entry-level practice, operationalize these professional components in the form of learning objectives, provide opportunities for students to achieve these operationalized objectives in the curriculum, and ensure the mastery of these objectives through evaluations of students.

Fieldwork education is based on the principle of development that is ordering the learning experience in increasing levels of competency, knowledge, skills, and practice.

The principles and methods of social work are not be taught or learned in the abstract. Social work studies cannot be confined to the intellectual atmosphere and theoretical approach developed in classrooms, but it has to be necessarily augmented by a practical programme of Fieldwork. This alone can properly initiate social work trainees into the field of social work, with a realistic and 'down to earth' approach to the many problems to be met within the field. The analysis of the theory-practice relationship in Social Work *vis-à-vis* the curriculum, the pedagogy, the evaluation process, and the Fieldwork practicum, reveals the central role that ideology plays in influencing this relationship. Social work practice includes a wide range of activities such as individual counselling, generating awareness about social issues, mobilizing resources to meet the needs of a community, and participation in social movements. Professions based on the human relationship such as social work must have its knowledge base truly reflecting values, culture, problems of society in which it has to be taught and practised.

Assessment of Social Work Students during Fieldwork Training

The means by which students are evaluated is *via* positivistic methods and the use of competencies. This approach to valuation considers that the evaluator is successfully an intellect, divorced from identity, gender, race, class and culture, which can provide a 'value-free' assessment of the student's performance.

Normally, the course regulations shoulder that the assessment of social work students should be the responsibility of the University. It is significant to evaluate not only the students' performance, but also the process of the Fieldwork learning experience to ensure that they are being given optimum opportunity to develop professional knowledge and skills. Now, it is time to attempt for self-assessment by students which may also bring responsibility among the students?

The comprehensive changes force social work educators to reassess their fundamental assumptions and take risks in changing the face of Fieldwork education to fit the current practice environment.

New Methods can be Employed to Assess the Students in Fieldwork

- Replacing the viva voce to theory exam. Or
- 50 per cent weightage to theory exam and Viva Voce.
- Marks for seminars, Attendance and Assignments on Fieldwork curricula.
- Linking marks to the practice of social work methods in Fieldwork.

The Changing Components of Fieldwork Practice

Social Work should address the concerns of marginalized, oppressed, suppressed, depressed, disempowered, destitute, exploited, abused, unsupported, weaker and vulnerable sections of society.

Change in Social Work intervention needs to be three dimensional — in height, breadth and depth as a profession.

- Firstly, in terms of height, SW has tremendous potential for contributing to social development and social welfare provision in all countries.
- Secondly, in terms of breadth, we should reach the unreached.
- The third dimension is that of depth, i.e. the depth of our knowledge, skills and commitment.

Ours is a profession in which service is supreme which is beyond self-interest. This necessitates the role of Social Workers, who act as change agents in transforming the lives of people in the global context integrate theory with practice.

The Fieldwork in social work must also focus on the process to educate the students to evaluate the effectiveness of interventions, Contend with the realities of social, political and economic injustice, Strive for cultural sensitivity and competence, Deliberate on the choices posed by ethical dilemmas, Develop a sense of self in practice; and Build a connection to, and an identity with the profession

Global Consciousness in Social Work

The impact of globalization has entered into the Family structure, Marriage values, and Social values. Globalization has also contributed to the Adultery, Food, Clothing, Employment and the Agricultural sector.

Global Outsourcing provides jobs to one country and takes away those jobs from another country, leaving many without opportunities. It has also impacted in the increase of environmental damage and erosion of traditional culture. Terrorists are now globally interconnected and empowered with knowledge. A direct consequence for the safety of people and the environment is on the threat.

Just like the Industrial Revolution, globalization entails radical change. Experts emphasize different features of globalization to stress the kind of changes that globalization brings. Globalization is a Solution, Communication allows the world to be a global village; free movement of capital/investment allows for well-needed funding of underdeveloped industries in underdeveloped countries, and Globalization is also a problem, which ruins Third World economy; international division of labour; increase the economic discrepancy between classes; monoculturalism. We the social workers must have the concern on the impact of globalization and take the positive and negative issues to the concerned curricula and for field practice.

Conclusion

The problem in the Fieldwork is that the sense of learning is being a university requirement rather than an aid to practice, a hindrance rather than a help. So, the universities must attempt to make Fieldwork learner friendly rather a formality. Agency supervisors must become partners of theory and classrooms and to improve the theoretical base for the theme.

Assessment tools of the Fieldwork must be redesigned at the

quality level and should be a self-check to the social work students and schools. Social work students must also be involved in their own assessment. Fieldwork training and theory are viewed as two different worlds by agency-based supervisors and social work students. So, the process of linkage to bridge theory and practice should be the priority of social work schools. The Departments of Social Work should organize workshops for agency-based supervisors to update their theoretical knowledge base. The faculty supervisor should conduct regular field visits during the field placement of the students. Communication channel should be established between agency and schools.

This is high time to redesign the pattern of Fieldwork in social work with quality perspectives. University, Social work Schools, Fieldwork agency and Social work students should be equally concerned to uphold the quality in Fieldwork.

References

Cox, D., Pawar, M., and Pawar, M.S. (2006). *International Social Work: Issues, Strategies, and Programmes*. Sage.

Dilshad, M. (2011). *Integrated Social Work Practice*. New Delhi: Anmol Publications Pvt. Ltd.

Evaluation of Fieldwork Practice in Social Work Education at The University of Limpopo: (Turfloop Campus) Aligning Theory and Practice, by Peter Masibinyane Dimo.

Garber, R. (2000). World Census of Social Work and Social Development Education Interim Report. *Canadian Social Work Review*, *17*, 198-215.

Guha, R. (2011). *Communication in Social Work*. New Delhi: Centrum Press.

——*Field Instruction in Social Work*. New Delhi: Centrum Press.

Hokenstad, M.C. and Kendall, K.A. (1995). *National Association of Social Workers, Encyclopedia of Social Work*, pp. 1511–20. Washington, DC: NASW Press.

International Federation of Social Work. (2014). Global Definition of Social Work. Retrieved from Http://Ifsw.Org/Get-Involved/Global-Definition-Of-Social-Work/.

Jagadish, B., and Siddegowda, Y.S. (2014). *Fieldwork in Social Work—Learning by Doing*. Jaipur: Pratheeksha Publications.

Khan, A.A. (2011). *Training for Social Work*. New Delhi: Anmol Publications Pvt. Ltd.

Midgley, J. (1981). *Professional Imperialism: Social Work in The Third World* (Vol. 16). Heinemann Educational Books.

Midgley, J. (2001). The Critical Perspective in Social Development. *Social Development Issues*, *23*(1): 42-50.

Salamone, F.A. (1979). Epistemological Implications of Fieldwork and Their Consequences. *American Anthropologist*, *81*(1): 46-60.

Singh, K., and Singh, R.S. (2011). *An Introduction to Social Work*. New Delhi: ABD Publishers

Singh, S. (2013). *Modernisation of Social Work Practices*. New Delhi: Centrum Press.

Smalley, R. (1968). Social Work Education: A World View. *Social Work/ Maatskaplike Work*, *27*(3-4), 339-346.

Subhedar, I.S. (2001). *Fieldwork Training in Social Work*. Jaipur: Rawat Publications.

Yu, S.W.K. (2018). The Contributions of Welfare Typologies to International Social Work Practices. *Asian Social Work and Policy Review*, *12*(2): 66-74.

11

Community Development Initiative Through *Swadhyaya*

A Case Study

Molankal Gangabhushan M.

Introduction

Swadhyaya initiative by Pandurang Shastri Athavale has been an important initiative towards addressing the problems of poor/underclass villages, which has transformed communities through collective action. '*Swadhyaya*' literally means the study, knowledge, and discovery of the self. According to proponents, it is a "journey to work out a unity in a multiverse of cultures and worldviews, of harmonizing the self with a network of relationships, of creating and maintaining vital connections between self, society, and God, of knowing and enriching human action with sacredness." The goal of *Swadhyaya* is to restore respect for a greater power and the creations of that greater power, especially respect for one's self. In this process of individual transformation, societal transformation occurs as a by-product. *Swadhyaya*'s discourse is centred on the idea that a divine force, an "indwelling god", resides in all human beings. The recognition of an inherent divinity is perceived as a strong foundation on which to build personal dignity and as a universal link between the self and others. The notion of an indwelling God is not new in the history of Hinduism; however, *Swadhyaya* puts it to novel use, actively attempting to refashion individuals for the purpose of redefining and strengthening human dignity and human relations. *Swadhyaya* insists to build bonds of brotherhood and community across the socio-economic and caste spectrum in India has social implications. The contribution of *Swadhyaya* has been immense as it tackles three of our most intractable social problems: caste, religion, and gender inequality. *Swadhyaya* is unique because its theory and praxis of self-fashioning are not concerned with the transformation of the self-alone. Instead, it seeks to redefine the self in terms of its relationship with the other through concrete practices rooted in the notion of devotion and aimed at creating bonds of brotherhood between selves. One of the things that made *Swadhyaya* so unique and so effective was that it offered a way of translating theory into practice. *Kriti-bhakti*, by its very definition, implied a devotion, which was expressed through action. *Swadhyaya* focused more on the rural people targeting the downtrodden sections of society such as fishermen and tribals in Maharashtra and Gujarat, especially in Gujarat. The thrust of *Swadhyaya* is on moral development—cultivation of the self towards higher and higher moral and spiritual levels, not by isolating oneself, but in active association with others, by improving relations with others and spreading selfless happiness all around.

Historical Background

Historical background of *Swadhyaya* movement goes back to 1980s in India and eventually has also percolated to different countries around the world. In the early years of *Swadhyaya's* urbanization, it created a needed space for critical thinking and personal commitment to non-denominational spiritual progress. The impetus for social transformation in India comes from its religious and spiritual traditions. Almost all the major reform movements of the 19th century drew their inspiration from religion and acted on it. Raja Rammohun Roy, Swami Dayananda Saraswati, Sri Ramakrishna Paramahansa were all religious leaders. Further back in Indian history, again and again, we see that religion is the source of social transformation. The whole *Bhakti* movement is an example.

Swadhyaya movement has given an impetus to the overall development of the communities cutting across caste, class and religion. *Swadhyaya* is a way of bringing diverse people together in such a manner that they can learn from each other and share each others' talents. Human beings need is dignity and recognition, which can only come from genuine mutuality and care, which is very well recognized in the *Swadhyaya* process.

Foundation of *Swadhyaya*

The philosophical foundations of *Swadhyaya* are inspired by the *Bhagavad Gita*. *Swadhyaya* makes the idea of indwelling god residing in everybody's heart and working for everybody, as the case of its vision and practice. There are a universal connectedness and sharing to which one has to awaken through '*Bhakti*' (devotion). The concept of devotion has two important aspects in *Swadhyaya*: one of self-exploration, with a view to becoming closer to God (*Bhava Bhakti*), and an active and creative principle of devotion to promote communal good (*kriti bhakti*). *Swadhyaya* emphasizes the need for both, i.e. emotional devotion and devotion associated with the action. Therefore, in *Kriti Bhakti* one exemplifies one's devotion to concrete acts of labour and love for and with the other, which has the potential to solve the socio-economic problems. The process of self-cultivation, realising one's full potential, cannot be done in isolation, but essentially in relation to others whose self-development too has to be cultivated. *Swadhyaya* emphasizes the need for "self-cultivation as means of both personal development and social reconstruction".

Swadhaya believes in the cultivation of self is the prerequisite for both personal development and social transformation. In other words, development is not confined to economic growth and political empowerment. However, it is primarily an initiative in developing one's intellect and heart. The real development is sustainable only when it is fundamentally a work towards inner transformation. The transformation is manifested in the change in perspective of the people. The *Swadhyaya* perspective emphasizes the brotherhood of all human beings and regards others as an integral part of one's own development. *Swadhyayees* believe that one's own valuation can be affected by the quality of social relations with others. While self-development certainly does not exclude economic development, it is incidental to one's development on moral, intellectual and knowledge planes. In the process, *Swadhyaya* movement imparted a sense of dignity and self-respect even to the lowly and downtrodden sections in the society, who regarded themselves as equal members of the *Swadhyaya* family. In a nutshell, the fundamental characteristics of *Swadhyaya* are given below:

1. *Swadhyaya* aims at spiritual mobilisation.
2. The primary stress of *Swadhyaya* is an individual's spiritual self-development.
3. Those who come to *Swadhyaya* do so for greater understanding of their own selves and self-cultivation in harmony with the self-development of others.
4. *Swadhyaya* is more egalitarian in outlook, selflessly interested in promoting the welfare of lower castes.
5. *Swadhyaya* is a loosely knit organisation of like-minded people with no formal membership.
6. The driving force behind *Swadhyaya* is *Bhakti* (love, devotion).
7. Towards other religions, *Swadhyayees* feel much more tolerant, understanding and friendly.

Activities

Swadhyaya has motivated the followers to express their devotion through their action (*Bhakti*). This individual transformation eventually can lead to wider social change through their collective actions scheduled in *Swadhyaya* as stated below:

Bhaktipheri: The primary practice in *Swadhyaya* for cultivating selfless love and affection for others is known as *bhāvpheri* and *bhaktipheri*. *Bhāvapheri* refers to local devotional visits involving meeting other people with the understanding of divine brotherhood and connectedness. The basis of the visits is to build a relationship of trust and to bring people to the realisation that each individual, each living thing is divine. Selfless work and selfless love is the only motive to meet others simply for the sake of meeting them and not for any selfish purpose through the practice of *bhāvapheri*. *Bhaktipheri* involves going to another village or town. *Bhaktipheri* provides an opportunity to experience homelessness voluntarily, establish new relationships, and collectively touch the transcendental dimension common to all. By continually talking about the messages and the basic concepts of *Swadhyaya*, *Swadhyayees* begin to understand, believe and follow.

Bhaktipheri abroad had to be mainly from one city to another city, in the Indian context, it has been from one village to another. In the meeting between villages, there takes place a critical reflection on the state of life and well-being, which translates itself into a series of projects where people can come together to share their time and labour towards collective welfare. Such projects are called *prayogas,* i.e. experimentations namely— *Yogeshwar Krishi, Matsyagandha etc.* They are tailored to the needs of local villages and conditions there.

Yogeshwar Krishi (Lord's Farming), where *Swadhyayees* of the village take a piece of land on lease and cultivate it through own labour, even while working on their own individual farms. It is a cooperative farming in which volunteers from one or several villages participate, each person subsequently, one day a month, works on cultivating that particular plot of land. They participate not as farmers, but as *pujaris*, or worshippers. What is produced from community farming is considered as impersonal wealth (*apourusheya Lakshmi*), one-third of which remains in the village for collective well-being, and two-thirds is deposited in the name of the village in a trust in the *Swadhyaya* headquarters in Mumbai.

This wealth is then used to help and support those who are the neediest, yet it is not seen as charity or dole. It is the *prasad* of the worshipful work of the whole community and can, therefore, be given and accepted in a manner as impersonal as that with which it was created. *Yogeshwar Krishi* is confined to one village; *Shri Darshanam* is the combined effort of 15-20 villages; while a *Vriksh Mandir* involves an even greater number. The sizes of the communes vary, ranging from two or three acres in a *Yogeshwar Krishi*, to dozens of acres in *Shri Darshanams* and *Vriksh Mandirs*.

Matsya Gandha: There is a similar experiment for fishermen in the form of a community boat. The same idea of creating impersonal wealth and building communities informs projects like *Matsya Gandha*. Here, instead of community farming, they have community fishing. Likewise, there are community vegetable carts, where the same concept of cooperative volunteerism is employed.

Voluntary time and labour given to such projects are called *shrambhakti* (devotional labour or simply labour of love). Projects to increase water supply in the village through the construction of clean water ponds (*Nirmal Neer*), well-recharging and other water conservation measures and soak-pits for improving village sanitation, are also executed through *shrambhakti*. There is disinclination towards the construction of roads as a *prayog*, as it is considered best done by the government, though *Swadhyayees* may induce the government to take it up in their areas. Doctors, traders and businessmen like diamond merchants are also involved in *shrambhakti*. Doctors give their precious time and skills for consultation, and medicines are given through health centres of *Swadhyayees*.

Other experiments include recharging wells, building or rebuilding tanks and water bodies, organic farming, etc. All these are meant to redress the ecological damage caused by the over-exploitation of the earth. Indeed, water management is the key to sustainable agriculture and rural reconstruction.

Amritalayam: Amritalayam is the hub of such community interaction, which is mainly a meeting place, including a place where collective worship is done. There are also *kendras* (centres) for providing free school education up to the fifth standard, crèche for younger kids, for women's interaction among themselves, youth centres and sometimes even centres for the elderly people. Such centres have come up even in tribal and *Dalit* colonies. Community singing and cultural activities, involving particularly children and women in the commonplace. In addition to such routine activities through village resources, *Swadhyayees* have risen to the occasion when calamities struck, such as when Gujarat was hit by a devastating earthquake.

Shrambhakti is normally offered where it is more difficult to raise resources in the form of money, but easier in the form of free voluntary labour. In such cases, *shrambhakti* is a potent form of community mobilisation for common good.

Bhavlakshis and Others

Bhavlakshi refers to the new name given to *Harijans* or Scheduled Castes. Rechristening the downtrodden communities with invitational new names which embody a new aspiration, are only first steps. But the realization of the potential of these words also calls for the structural transformation of bases of caste, class and gender which produce caste deprivation. Though there is a limit to this in *Swadhyaya,* but has changed the outlook of the downtrodden. Before *Swadhyaya*, this used to be like most other untouchable colonies — filthy, impoverished, neglected; the residents had a low self-esteem; drinking, gambling, wife-beating were rampant; very few children went to school; though the reservation policy had ensured jobs for some, there was terrible social discrimination and contempt for these people. After *Swadhyaya*, everything changed. The drinking and wife-beating stopped, as did the petty quarrels. Marriage customs were reformed; injurious and expensive superstitions were abandoned; children started going to school; the houses became clean and tidy.

The empowerment that comes with *Swadhyaya* is not external; it is not brought about by economic or social prosperity. It is not based on subsidies given by the Government. *Swadhyaya* transforms a person's concept of self from seeing himself as helpless and weak, a person begins to see himself as self-sufficient and strong. Communities which have been alienated from society are reintegrated by revitalizing relationships.

Outcome of Swadhyaya

The collective activities in the villages covered by *Swadhyaya*, which enrich social life and interaction and improved interpersonal relations within families, between families and between villages. *Swadhyaya* gives a fairly prominent role to women, insisting on giving due respect to them in all gender relations. Softness of speech, humility, affectionate and genuine concern for others, and readiness to help selflessly are insisted upon. Many families, treated as untouchable earlier, rose in social status as a result of their association with *Swadhyaya*. *Swadhyayees* have been helpful to small farmers who did not have irrigation wells of their own by giving them irrigation water. *Swadhyaya* has insisted on communal amity and brotherhood across religions too. Muslims have not hesitated to participate in *Swadhyaya* collective activities such as sports, and have even attended meetings in *Amritalayam* (pp. 138-39).

The changes were brought to the followers of *Swadhyaya* as a result of their participation in the movement was an impressive increase in the education of children and women, and in reading habit, improvement in husband-wife relations, in cleanliness, greater respect for people of other castes and religions including lower castes, and readiness to contribute labour and skills for community work. There was a spill-over impact even on families within the villages who were not *Swadhyayees* as such, in the form of village sanitation and cleanliness, social relations, more youth activities, centres for kids, health centres, and even through a general, if not conspicuous, improvement in economic well-being (pp. 24-25).

The *bhakti pheri* is a combination of a pilgrimage and a vacation. The emphasis on the family means that the husband and the wife get to do things together. Children are involved in the process from an early age. There is a special programme for youth and for women.

Thus, everyone is involved. What time might have been wasted in trivial socializing or gossip is now channelled for a higher cause. Everyone is constantly learning; this adds to the participants' self-esteem. The participants feel ennobled by the productive work that they are doing.

Conclusion

Thus, to sum up, *Swadhyaya* has initiated a relational revolution which has its multidimensional impacts, most notably in the emotional and the social fields. Emotionally, *Swadhyaya* has inspired its participants to discover the soft and subtler dimensions of life and in the social field; it has created manifold relationships across boundaries of caste and gender. *Swadhyaya* has impacted upon the economic life of people by creating new opportunities through social networks, by instilling a respect for one's labour and time, by cultivating the art of working together, by helping people realize their inherent and God-given potentiality. The success of *Swadhyaya* is based on the utter dedication and sincerity of its workers, because of innovative planning and vision, but most of all because it offers a holistic and total approach to the needs of its practitioners, nourishing their physical, vital, mental, and spiritual being. *Swadhyaya* works because it is practical and pragmatic, not unrealistic and other-worldly. It does not make impossible or unreasonable demands on its adherents. The extent to which they want to be involved is left entirely to each individual. Its structure may be hierarchical, but it is totally egalitarian in its approach to problem-solving. The changes brought about by it are gradual and self-motivated, not sudden and externally imposed. *Swadhyaya* provides a meaningful orientation to life, an orientation based on our own cultural patterns and resources. Ultimately, what makes *Swadhyaya* work is the yearning within each of us to improve our lives and to contribute our might to the betterment of the world. Each of us has this desire, but does not know how to fructify it. *Swadhyaya* shows the way.

References

Babb, L.A. (1991). *Redemptive Encounters: Three Modern Styles in the Hindu Tradition* (Vol. 1). University of California Press.

Fisher, M.P. (1997). *Living Religions: An Encyclopaedia of the World's Faiths*. IB Tauris.

Giri, A.K. (2009). *Self-development and Social Transformations?: The Vision and Practice of the Self-study Mobilization of Swadhyaya*. Lexington Books.

Jain, P. (2016). *Dharma and Ecology of Hindu Communities: Sustenance and Sustainability*. Routledge.

Katz, A.H. (1993). *Self-help in America: A Social Movement Perspective*. Twayne Publishers.

Shah, V.P. (1998). *Role of the Swadhyaya Parivar in Socio-economic Changes among the Tribals of Khedasan: A Case Study*. Gujarat Institute of Development Research.

Srivastava, R.K. (1998). *Vital Connections: Self, Society, God: Perspectives on Swadhyaya*. Weatherhill, Incorporated.

Tyndale, W. (Ed.). (2006). *Visions of Development: Faith-based Initiatives*. Ashgate Publishing Ltd.

12

Local-Governance

Revisiting Indian Indigenous Perspective

Yugal Jha

Introduction

The eighteenth century India witnessed cautious imperialism coupled with a number of religious reformation and movements. Apart from important reformation movements in the country like Arya Samaj, Prarthana Samaj, Brahmo Samaj, Satya Sodhak Samaj, Wahabi Movemnts and Kherwarism are the curtain raisers under the great leaders, saints and the creative genius of Indian mind who knocked the bemused mind of millions people to brood over their misery and shook the shackles of pedantic angers, old thoughts, superstitions, castes, creed and feudalistic segments for a new vibrant India. The Indian soil has been bequeathed by the great saints like Sur Das, Kabir das, Tulsi Das and Ravi Das, Chaitanya Mahaprabhu and Bhagirath Manjhi who have changed the mindset of the Indian people with their *mantras*, songs and slogans for the creation of a benevolent society throughout the country. Saints are philosophers and philosopher is born free.

The *mantras* of Chaitanya Mahaprabhu '*Hari Bol*', '*Krishna-Krishna*' has earned the long impress on the people of Bengal. The Sapahor movement or Kherwarism laid by Bhagirath Manjhi got electric spell on the indigenous people of Jharkhand and the people of rest India has been arrested in the soothing balm of the fiction of the great historical legacy of Murli Manohar, Sita Ram who enthralled the ecstasy of the cultural mosaic of Indian nation by Sur Das, Ravidas and Tulsidas. Sant Kabirdas has revolutionized the Indian people for the new order of the society which prepared the 'thought processes' in the Indian mind for the new set of Indian nation. Swami Dayananda has enriched the greater philosophy of Vedic India for the unification of Indian people. In brief, the Indian society was emerging as a nation for their democratic rights—the credit goes to these saints and philosophers for preparing the Indian soil for fraternity, equality and liberty. As Vinoba Bhave says that to strengthen the people's democracy "no rajniti but lokniti' is the single motto of *gram raj*. Supporting the system of 'village government' no party, no elections, no parliament, but the implementation of participating or communitarian democracy involves the devolution and genuine decentralization of political and economic power at all levels.

The great revolutionary Sido-Kanhu became the harbinger of the freedom call for the millions of slave India and gave a new spark of liberty in the strong voice of Hul against the imperial raj and became the founder of *Abua Raj*. In history, the Hul is known as Santhal Rebellion 1855—that charged the first war of indendence of 1857 all over the nation. The proposal of *Hind Swaraj* is the edition of *Abua Raj* proposed by Mahatma Gandhi in the freedom struggle of India. The Sapahor movement has been the further vindication of *Abua Raj* as the witness of mass support for the Quit India movement in the entire range of Santhal Pargana and Jharkhand as well. So, *Hind Swaraj* is the challenging inspiration of *Abua Raj* in the vision of Mahatma Gandhi that he released and uttered many times to the adoration of cultural ethos of the primitive India—the custodian of Vedic India in their habits, beliefs, customs and their abode of life. Specially, the Santhal society forms a part of pan-Indian cultural and belief-system continuum where as a large number of cultural and belief system usages conform to the same followed by most of the other tribes and castes of India. Our discourse used the world 'tribe' in a positive sense.

They live in the Santhal Parganas, Dhanbad, Hazaribag and Singhbhum districts of Jharkhand, and an entity as a state carved out from Bihar.

Although Santhals have a language of their own but because of their physical distribution, they write in different scripts like Oriya, Bengali, Roman and Devnagri. One of the experts of Santhali literature Sri Raghunath Murmu revolutionized the new script and invented it as 'Alchiki' with his innovative skill. Gradually, it is gaining its wide range in the field of writing and publications. Santhals are a homogenous group both biologically and linguistically and to a great extent even culturally. Like the ancient oral tradition of Vedic India, the Santhals too nursed and preserved the system of folk songs to their habits, habitations, description of their journey through time, record of their agricultural life, information about various occasions when these songs were to be sung either in private or in community life. All ancient civilizations have expressed their history in the form of oral modes reflected in their folk songs which also provide rich materials to know how they acknowledge their political, social and cultural togetherness with the co-existence of the ecology as an integral part of their philosophy of life.

Moral Institutions

Binti—The Santhali narratives of moral consciousness by the feminist clot of maternal power in the divine presence. The acceptance of the natural order constitutes an integral element in Santhals' view of life. The significant categories of Santhal consciousness are running hold in their daily walk of life. First, the Binti, the creative narratives and the Jaher-than. Central to the Santhal consciousness is the motion of Jaher-than, the sacred grove which reflects the women/nature complex in the Santhal worldview and worship. Both these need considerable elaboration for a full focus of self-system of governance of the village republic of the tribal society.

These narratives define the individual's social, psychological, cultural and gender position in a community. It focuses on a myth and presents a mechanism of self-representation and also includes the cosmic and trans-cosmic world of the gods, spirits, super-sensible beings, cosmic spaces and their total worldview.

Legends hold that Marnag Buru while wandering on the earth (Monchapuri) at different places from Harata to Chai-champa for more than one decade, he has to face hardships and sinful living. Their narratives known as '*sangal-jari*' rain fire destroying sins and '*Sangal Dha*' to recover the burnt jungles, trees and animals. The next narrative '*Thakur*' includes as '*sausabonga*' where he observed "the earth becomes dry and the sky red" due to the undue producing system on the earth. After the great destruction they entered the seven river valley called Champa where the soil was fertile and the plants and seeds thrived and the birds sang. After that they made this place their abode for twelve years and named this blessed and prosperous region *Chai-champa*. It was the land of light and happiness where the seed could be sown. Whenever the Santhals identify a settlement, they must locate the presence of a tree (*sarjom*), a bird (*sim*) and grass seed (*erierbe*) in a forest as an auspicious sign.

Thus, the narrative creation unfolds the story of the history of earlier migration and unsettled life. Several versions of the narrative have been recorded. The readings of the myth do not reflect the theological variations, but is limited to descriptions and episodes. Traditionally, santhals' belief centred on a supreme deity whom they called Thakur: By the order of Thakur, Lita (Supreme Goddess) informed him that earth (*monchapani*) is a beautiful place for the consort to live in. After that Thakur descended on earth with the help of gossamer thread (*toresutam*) and began to live there. Thakuran (goddess) on her part created a pair of male and female geese/swans and named Has and Hasal. After some time they laid two eggs in the care of Jaher-era and from which a pair of men and women called *pilchuharam* and *pilchubuddhi* were born. They became the ancestors of human race. Seven descendants of the earliest couple were the forefathers of the seven Santhal clans. Some of the place names that find mention in their myths of migration and folklore are Khos Kaman, Harata, Sansabeda, Jarpidisom, Ayrondisom, Kayandaydisom and Chai-champa disome. Legends hold that an important occasion is in times of crisis when the community recovers its collective memory to reaffirm clan solidarity. As the legends define that this clan was a short of demarcation of the domain as divided on the basis of their vocation. Each of them is assigned a geographical location.

1. Kishku—who enjoyed the status of a king located in Champanagar.
2. Hembram—the noble man given the region of Pouwagulin.
3. Marandi—a wealthy person whose shelter is Ajodya.
4. Siphahi—warriors who are not allotted any particular region.
5. Tudu—whose shelter is Dusianagar.
6. Hansala—the agriculturists who have their abode as Tatijhari. Besra—famous for performing dances, are given Bethlnagar.
7. Basky and Murmu are known as Thakur. The Murmus are blessed with the power to read and predict human destiny. They are assigned Sagarpuri as their abode.
8. The last three groups, Chore, Dodika and Pouria, adopted

forbidden practices in family life. They inhabit Gagichowri, Diyen, Buru, Sitapuripara Pachitareas. It is well recognized that these groups enjoy their equal status in the cell of their systems. God Moreiko (five primal of males) established the Santhal village. Turuiko (six males) are responsible for the succeeding generation of Santhals and Gosai-era, the spirit of motherhood.

One of the expert of Santhali literature. C.R. Manghi refers that 'Jaher' is the symbol of memory as women in the Santhal society. The relationship to nature is perennial and can be traced in many ancient cultures of the world. In the case of the Santhals, thus relationship is exposed as the adoration of the feminine principle in the form of a grove with Jaher-era, the lady of the grove with presiding deity. This Jaher is the residence of four other deities. Apart from Jaher-era, there is Marangburu (literally the highest mountain) who is regarded as this creator God, a source of knowledge, water and human acts. With the help of Jaher-era the presiding mother goddess is consistently involved throughout the year for protection, abundance and for good fortune of the community, animal kingdom, forest, plants, rivers, mountains and the whole of nature. The whole of nature is holy and sacred. This perception of wholeness is echoed in the invocations and prayers to the mother goddess in the Santhal literature.

Traditional institutions: As per the opinion of Lt. Basudeo Besra, renowned pleader of Santhal Pargana Court, explained in one of his articles "Traditions and Institutions of Santhals" brilliantly as follows—

The Santhals have a well-organized social political structure which is responsible for the discipline in the community. It is widely known that the British administration was highly impressed by the well-knit social organization of the Santhals. The smallest social organization of the Santhal village consisting of five persons was responsible for regulating day-to-day life, each with a distinct function. The headman of the village is known as Manjhi. He is assisted by Pramanick. Then comes the village priest known as Naike who is the ritual specialist responsible for conducting the yearly rituals and other celebrations; the next is Joga Manjhi, who guards the conduct and morals of the tribe, the last is Godet, the messenger whose job is to inform the villagers, the place and time of the meetings.

The next level of the administration is known as Pargana,

consisting of ten to twenty villages, with the Parganait at its head and several Manjhis below him. The third and highest level of administrative unit is the Shikar Parishad or Lobir which is the sheet of the traditional form of Supreme Court of the Santhals that mainly deals with cases of break-down of morals. The agency has the authority of 'Bithlaha' or pronouncing as a Santhal from their community as an out-caste, a punishment usually granted to over-indulgent men or women who have entered into an illicit relationship with an alien.

This well-established long standing system of authority has undergone changes under the police administration of the Indian Constitution. The Santhals as the citizens of the state have had to adhere to government rules with local panchayats having judicial powers. The traditional structure of the village councils is sometimes undercut and even rendered inefficient due to the malpractices of British administration. The independent India has revised the preamble of the constitution with the brilliant structure of the traditional institutions of the indigenous society. These indigenous institutions have played the role of a unifier and an integrator to build a self-reliant village republic in the tribal society. In fact, the Vedic culture of India depicts the indigenous approach of the Indian village system where the community life has been the backbone of the society. The feminine system of governance in the perception of wholeness for the complete configuration of the village autonomy for good fortune of the community that can be an example of an after alternative knowledge system from which we can learn something about the reorganization of the society and a reorientation to sublime thought of life.

It is interesting to observe that in time of need, these indigenous women have shown a remarkable resilience and have risen to the occasion. The Santhal women have been the part of reformation movement. The *Abua Raj* (Self-Rule) which has been the manifestation of Santhal rebellion of 1855, nearly 50 per cent were women and children. Many of them fought the British, some of them acted as informers. In the tribal tradition of '*Janishikar*', there is a custom where women in men's guise go for hunting, or to fight enemies. The story of Saini Dai, Kaili Dai and Debayani sisters who gave brilliant fight to the alien rulers was the great victory of Jharkhandi women in escorting the fort of Rohtasgarh during the imperial period. Not only were that women the part of Birsa

Movement—the vibrant phase of Ul-gulan which became the part of liberty on the broader past of Jharkhand movement. The great participation of those women in the tribal cultural movements linked to the preservation of adoption of Santhali language and script has played an active role in the social, political and cultural breakthrough of the Jharkhandi society.

But after seven decades, the persisting nexus of the present administration has disappointed and ruthlessly crushed the legacy of '*Jal, Jungle, Jameen*' for which the new state of Jharkhand paid their great sacrifices and contributions.

Its Impact on Making of Modern Indian Polity

In the period of Quit-India movements Mahatma Gandhi made several visits to make the indigenous people vibrant and recapitulate their brilliant past for the indomitable courage against injustice and slavery. In the open session of Ramgarh Congress, 1940, he honoured the great freedom fighter Birsa Munda as 'Bhagwan' of our society who has revolutionized the foundation of *Abua Raj* in his voice of '*Ulgulan*' on the broader past of Jharkhand Movement. The world philosopher Karl Marx has sketched the intensity of that 'Santhal' insurrection, 1855 as the 'Agrarian revolt' of Asian sub-continent. The strong spell of indigenous society has painted the pages of history as the first phase of socio-economic transformation for the deprived society and turned it into an agrarian unrest that impressed the emerging personality of Dr. B.R. Ambedkar in the thought process of social engineering before getting the political independence of India. Dr. B.R. Ambedkar was not new but the champion of establishing a new society out of caste, creed and orthodoxy of feudal order of the Indian society. He was impressed by the philosophers, social reformers and poetic genius of India like Mahatma Jyoti Rao Phule, M.G. Rana Dey, Subramaniam Bharati, Raja Ram Mohan Roy, Ravindra Nath Tagore, Bankim Chandra Chatterji and Nazrul Islam. These were the jewels of Indian society who had been propagating with their academic and social flight of thought at the set of finest creative compositions for the new democratic structure of the socialist secular and pluralistic form of emerging sovereign India.

Mahatma Gandhi's philosophy of *Hind Swaraj* was the standing pad to recapitulate the genius mind of Dr. B.R. Ambedkar at the conciliation point for the building process of modern India. Not only that it was the great ocean of all the riddles that was running throughout the nation either regional or national to nurture and furnish the pluralistic mind of Indian nation at the set of hundred and thousand socio-religious movement to liberate India against all the narrow domestic walls with the guarantee of democratic polity as a sovereign state of the world. After that, he requested Dr. Ambedkar to design the Constitution of Indian Republic to be the living organism of participatory democratic polity. Mahatma Gandhi quoted, "India's tryst with the democratic destiny would not be complete for the reach of human rights to attend the last strata of the society unless political democracy is supplemented by social and economic democracy". This point was vividly underlined by Dr. Ambedkar, the great visionary of human right claims and the Chairman of drafting committee in his last address to the constituent assembly.

The founding father of Republican Indian Polity has cemented the Indian Constitution with strong bricks of Democratic rights as the provision of Fundamental Rights in chapter 3 and the Directive Principles of State Policy in the 4th for the citizen of India. The Right to primary education to the children has been made afresh new add to the urgent part of fundamental right rather the normal one. The Fifth Schedule makes provision for the tribes' advisory council for administration for the scheduled areas and Scheduled tribes in other states of India. The Sixth Schedule of constitution also makes a special arrangement for the seven sisters of Northern states like Assam, Meghalaya, Manipur, Tripura, Nagaland, Mizoram and Arunachal Pradesh.

The Indian Constitution is the visionary ground of *Hind Swaraj* as quoted by Kenneth Kaunda, the veteran Gandhian, 'the right signal for the choice of strategy best suited for the needs of community life and for the individuals is the right place in the legitimate society for their civil rights which has still to achieve for the decades'. The Gandhian view of life commands the full canvas of involving the pluralistic set of society where the legacy of community life for which the artisan communities, and the primitive society fought many insurrections has been taken granted in the constitution but the real picture is different. The subjugated community are still running in anguish and frustrations after the provisions made for them in the constitution since more than half century. The *Abua Raj* is the great pedestal of *Hind Swaraj* that has been incorporated in its spirit and vision in the preamble of Indian constitution. Mahatma Gandhi has explained the brilliant structure of traditional institutions as the inherent character of self-reliant *gram swaraj* of Indian Republic. These indigenous institutions has played the role of unifier and an integrator where the company raj and its nexus has ruthlessly crushed the brilliant legacy of *Jal-Jungle- Jameen*— for which great revolutionary *Tilka Manjhi*, sacrificed his life in the Rajmahal hills. His martyrdom has been the source of inspiration for the coming generations who fought bravely against the British rule and still burning like the torch to focus on the taboos that still hurdles the herald of indigenous society. The indigenous society has been breathing with the philosophy of co-existence, which led us to think about the other great oral tradition of Vedic literature where the earth has been equated with mother— *Mata Bhoomi, Putro Aham*. That Vedic thought has been expounded by Swami Vivekananda as a visible expression of a divine mother that is 'Mother India' that regulates the livelihood of the people. This resemblance has opened the traditional resource inventory of traditional farming of the peasantry set of agricultural input, which has been the verdant vista of feminist civilizations that has been hampered by the maladministration of exploitative colonial regime. The specific feature of the indigenous society has been sketched in the book of '*Santhal Village Government*' by W.W. Hunter, 1868 and by then settlement officer John Reed in the report of Irrigation and Canal Commission 1901-03.

Thus, the self-reliant village of indigenous society as in the vision of '*Abua Aato Re: Abua Raj*' is the finest replica of *Hind Swaraj* with its traditional set of Institutions like Manjhi, Pargana, or disom pargana in the lap of mountain, river and long range of forest cover. In the 17th chapter of *Santhal Pargana Gazetteer* it has been written, "the people themselves are final authority, the officials are only their representatives appointed to perform certain duties and to keep order and to represent them generally." But, the rein of imperialism ruined the entire set of indigenous India and established the colonial rule of British Raj. The persisting regime of British administration has been in constant feud and in turmoil at its root by the uprisings and revolt of indigenous people.

Conclusion

The genesis of any renaissance movement lies in the helplessness of community to meet the onslaught of the machinery of operations.

While severe ecological and politico-economical stress associated especially with colonial conquests and intense class exploitation beliefs and rituals tends to be concerned with achieving a drastic improvement in the immediate condition of life and/or in the prospects of an afterlife. The entire regime has undergone in the same condition. But their sufferings, sacrifices and martyrdom herald the horizon of societal change for the new road of national building under the umbrella of constructive social-cultural reconstructions for a sovereign nation that India achieved gradually after decades. Thus, the democratic republic of India, which has been bestowed by revolution, revolt and the formative movements is the real creation of great visionary of leadership from generation to generation from *Abua Raj* to *Hind Swaraj* and being carried out in the present form of Panchayati Raj Institutions— a counterpart of the continuous journey for participatory decentralized democratic polity of the modern India. The Panchayati Raj system was envisaged as reintroducing method of *gram swaraj* by empowering the people to deal with their problems as per the hierarchy (District, Block and the Village panchayat) of the system. The development plan and schemes can be attributed to top-down planning and approach towards the people. District or block level planning can be only generic, while the specific plan for the development of village should be the domain of panchayats. People participations through panchayats will prove to be panacea for all miss-governance and they have the potential for good governance at the local level provided them institutionally, financially and legally are supported by the existing power structures. Due to the shockingly poor state of implementation, the entire set of system needs to be squarely placed at the door of the top structures. There should be a national level authority which has to work as a watching dog to check the proper implementations of the entire human development programmes. The gist of these indicators drive one to conclude the main objective of the good governance is to maximize the well-being of the people. Gandhian concept of *Hind Swaraj* is the real foundation of good governance. His global vision of liberty for the human society is the village republic system based on the autonomous rural economy, signifying with the full sense of social justice and peace. The Panchayati Raj Act, passed by Parliament in December 1992, easily constitutes a milestone in the history of '*Gram Swaraj*' as Gandhi Spoke "freedom from meanest of our countrymen". The amendment, in-fact aimed at enhancing the capabilities of the rural people to evolve themselves in the planning process with respect to their priorities. It also exercised decentralization of the execution of all types of development activities with the active participation of the rural masses. In nutshell, the purpose of the amendment has to bring good governance at the rural local level through decentralization.

References

Akbar, M.J. (16 February, 2008). Towards a Global India. *Times of India.*

Bodding, P.O. (1942). *Traditions and Institution of Santhals Bulletin, Auslo.*

Choudhary, P.C.R. (1935). *Santhal Pargana Gazetteer.*

Dutta, K.K. (1988). *The Santhal Insurrection: 1855-57.* Calcutta: University of Calcutta.

Gandhi, M. (1924). *Young India.* Swami Anand, Navajivan Press.

Gandhi, M.K. (1939). *Hind Swaraj.* Ahmedabad:

Haeke, E.H. (1866). *Ancient Wisdom and Ecology.* Chicago: Loyola University Press.

Hansda D., and Sahu, D. (1998). *Sameer Santhal Sahitya Academy, Language and Literary Profile.* Jamshedpur, Jharkhand.

Hembrom T. (1996). *Theological Reflection of Santhals.* 10-11.

Nawedker, B.M.(1984). *History of Indian Philosophy.* Delhi: Motilal Banarasi Dass.

Saha, C. (1996). *The Santhal Women.* Delhi: Delhi Book Depot.

Santhal, B.B.K. (2012). Culture and the Traditional Belief System in Pan-Indian Continuum Frame, National Seminar, Dumka, 2-3 October, 2012. Dumka: S.K.M. University.

13

Overview of Information and Communication Technology (ICT) Integration in Social Work Education and Practice

Ushvinder Kaur Popli and *Payal Poddar Singhania*

Introduction

Information and Communication Technology (ICT) has brought revolution not only in the technological arena, but also in human development. ICT plays a pivotal role in providing education for all students. With the integration of ICT in social work education, its horizon is expanding. Information and communication technologies (ICTs) are broadly defined as technologies used to convey, manipulate, and store data by electronic means. This can include e-mail, SMS text messaging, video chat (e.g., Skype), and online social media (e.g., Facebook). It also includes all the different computing devices (e.g., laptop, computers and smartphones) that carry out a wide range of communication and information functions. ICTs are pervasive in developed countries and considered integral in the efforts to build social, political, and economic participation in developing countries. For example, the United Nations (2006) recognizes that ICTs are necessary for helping the world achieve eight time-specific goals for reducing poverty and other social and economic problems. Despite this interest in technology, the attention that the field of social work has given to ICTs in research, education, and practice does not match the efforts of other national and international organizations that view ICTs as critical to improving the lives of disadvantaged and disenfranchised persons, and necessary for all forms of civil engagement. The Council on Social Work Education (CSWE) calls for the integration of computer technology into social work education, but there are no explicit standards for integration or student learning (CSWE, 2008; Beaulaurier and Radisch, 2005). Asking other social workers, social work students, and social work educators can easily reveal that many are unaware of the NASW technology standards. A review of syllabi of social work courses will also show that ICTs, beyond e-mail communication, are generally not present in the educational environment. Consequently, social work students are not being adequately prepared in the use of ICTs, which are integral in the workforce today and will become even more important over time.

Concept of ICT

The term Information and communication technology consists of three components, they are 'Information', 'Communication' and 'Technology'. In general, it is said that the purpose of all communication is to bring about the change for the better, to influence some action in order to promote the common welfare of a group or an organisation. Communication refers to impart, transmit, interchange of message, fact, ideas, opinion or emotions of two or more persons. The method, tact, and the devices used in effective communication are called the technology.

Informatics (computing science): UNESCO defines informatics as the science dealing with the design, realization, evaluation, use, and maintenance of information processing systems including hardware, software, organisational and human aspects, and the industrial, commercial, governmental and political implications of these.

Informatics Technology: Informatics technology is defined as the technological applications (artifacts) of informatics in society.

Information and Communication Technology: ICT is defined as the combination of informatics technology with other related technologies especially communication technology. The definition implies that ICT will be used, applied, and integrated into activities of working and learning on the basis of conceptual understanding and methods of informatics.

ICT in Education

Information and Communication Technology (ICT) can contribute to universal access to education, equity in education, the delivery of quality learning and teaching, teachers' professional development and more efficient education management, governance and administration. Organizations like UNESCO take a holistic and comprehensive approach to promote ICT in education. Access, inclusion, and quality are among the main challenges. ICT has permeated in every walk of life. Year by year it is becoming simpler to use devices such as desktop, iPad, iPod, and mobile. Due to the emergence of a knowledge-based society, today, information is flooded in different forms.

The impact of ICT on education in India, however, has been far less and slow. The most fundamental cause seems to have been the deep-seated belief that teaching is an art or at best an imperfect science with no role of technology in the design or delivery of instruction. Now, time has changed and the paradigm of education and learning has changed from art or science to technology-mediated instruction and learning. ICT can, therefore, be perceived as a big change agent for education.

In case of Open and Distance Education (ODE) system where "Anyone, Anywhere and Anytime", that is, 3As is the main philosophy, ICT- enabled education can do wonders that no one can imagine and help pave way for the creation of virtual universities in the long run. ICT can also significantly contribute to efficiently managing the governance in the universities and colleges. ICT in education is the need of the hour. It has the potential to provide a solution to many of the challenges of higher education faces today. The common fear that ICT shall replace a teacher is totally unfounded. Realization now seems to be slowly dawning on the teaching community that ICT is primarily to empower them and not to replace them. ICT is, therefore, not to be feared, but to be embraced so as to empower our future generations by providing them high-quality ICT-enabled education.

Role of ICT in Rural Development

Rural areas and villages are among those areas that need information technology development. Information technology can have an important role in promoting the prosperity in economics, social, cultural, and political aspects of rural areas. ICT has helped in infusing the knowledge with the technology rendering the easy access to information by the rural population. Knowledge is information for an individual, but it is an asset for the whole society. Information sharing on new production processes with farmers was prominent in the sixties, which was the key to the success of the green revolution. Rural economies can be benefited from ICT by focusing on social production, social consumption, and social services in rural areas. In India ICT applications such as Warana, Dristee, Sari, Sks, E-Chaupal, Cybermohalla, Bhoomi, E-Mitra, Deesha, Star, Setu, Friends, E-Seva, Lokmitra, E-Post, Gramdoot, Dyandoot, Tarahaat, Dhan, Akshaya, Honeybee, Praja are in functioning for rural development. ICTs can play a significant role in combating rural and urban poverty and fostering sustainable development by creating information-rich societies and supporting livelihoods. If ICTs are appropriately deployed and realize the differential needs of urban and rural people, they can become powerful tools of economic, social, and political empowerment. The role of ICT to enhance food security and support rural livelihoods is increasingly recognised and was officially endorsed at the World Summit on the Information Society (WSIS) 2003-2005. This includes the use of computers, internet, geographical information systems, mobile phones, as well as traditional media such as radio or TV. Although, it is a relatively new phenomenon, evidence of the contribution of ICT to agricultural development and poverty alleviation is becoming increasingly available.

ICT and agriculture

The vast majority of poor people lives in rural areas and derives their livelihoods directly or indirectly from agriculture. Increasing the efficiency, productivity, and sustainability of small-scale farms is an area where ICT can make a significant contribution. Farming involves risks and uncertainties, with farmers facing many threats from poor soils, drought, erosion, and pests. ICTs can deliver useful information to farmers about agriculture like crop care and animal husbandry, fertilizer and feedstock inputs, pest control, seed sourcing and market prices.

ICT for Economic Development

Information and Communication Technology has a vital role in connecting the rural community to the outside world for exchange of information, a basic necessity for economic development. Effective use of ICT can demolish geographical boundaries and can bring rural communities closer to global economic systems and be of meaningful help to the underprivileged.

Employment Opportunities

Poor people in rural localities have lack of opportunities for employment because they often do not have access to information about them. One use of ICTs is to provide online services for job placement through electronic labour exchanges in public employment service or other placement agencies.

ICT in e-Governance

The poverty can be adequately addressed by effective use of e-governance and ICT application in environmental management. Improved governance by using ICT can have a direct impact on reducing poverty and improving the environment. ICT can contribute in a large way by making government processes more efficient and transparent by encouraging communication and information sharing among rural and marginalized people. A role is also played by ICT in making processes more efficient and transparent. It helps in making laws and land titles more accessible. Global Positioning Systems (GPS) linked to Geographical Information Systems (GIS), digital cameras and internet, help rural communities to document, and communicate their situation. Rural communities benefit from better access to credit and rural banking facilities. Recent mobile banking initiatives offer further scope to reduce costs and stimulate local trade. The Indian AMUL programme automates milk collection and payments for its 5,00,000 members, thereby enhancing transparency of the milk volume and quality collected and ensuring fair payments to farmers.

ICT and Service Delivery Mechanisms

There is a huge gap between information residing in agricultural knowledge centres and rural communities. At the local level, multi-stakeholder mechanisms are important to make relevant information accessible to end users. Intermediary organizations have to connect rural communities to available knowledge. Users will increasingly want tailor-made, quality answers to their questions. In the Agricultural Clinics in India, customers get answers within one to two days. Mobile Q&A services are being piloted in India. At the national level, mechanisms need to be in place to ensure learning and information sharing. The type of ICT used by local communities is subject to rapid change. However, broadband internet access is seen as central for societal innovation because storing large datasets and live communication requires good connectivity. Until recently, connectivity in rural areas was limited to slow dial-up lines. Satellite connections now make broadband access possible in remote areas. Use of mobile phones has seen an enormous increase in recent years. Nevertheless, big differences still exist in broadband access between developed and developing countries. New wireless technologies such as MESH and WiMAX, and new-generation mobile phone networks, will provide high-speed internet services at sharply reduced costs, thereby dramatically increasing internet coverage in rural areas.

Role of ICT and Healthcare system

Health care is one of the most promising areas for poverty alleviation. ICTs are being used in India to facilitate remote consultation, diagnosis, and treatment. Delivering health care with ICTs enables healthcare professionals and institutions to address the critical medical needs of rural communities, especially those in remote locations and those that lack qualified medical personnel and services.

E-Health, broadly defined as the use of Information and Communication Technology (ICT) in health, e-Health is that it is enabling the transformation of the health system from one that is narrowly focused on curing diseases in hospitals by health professionals, to a system focused on keeping citizens healthy by providing them with information to take care of their health whenever the need arises, and wherever they may be.

Public health service run by the Government is overburdened and collapsing. Large geographical size, increase in population density, lack of transport, inaccessibility, illiteracy, poverty, poor nutritional status, low budget for health, lack of funds and coordination and diversity in food habit and lifestyle are various challenges that have triggered downtrend in health services.

Web services are essential for medical professionals, administrative members, and patients to organize, share and access medical services. Improving health care involves not only improving the knowledge and skills of medical Professionals, but also empowering people with the knowledge needed to make informed decisions about how to live healthier. ICT offers a plethora of alternatives to communicating important health messages to the public.

The application areas of ICT in healthcare are broadly classified into Health Research, Hospital Management System, Management of Health data, and Health Education. The highlights of some of the initiatives taken by the Government of India and by various State Governments in India to provide a quality and sustainable health care services using ICT. Some of the initiatives are e-Aushadhi, BADEA (Birth and Death Entry Application System), E-Mamta (MCTS) and CHRIS – Computerized Human Resource Information System, e-Vidya is an electronic primary healthcare amenities in the rural area.

Background of Social Work Education

Social work is a discipline that grew out of humanitarian and democratic ideals and its values are based on equality, worth, and dignity of all the people in the society. (www.ifsw.org). Human rights and social justice are the main motivation behind the social action. Social work as a profession strives to alleviate poverty and uplift the vulnerable and oppressed people in the society in order to achieve the social inclusion and development.

Social work education in India began with the establishment of the Sir Sorabji Tata Graduate School of Social Work in 1936. The development of social work in India took a societal approach, in contrast to individual approach applied in Western social work. Social work education expanded its scope and includes other fields, such as family, child, youth welfare, rural and urban development, and medical and psychiatric social work with both training as well as methods are available.

The major goal of social work is to enhance the well-being of people to develop their capacities to become participating and contributing citizen[s] developmental tasks of the profession are related communities in problem solving and bringing about change in institutional structure and processes which retard, block or deflect development (University Grant Commission, 1980: 41). Implementing a uniform syllabus across all universities in the country represented a great challenge, and, indeed, the social work curriculum and patterns of fieldwork practice still differ among universities (Thomas, 2010: 57).

Implication for Social Work Education

It is the fact that technology has transformed the practice of social work today, and, as predicted by the NASW and the ASWB (2005), we may have automated interventions in the future. As Dragon (2006) rightly observes, applying technology to practice is good, but one should remember that technology is just a tool one utilizes to facilitate care or service delivery. Three fundamental questions should entail critical reflections when deciding on incorporating technology into social work education and practice. These questions include: (1) Will technology improve social work education and practice? (2) Will technology ensure quality services for our clients? (3) Given the reality of digital inequality or divides (Aqili & Moghaddam, 2008; Mellander, 2011) and owing to the fact that social workers have historically worked with individuals living in poverty (NASW, 2008), will incorporate technology into social work foster timely access to services? The practical implications of these questions must always be considered as one adapts and deploys technologies in social work. The Council on Social Work Education (2008) recognizes the importance of technology in social work education and acknowledges this in its Educational Policy and Accreditation Standards Policy 1.2. Both the National Association of Social Workers (NASW) and the Association of Social Work Boards (ASWB) (2005) equally recognize the centrality of technology to social work practice, maintaining that technology has transformed social work practice and offers new ways of providing services.

Threat/Challenges

There are possible threats and challenges for developing the ICT based knowledge and using it. Some of the threats and challenges are as follows.

Cost of good quality content creation is very high and costs of infrastructure investment for developing such content and for use of the content is also high. There is also lack of sufficient Internet connectivity in rural and small town areas. Teachers must believe and get convinced that ICT is helping them and students in the teaching-learning process because teachers feel that they will be replaced by the ICT based knowledge in future (which is not a fact. Traditional teaching-learning process will last long). Lots of information/content is available on the Internet, but students get confused in referring to the right content. Therefore, efforts are required by the teacher to curate the content and guide students.

Problems of Developing Quality E-Content

As a part of the Ministry of Human Resource Development Mission of NME– ICT, the researchers are developing e-Content for Business Management, Human Resource Management, Office Management and Secretarial Practice and Indian Classical Music courses for undergraduate. Till now, they have developed about 350 programmes out of approximately 1100 programmes. The content has different components like Objectives, Synopsis, Transcript, Power-point Presentation, Academic Script, Frequently Asked Questions (FAQs) with answers, Multiple Choice Questions (MCQs) with answers, Tutorials, Assignments, Case Studies, Glossary, References, Authentic Web Links, and Misconceptions. While developing these programmes, the researchers came across many problems. Some of the problems are mentioned below—The biggest problem is that the good teachers are not ready to come forward and prepare the material required for developing the content. There is lack of initiative of developing since it requires a lot of components as mentioned earlier like transcript, Academic Script, FAQs, MCQs, and Tutorial etc. Developing the content requires original thought. The tendency of downloading material from the Internet is killing original thinking. The good teachers are also required to have good presentation skills and have voice modulation. The lecture of about thirty minutes should build interest in students to learn the topic. Studies show that these teachers are camera conscious (shy). They fear to face the camera. In future, more and more interactive modules are required to be developed for which the trainer/teacher should have the in-depth domain knowledge to explain different queries from different students and to have more interaction. The template should be easy to browse/move around and should have a good colour scheme, so, that while using these programmes, students must feel comfortable and should continue using it repeatedly. For this, proper 'Instructional Designers' are required to be trained properly. They have the knowledge of developing these interactive e-Content modules. The support technical staff also should know the subject or at least try to understand the subject. Therefore, while developing the content he/she can contribute creatively. Finally, all involved must keep a view that "ICT must be of the best Quality".

The Impact of Technology on Social Work Practice

Technology has played and continues to play a significant role in social work. Social workers and other professional service providers are using the internet to interact with clients regularly (Farley, Smith, & Boyle, 2003). Such interactions or Internet services may be question-and-answer chats, e-mails about appointments, or weekly group-counselling sessions, which may be very helpful to homebound clients with small children, people with debilitating illnesses, or rural clients. The National Association of Social Workers and the Association of Social Work Boards (2005) equally underscore the impact of technology on social work. They acknowledge that technology has impacted every aspect of social work practice, ranging from direct practice to macro or community practice. At the level of direct practice, the use of electronic mail (e-mails) facilitates with fewer cost communications among workers as well as between workers and clients (Bradley & Hendricks, 2009). The Web has made it easy for online support groups to be established and for both workers and clients to interact as well as to access and retrieve information and needed resources online (Kaplan, Wade, Conteh, & Martz, 2011; Art, 2009). At the agency or organizational level, technology has of social media work if one should address issues of privacy on social networking sites (Zur, 2011). Second, workers should not shed traditional practice models; instead, traditional protocols should be adapted to the new reality. Third, practitioners should adjust to the demands of new technologies. Finally and most importantly, workers should always refer to the deployment of technology in social work practice.

Conclusion

It must be remembered that the integration of ICT into social work education and practice cannot be accomplished overnight. It takes years of planning and preparation, refining and retuning the systems. The other thing to keep in mind is the rapid change and development in technology. It is not uncommon to find innovative tools and practices once very much in vogue quickly losing grounds to newer inventions. Any investment made in the now "outdated" technology could, therefore, be lost – a situation to be avoided at all costs especially in view of limited resources. This certainly creates a dilemma. On the one hand, development of ICT for learning is a long-term project; on the other, the ICT sector advances too fast to permit ponderous consideration and decision-making. The field of social work education, research, and practice is surrounded by rapid developments in ICTs. In order to ensure that social work practice upholds the standards and values of social work ethics, it is necessary that social workers are competent and literate in ICTs. This will position social workers at all levels of practice to help advance the lives of disenfranchised and disadvantaged persons through greater access to education, knowledge and other resources. While numerous ICTs have failed to realize their expected potential, the ongoing rapid growth of ICTs has created a context in which social workers cannot resist technology, but must understand the role it plays in everyday life.

References

(n.d.). Retrieved from: http://www.e-aushadhi.rajasthan.gov.in/DWH/startup/loginAction

Alden, C. (2004). For most Africans, Internet access is little more than a pipe dream. Online Journalism Review. Retrieved online August 20, 2009, from: http://www.ojr.org/ojr/workplace/1079109268.php

Bargh, J.A., and McKenna, K.Y. (2004). The Internet and social life. *Annu. Rev. Psychol.*, *55*, 573-590.

Bargh, J.A., McKenna, K., and Fitzsimons, G.M. (2002). Can you see the real me? Activation and expression of the "true self" on the internet. *Journal of Social Issues, 58*(1): 33-48.

Bhatnagar, S.C. (n.d). *E-Government: From Vision to Implementation—A Practical Guide with Case Studies*. New Delhi: Sage Publications Pvt. Ltd.

Car, J., and Sheikh, A. (2004). Email consultations in health care: 2—acceptability and safe application. *British Medical Journal, 329*(7463): 439-442.

Chandrasekhar, C.P., and Ghosh, J. (2001). Information and communication technologies and health in low-income countries: The potential and the constraints. *Bulletin of the World Health Organization*, 79(9), Geneva. Retrieved online August 24, 2009, from: http://www.scielosp.org/pdf/bwho/v79n9/v79n9a10.pdf

Council.on Social Work Education. (2008). Educational policy and accreditation standards. Retrieved, January 10, 2016, from: http://www.cswe.org/File.aspx?id=13780

Dash, B.M. (2017). Revisiting eight decades of social work education in India. *Asian Social Work and Policy Review*, *11*(1): 66-75.

E-mamta.gujarat.glov.in. (n.d.). Retrieved from: https://server.easycounter.com/e-mamta.gujarat.glov.in

Finn, J. (1999). An exploration of helping processes in an online self-help group focusing on issues of disability. *Health and Social Work, 24*(3): 220-231.

Gujarathi, D.M. and Patil, R.S. (2009), Role of ICT and e-governance for Rural Development, *International Referred Research Journal*, 1(9).

Health & Family Welfare, Government of Rajasthan, Jaipur. (n.d.). Retrieved from: http://chrisnrhm.org/

ICT in Education. (n.d.). Retrieved from: http://ictcurriculum.gov.in/

Information and Communication Technology. (n.d.). Retrieved from: http://mhrd.gov.in/ict_overview

Information and Communications Technology. (2018, September 01). Retrieved from: https://en.wikipedia.org/wiki/Information_and_communications_technology

Kinesics. (2018, August 28). Retrieved from: https://en.wikipedia.org/wiki/Kinesics

Nadkarni, V.V., and Desai, K.T. (2012). *Report of the national consultation on national network of schools of social work for quality enhancement of social work education in India*. Mumbai: Tata Institute of Social Sciences.

Pandey, S. (2013). Social work through distance education: Commitment for justice, equity, and inclusion of the marginalized. *Perspectives in Social Work*, 28(1): 47–64.

Pradhan Mantri Swasthya Suraksha Yojana (PMSSY). (n.d.). Retrieved from: http://pmssy-mohfw.nic.in/

Primary, Secondary and Tertiary Health Care. (n.d.). Retrieved from: http://www.arthapedia.in/index.php?title=Primary,_Secondary_and_Tertiary_HealthCare

Thomas, G., and Varghese, J. (2012). Social work education around the world. In S. Singh (Ed.), *Encyclopaedia of Social Work*, Vol. 4 (pp. 1385–96). Lucknow: New Royal Book Company.

University Grants Commission (1980). *Review of Social Work Education in India: Retrospect and Prospect*. New Delhi: UGC.

14

Dalits, Human Rights and Social Work Practice

Pratap C. Behera

Introduction

Human rights are not static; they continuously evolve in time and space. Though universal in its initial character, it stands for equality and non-discrimination. Bases of discrimination are many. Identity and difference are important among them. Human rights practice addresses disparities that arise because of the identity of groups. The difference is materially and socially shaped. Often, materiality is the cause. Therefore, material disposition leads to the social. There is a dialectical relationship between identity and difference. Identity and difference are the values and social realities. Human rights protect the identity of a cultural and social group. Addressing the identity concerns minimises the differences and subordination. Social work, as a caring and helping profession, takes the side of subordinated and subjugated. Social work worked with these sections of society employing different models of practice. For the last couple of decades, social work treats the concerns of the subordinated groups as matters of human rights. The imperative is to adopt an empowering, anti-oppressive and emancipatory practice model.

Human Rights Discourse

Human rights are dynamic in nature and constructed, rather than objectively existing. They emerge and vary depending on the varying cultures and political contexts over time (Ife, 2008). In this context, Ife (2008) poses a number of important questions:

> "...Whose voices are privileged in the human rights discourse, and whose are not? How can other voices be heard, and are there other ways in which human rights might be conceptualised? Are some rights privileged over others, and does the way in which we have conceptualised human rights value some sorts of human action and marginalise others?" (Ife, 2008: 11)

The age at present is variously known. This is the age of globalisation and neoliberal era. It is 'the age of rights' as well (Baxi, 1997: 142). Baxi further highlights the confrontation between 'emerging cultures of rights' and 'entrenched cultures of power'. The underlying principle, according to Professor Baxi, is the 'right to be human and to remain human' (*Ibid*). Drawing from the works of Zajda & Ozdowski (2017), we do have a number of questions. Some of them can be articulated as questions as they follow here. How can we create a more equitable, respectful, inclusive, and just society for everyone? How do we address the challenges of globalisation while promoting human rights education? Baxi (2008) describes the contemporary scenario as an "era of post-development and of hyperglobalization". In this period, "social and cultural pluralities are seen to pose an obstacle, rather than an asset, for human and social development" (p. 49). His emphases are to "privilege the voices of the suffering and rightless people and the communities in resistance" (p. 51).

The philosophical deliberations make the human rights polemic, particularly its universal concept. The individual rights *versus* group or collective rights are matters of serious concern. There are also questions related to the origin of the ideas articulated in human rights declarations. There are views that the conception of human rights are "hegemonically Western and spread colonialism or imperialism in a very indirect way" (Baxi, 1997: 148). Accordingly, it promotes the colonial and capitalist agenda. It has a homogenising effect. The decolonised nations, indigenous cultures, socialistic nation-states and eastern culture and societies have different conceptions of rights. Therefore, promotion of human rights and human rights education should address the cultural diversity. To have a pragmatic approach, it "requires that like cases should be treated alike and that there should be a differential treatment only where there are relevant differences" (Milne, 1986: 43).

Dialectics of Difference

We need to have some operational sense of the concept of difference before deliberating on its practical significance, more specifically its human rights connotations. Fiona Williams (1996) discusses the concepts of diversity, difference and division in her emphasis to address the concerns of the subalterns. According to her, diversity is the "difference claimed upon a shared collective experience which is specific and not necessarily associated with a subordinated or unequal subject position"; difference would refer to "a situation where a shared collective experience/identity forms the basis for resistance against the positioning of that identity as subordinate"; and division would mean "translation of the expression of a shared experience into a form of domination" (Williams, 1996: 70). This is the objective reflection of an unequal hierarchically stratified social order in a society. In Indian scenario, differences can be prominently seen in the domain of caste, class, gender, religion and language.

There is also a dialectic relationship between social identity and social difference. According to Eisenberg (2003), differences among people "play a constitutive role in shaping their identities. The approach is predicated on the fact that the shape and health of identity largely depend upon how societal institutions treat differences amongst people" (p. 51). The different approach asserts the historical facts, "paying close attention to the role played by particular practices and by the histories of distinct groups" (Eisenberg, 2001: 165). People's histories and different perspective, together, see the necessity of rights to protect their distinctive values and cultures.

Imre (2010) discusses the ideas of Alain Badiou. For Badiou, the material realities of a social group are not so important which is quite problematic. To make it clear, Imre cites the example of Maoists. Often, they are 'the other', in a society. Across societies and nation-states, the other is numerous, different and diverse. Often, there are contesting positions of the other. And, we can comprehend that without looking at the material deprivation of the communities, our understanding of their social position and reactions would be incomplete and would have shortcomings. In a way, the material condition shapes the social. The crux of his views can be discerned from the following:

> "...There are clear differences and measurable 'better' and 'worse' conditions of existence in which material needs can be discussed and compared. If we want to reinvigorate social work practice, then why not (re)politicise it by demanding that our own nation-states look at the successes of other nation-states and think about employing similar strategies at home? This is a deeply politicised practice, and would most certainly raise the ire of those governing the discourse around the diversity and difference problematic..." (Imre, 2010: 256).

Unless difference leads to a subordinated position, the difference is closer to diversity. Diversity is to be cherished. More often than not, this is not the case. Those sensitive to concerns of subaltern social groups and communities, they count difference seriously. It becomes a larger agenda to address. However, we do see counter views. In an article titled "*Against Difference and Diversity in Social Work: The Case of Human Rights*" Webb (2009) says, " Social work should be 'indifferent to differences' by transcending the politics of difference." (p. 309). This happens to be a problematic statement and attracted reactions. His argument is that social work should be with inequality and injustice but not with difference. However, one aspect of difference is that it is a manifestation of social and material inequalities. The other aspect of difference is not because of inequalities, but because of culture and belief systems which developed through evolutionary processes. When the social differences are social facts, a neutral or an indifferent stance to the differences would not be logical and would go against the basic tenets of social justice. Therefore, Fierlbeck would say: "to respect individuals within distinct cultural groups may in this way require differential rights; rights which protect cultural or group-specific traditions and institutions prior to the uniform rights propounded by the proponents of a more traditional democratic liberalism" (Fierlbeck, 1996: 3). However, the extent of differential treatment may vary. The reasons for this, she would say, are "philosophically unconvincing and possibly politically dangerous" (Fierlbeck, 1996: 22). Eisenberg (1994) looks at the values underlying the rights. Then, she goes on to reflect on the identity-related differences and the conflicts between individuals and communities. For example, an individual can have a dissenting voice, beliefs or lifestyles. Even, it can include such things as unique literary or creative expressions. These individual stances may be in conflict with community values and belief systems. Language, culture, gender, caste, tribe and religion, among many others, are the bases of group identities and differences. The thrust areas of protecting individual and group differences, therefore, would vary. Individuals may have certain advantages, privileges, power and rights. However, the rights would serve the values that are the bases of expressing differences. Measures of protecting individual differences may not address the concerns of group differences. What would it mean to protect individual difference? Eisenberg elaborates, it would mean:

> ...allowing individuals the opportunity to voice their opinions, to choose their beliefs and generally to be the authors of their own lives and identities as long as their choices do not cause harm to others. A politics that values individual differences may set parameters to community decision-making by employing rights as devices to protect the interests which are crucial to the preservation of individual identity. (Eisenberg, 1994: 11).

Differences do Matter

Differences can pertain to individuals and social groups. The nature of difference would vary when it applies to social groups. Therefore, group differences require separate contextualisation and approach. The differences are construed between an individual *versus* a group or between groups. When it comes to preserving or protecting a group difference, the focus would be to "protect a group that dissents or differs from all or some of the practices of the larger community, just as the politics of individual difference protects individual dissent from the community" (Eisenberg, 1994: 12). Hence, addressing the difference and recognizing rights would go hand in hand. Green (2000) summarises the discussions of Eisenberg and Fierlbeck. Eisenberg discusses the case of Aboriginal peoples in Canada having their identity and identity-based differences. There is inherent value in difference. Eisenberg advocates protecting identities whereas Fierlbeck differs.

Here, Fierlbeck takes a stand that identity is to be construed as "private and personal and therefore indeterminate and idiosyncratic; Identity is not an appropriate source of rights; drives people to focus on difference rather than on commonality" (Green, 2000: 134). In a rejoinder, Eisenberg makes her position more clear. In the case of aboriginal communities, the rights are not just to protect their identities. Rather, these rights pre-exist the Canadian nation-state. Colonialism added the elements of domination and exploitation (Baxi, 1997). At times, unless we become critical, the so-called rights can be wrongs. Therefore, a moral stance is often a necessity (Audi, 2005).

Both Eisenberg and Fierlbeck deliberated upon difference and its human rights interface (Eisenberg, 1994, 2001, 2003; Fierlbeck, 1996). Similarly, if we look at the academic exchange between Eisenberg and Green, we also see the nuances related to difference and human rights (Eisenberg, 2001; Green, 2000). Because of historical reasons, different social groups in a society or nation-state enjoyed varying quantities of social and material benefits. It often or always favoured the dominant groups and marginalised the remaining groups. In this context, Fierlbeck questions the fair and neutral principle. She would say, "some groups have, statistically, remained relatively disadvantaged in the face of ostensibly fair and neutral principles has increasingly led theorists to question whether it is our perception of what constitutes "fair and neutral" which has exacerbated the marginalization of certain identifiable groups" (Fierlbeck, 1996: 3).

Difference and *Dalit* assertions

Let us think about the *Dalits* who suffered human rights violations, in spite of several safeguards in the Constitution of India. As we have discussed earlier, the economic context of the *Dalit* families shapes their social realities. We can bring in the perspective of *Broken People*. With emphasis, the summary note of the publication describes the context of economic conditions affecting the *Dalits*. The excerpts worth reading as given below:

> Most *Dalits* continue to live in extreme poverty, without land or opportunities for better employment or education. With the exception of a minority who have benefited from India's policy of quotas in education and government jobs, *Dalits*

> are relegated to the most menial of tasks, as manual scavengers, removers of human waste and dead animals, leather workers, street sweepers, and cobblers. *Dalit* children make up the majority of those sold into bondage to pay off debts to upper-caste creditors. *Dalit* men, women, and children numbering in the tens of millions work as agricultural labourers. Their upper-caste employers frequently use caste as a cover for exploitative economic arrangements: social sanction of their status as lesser beings allows their impoverishment to continue (Narula & Human Rights Watch, 1999).

Historical positions and current human development scenario of the *Dalits* have been extensively deliberated (Irudayam, Mangubhai, & Lee, 2006; Mangubhai, 2014). We can have a look at the figures relating to the poverty rate among the *Dalits* (Government of India, 2005). At least in six Indian states, the poverty rate among the *Dalits* is more than 50 per cent. The Millennium Development Goals had an agenda to reduce the poverty by half (United Nations, 2000). *Dalits* is both an identity and a subjugated category representing differences among castes. In a narrative, Bob (2007: 167) raises the following questions: "Why are certain problems recognized as human rights issues, while others are not? How do historically marginalized groups transform long-standing domestic grievances into internationally cognizable human rights claims?" (p. 167)

An ironic point is that the atrocities against *Dalits* were never treated as human rights issues until the late 1990s. Caste is different from race. So, the provisions of the International Convention on the Elimination of All Forms of Racial Discrimination (ICERD) did not apply. The first article of ICERD talks about the meaning of racial discrimination.

> ...the term "racial discrimination" shall mean any distinction, exclusion, restriction or preference based on race, colour, descent, or national or ethnic origin which has the purpose or effect of nullifying or impairing the recognition, enjoyment or exercise, on an equal footing, of human rights and fundamental freedoms in the political, economic, social, cultural or any other field of public life.

Here, descent meant racial decent and, therefore, caste-based descent in India was excluded. In 1996, as a result of the constant lobbying of the *Dalit* groups, ICERD refined the meaning of the term descent. The limited meaning of descent changed from descent solely based on race. It implied also the descent based on caste and tribe in India (Bob, 2007). This has repercussions on education and human rights education. What is apparent or not so apparent is a challenge for the educators as well as practitioners. A vulnerable community is voiceless or silenced; therefore, they themselves and their concerns remain invisible. It requires a sensitivity and competency to question the everyday happenings. They look so normal. Questioning and critical analyses can open up the issues. Or else, they do go unnoticed.

Social Work Practice and Human Rights

We have an unequal world. There are human oppression and suffering, mainly with the marginalised and the vulnerable. There is a need to promote social justice and human development. That is the reason of social work practice (Dominelli, 2002). We may start with the latest definition of social work as shared globally as given below:

> "Social work is a practice-based profession and an academic discipline that promotes social change and development, social cohesion, and the empowerment and liberation of people. Principles of social justice, human rights, collective responsibility and respect for diversities are central to social work. Underpinned by theories of social work, social sciences, humanities and indigenous knowledge, social work engages people and structures to address life challenges and enhance well-being" (IFSW, 2014).

From this definition, as from the historical narratives, it is clear that the human rights perspective is integral to the social work. Since its inception, its practice mainly revolved around issues which later came in the purview of the declarations and covenants on human rights. Recognition of human dignity and worth of individuals are embedded in the Universal Declaration of Human Rights are at the core of Social Work Profession. The concern for human being would be there irrespective of the material or social status of an individual (Gore, 1969; United Nations, 1948). Gore (1969) describes the nature of social work as "an interventive action for the enhancement of the social functioning of individuals and groups... It will additionally identify and promote values and practices necessary for the realization of human rights... consistent with the rights of other individuals and groups." (p. 67).

In India, we have a constitution which reflects our diverse culture, principles of justice and human rights. India is also a signatory to the Universal Declaration of Human Rights and has ratified its rules and Acts as expected in several covenants and treaties on human rights. The uniqueness of India is that it has several castes, tribes, religious and linguistic minorities, gender, persons with disabilities, refugees and sexual minorities. In each social category, there is a large vulnerable and marginalised constituency. Their problems have been shaped and exacerbated because of historical reasons. In the two to three decades, several incidences communal violence in India has undermined its secular character. Concerns for the protection of minorities and their human rights are key agenda before the polity (Sinha, 2005). Demand is growing to adopt rights-based approaches to address their woes (Nadkarni & Sinha, 2016). Adoption of human rights approach does not mean leaving the other models. Incorporation of human rights into existing model would make the approach more empowering (Skegg, 2005).

As Witkin (1998) would say, "...Social work's concern for meeting basic human needs, its respect for differences, and its social change orientation position it at the forefront of human rights struggles..." (p. 198) The problems in the community would require a reframing or reconceptualization. Instead of assigning the reason either to the vulnerable individual or to the state, a problem could be framed as a human rights issue (Witkin, 1998). This would increase the visibility of the problem, locally as well as globally.

United Nations Centre for Human Rights (1994) articulates the conceptual linkages between social work and human rights in much detail. Elements of human rights concepts and perspectives are integral to the core of the social work profession. Freedom and human rights are indivisible. Ideas of human rights are embedded in social work theory and practice (Witkin, 1998). The core values, principles and ethics of social work have a direct correspondence with human rights. With these, a social worker takes the side of the vulnerable in a society. The complicity of human rights problem gets further accentuated by the global structural environment. It produces and perpetuates the discrepancies in income and power; provides unequal access to wealth and opportunity in society (Salomon, 2008). In a similar fashion, Garrett (2002) looks at the relationship of poverty and social differences and expresses his concern that the integration of both is not yet accomplished. With an intent to move closer to human rights profession, Steen, Mann, & Gryglewicz (2016) support the infusion of human rights content in social work education.

We come across narratives giving perspectives on anti-oppressive social work practice (Clifford, 1992, 1995; Clifford & Burke, 2001). They address the interests of the people who are marginal, poor, minorities, lower caste communities, especially those who have been subordinated and exploited by the dominant groups in the society. More specifically, it addresses the concerns of social divisions in society, especially race, caste, class, gender, religion, disability, sexual orientation, and age as matters of broad social structure. Clifford (1992) discusses the principles of anti-oppressive social work practice. Among them, one principle is to follow an anti-reductionist approach and locate the problem within a specific historical context. A subaltern group, may be with a colonial past, might be going through complex and multidimensional problems. Therefore, situating the problem in its historical context and following a holistic approach to understanding the problem are necessary. This process, which is also another principle of Clifford, would help in conceptualising the material dimensions of economic and political power structures in society. A thorough analysis of difference is crucial in his approach. The difference indicates the existing social divisions and the position of a subordinated group in society. It requires a separate pedagogy to address the concerns of subjugated and subordinated in a society. Perspective of conscientization and praxis of Freire would be quite relevant (Freire, 1993; Mies, 2014). Emancipatory social work is also discussed in the light of anti-oppressive practice. Instead of looking at liberty from interference from other individuals or the state, emancipatory practice would make efforts to increase people's autonomy and opportunity sets that would promote human well-being (Jordan, 2004).

Conclusion

Though social work education champions the cause of human rights, still there is a lot of scope for the social workers to develop competency in human rights (Steen, Mann, Restivo, Mazany, & Chapple, 2017; Reichert, 2015). Explicit involvement of social worker in the field of human rights is not very old. International Federation of Social Workers (IFSW) did not mention human rights as a social work principle in its ethics document until 1994. Now, human rights are part of social work principles. The process has just begun. The social workers require developing the ability to see human rights issues in the context of diversity and differences in society in terms of caste, class, age, gender, religion, language, and sexual orientations. These social constructs add to the heterogeneous composition of a community. Manifestations of problems in a community are embedded in key social institutions, structures, and policies. In this context, Libal & Harding (2015) emphasise the understanding of social conditions and how they interplay with various problems. This understanding would lead to becoming sensitive and empathetic to the apathetic situation of the subaltern groups. At the same time, it would enable community practice. This has bearing on the process of empowerment.

References

Audi, R. (2005). Wrongs within rights. *Philosophical Issues, 15*(1): 121-139.

Baxi, U. (1994). *Human Rights Education: The Promise of the Third Millennium*?

Baxi, U. (2008). Normative content of a treaty as opposed to the Declaration on the Right to Development: Marginal observations.

Bob, C. (2007). Dalit rights are human rights: Caste discrimination, international activism, and the construction of a new human rights issue. *Human Rights Quarterly*, pp. 167-193.

Clifford, D. (1992). Towards an anti-oppressive social work assessment method. *Practice, 6*(3): 226-238.

Clifford, D. (1995). Methods in oral history and social work. *Oral History, 23*(2): 65-70.

Clifford, D., and Burke, B. (2001). What practical difference does it make? Anti-oppressive ethics and informed consent. *Practice, 13*(3): 17-28.

Dominelli, L., and Campling, J. (2002). *Anti-oppressive Social Work Theory and Practice*. MacMillan International Higher Education.

Eisenberg, A. (1994). The politics of individual and group difference in Canadian jurisprudence. *Canadian Journal of Political Science/Revue canadienne de science politique, 27*(1): 3-21.

Eisenberg, A. (2001). Using Difference to Resolve Rights-Based Conflicts:

A Reply to Joyce Green. *Canadian Journal of Political Science/Revue canadienne de science politique, 34*(1): 163-168.

Eisenberg, A. (2003). Diversity and equality: three approaches to cultural and sexual difference. *Journal of Political Philosophy, 11*(1): 41-64.

Fierlbeck, K. (1996). The ambivalent potential of cultural identity. *Canadian Journal of Political Science/Revue canadienne de science politique, 29*(1): 3-22.

Freire, P. (1970). Pedagogy of the oppressed (MB Ramos, Trans.). *New York: Continuum*, 2007.

G.J. Andreopoulos and R.P. Claude (Eds.). *Human Rights Education for the 21st century.* Philadelphia: University of Pennsylvania Press.

Garrett, P.M. (2002). Social work and the just society: Diversity, difference and the sequestration of poverty. *Journal of Social Work, 2*(2): 187-210.

Gore, M.S. (1969). Social work and its human rights aspects. In *Social Welfare and Human Rights, Proceedings of the Fourteenth International Conference on Social Welfare* (pp. 56-68).

Government of India. (2005). Selected State-wise Percentage of Population Living Below Poverty Line (BPL) by Social Groups in Rural and Urban Areas of India (2004-2005). Retrieved from www.indiastat.com/table/economy/8/inciden%0D%0Aceofpoverty/221/443325/data.aspx

Green, J.A. (2000). The difference debate: Reducing rights to cultural flavours. *Canadian Journal of Political Science/Revue canadienne de science politique, 33*(1): 133-144.

Ife, J. (2012). *Human Rights and Social Work: Towards Rights-based Practice*. Cambridge University Press.

IFSW. (2014). Global Definition of the Social Work Profession. Berne: IFSW. Retrieved from: http://ifsw.org/policies/definition-of-social-work/

Imre, R. (2010). Badiou and the philosophy of social work: a reply to Stephen Webb. *International Journal of Social Welfare, 19*(2): 253-258.

J.D. Wright (Ed.). *International Encyclopedia of the Social & Behavioural Sciences (pp. 353–359)*. Amsterdam: Elsevier.

Jordan, B. (2004). Emancipatory social work? Opportunity or oxymoron. *British Journal of Social Work, 34*(1): 5-19.

Libal, K.R., and Harding, S. (2015). *Human Rights-based Community Practice in the United States*. Springer International Publishing.

Mangubhai, J.P. (2014). *Human Rights as Practice: Dalit Women Securing Livelihood Entitlements in South India*. New Delhi: Oxford University Press.

Mangubhai, J.P., and Lee, J.G. (2012). *Dalit Women Speak out: Caste, Class and Gender Violence in India*. Zubaan.

Marks, S.P. (Ed.). (2008). *Implementing the Right to Development: the Role of international law*. Friedrich-Ebert-Stiftung.

Mies, M. (2014). Freire's Method of Education Conscientisation in Latin America. *Economic & Political Weekly, 8*(39): 1764-1767.

Milne, A.J.M. (1986). *Human Rights and Human Diversity*. London: Palgrave MacMillan.

Nadkarni, V.V., and Sinha, R. (2016). Transforming Social Work Education in India: Integrating Human Rights. *Journal of Human Rights and Social Work, 1*(1): 9–18.

Narula, S., and Human Rights Watch. (1999). *Broken people: caste violence against India's untouchables.* New York: Human Rights Watch.

Reichert, E. (2015). *Human Rights and Social Work.*

Salomon, M.E. (2008). *Legal cosmopolitanism and the normative contribution of the right to development.*

Sinha, M.K. (2005). Minority rights: A case study of India. *International Journal on Minority and Group Rights, 12*(4): 355.

Skegg, A.M. (2005). Brief Note: Human Rights and Social Work: A Western imposition or empowerment to the people? *International Social Work, 48*(5): 667-672.

Steen, J.A., Mann, M., and Gryglewicz, K. (2016). The human rights philosophy: support and opposition among undergraduate Social Work students. *Journal of Teaching in Social Work, 36*(5): 446-459.

Steen, J.A., Mann, M., Restivo, N., Mazany, S., & Chapple, R. (2017). Human rights: its meaning and practice in social work field settings. *Social Work, 62*(1): 9-17.

United Nations Centre for Human Rights. (1994). *Human rights and social work: A manual for schools of social work and the social work profession.* New York and Geneva: United Nations.

United Nations. (1948). The Universal Declaration of Human Rights, 1948. Geneva: United Nations. Retrieved from: http://www.un.org/en/udhrbook/pdf/udhr_booklet_en_web.pdf

United Nations. (2000). GOAL 1: ERADICATE EXTREME POVERTY & HUNGER. Retrieved from http://www.un.org/millenniumgoals/pdf/Goal_1_fs.pdf

Webb, S.A. (2009). Against difference and diversity in social work: the case of human rights. *International Journal of Social Welfare, 18*(3): 307-316.

Williams, F. (2002). Postmodernism, feminism and the question of difference. In *Social Theory, Social Change and Social Work* (pp. 71-86). Routledge.

Witkin, S.L. (1998). Human Rights and Social Work. *Social Work, 43*(3): 197–201.

Zajda, J., and Ozdowski, S. (2017). Globalisation and human rights education: emerging issues. In *Globalisation, Human Rights Education and Reforms* (pp. 1-11). Springer, Dordrecht.

Annex–I

Selected State-wise Percentage of Population Living Below Poverty Line (BPL) by Social Groups in Rural and Urban Areas of India (2004-2005)

States/UTs	*Rural*				*Urban*			
	ST	*SC*	*OBC*	*Others*	*SC*	*ST*	*OBC*	*Others*
Andhra Pradesh	30.5	15.4	9.5	4.1	50.0	39.9	28.9	20.6
Assam	14.1	27.7	18.8	25.4	4.8	8.6	8.6	4.2
Bihar	53.3	64.0	37.8	26.6	57.2	67.2	41.4	18.3
Chhattisgarh	54.7	32.7	33.9	29.2	41.0	52.0	52.7	21.4
Delhi	0.0	0.0	0.0	10.6	9.4	35.8	18.3	6.4
Gujarat	34.7	21.8	19.1	4.8	21.4	16.0	22.9	7.0
Haryana	0.0	26.8	13.9	4.2	4.6	33.4	22.5	5.9
Himachal Pradesh	14.9	19.6	9.1	6.4	2.4	5.6	10.1	2.0
Jammu & Kashmir	8.8	5.2	10.0	3.3	0.0	13.7	4.8	7.8
Jharkhand	54.2	57.9	40.2	37.1	45.1	47.2	19.1	9.2
Karnataka	23.5	31.8	20.9	13.8	58.3	50.6	39.1	20.3
Kerala	44.3	21.6	13.7	6.6	19.2	32.5	24.3	7.8
Madhya Pradesh	58.6	42.8	29.6	13.4	44.7	67.3	55.5	20.8
Maharashtra	56.6	44.8	23.9	18.9	40.4	43.2	35.6	26.8
Odisha	75.6	50.2	36.9	23.4	61.8	72.6	50.2	28.9
Punjab	30.7	14.6	10.6	2.2	2.1	16.1	8.4	2.9
Rajasthan	32.6	28.7	13.1	8.2	24.1	52.1	35.6	20.7
Tamil Nadu	32.1	31.2	19.8	19.1	32.5	40.2	20.9	6.5
Uttar Pradesh	32.4	44.8	32.9	19.7	37.4	44.9	36.6	19.2
Uttarakhand	43.2	54.2	44.8	33.5	64.4	65.7	46.5	25.5
West Bengal	42.4	29.5	18.3	27.5	25.7	28.5	10.4	13.0
All India	**47.2**	**36.8**	**26.7**	**16.1**	**33.3**	**39.9**	**31.4**	**16.0**

Compiled from the statistics released by: Ministry of Tribal Affairs, Government of India. https://www.indiastat.com/table/economy/8/incidenceofpoverty/221/443325/data.aspx

Accessed on 14.3.2018.

15

Social Work Intervention with Single Parent Families

A Case Study of Half-Widows in Kashmir

Sumeera Nazir and *Dr. Shazia Manzoor*

Introduction

A single parent sometimes called a solo-parent is a parent that is not living with a spouse or partner, who has most of the day-to-day responsibilities in raising the child or children. A single parent is usually considered the primary caregiver. The primary caregiver is the parent the child have residency with the majority of the time (Dowd Nancy, 1997). If the parents are separated or divorced, children live with their custodial parent and have visitation or secondary residence with their non-custodial parent. (Benokraitis, Nijole, 2012, 2011, 2008). Single parenthood is a phenomenon that has always been in eistence and is as old as mankind. The demographics of single parenting show a general increase worldwide in children living in single-parent homes (Jayson, Sharon, 13 May, 2009). Single parenting has become an accepted norm in the United States and is an accepted trend found in many other countries. Debates concerning issues bothering on single-parent households, and more have risen. Recently, the numbers of single-parent families have increased drastically and it is gaining a global dimension. Parenthood is challenging enough even under the best of conditions. So, being a single parent in our society is tasking, to say the least. This is because, with one parent, the challenges are multifaceted. Single parenting in our society has been the focus of much interest and research in recent years. (Chiemelie Ezeobi, 2011). According to Funmilayo

Oriyomi (2011), a communicator, "The effect of single parenting are far reaching because it does not only affect the parents, it also affects the children. In fact, the effects are more devastating on the part of the children because single parenthood leaves them with deep scars. Being a single parent is a very tough and challenging task. Many of the problems that single parents have are similar to those of the two parents' family, but these problems seem more difficult to bear or manage when the home is being tutored by only one person. For example, all children feel hostile towards their parents as they grow up and try to be independent. But in a situation, where the anger and rebellion are all directed towards one person, it may seem worse, if there is only one to bear it, not for the two to share (single parent impact on children). The role of the single parent is challenging one especially when the family is headed by a woman. The problem of a single mother is linked with the upbringing of children, their future and setting down in life. The emotional life of the single mother was also affected by their single status. Majority of the single mother reported that they felt lonely, helpless, hopeless, lack of identity and lack of confidence. In the social sphere, majority of single mothers tried to avoid attending social gatherings and had changed their dressing style due to depression. They had developed poor food and eating habits. Majority of the single mothers found it hard to maintain discipline among the children due to the absence of male members. The mothers complained about loneliness, traumatic and depression and found it difficult to handle the responsibility of childcare and to establish a routine for her children.

The phenomenon of enforced disappearances emerged in Kashmir after 1989, after the outbreak of armed conflict gave rise to single-parent families. The heavily deployed security forces (more than six hundred thousand, the highest number of the army during peacetime anywhere in the world) during its campaign against combatant Kashmiris have resorted to different forms of human right violations like extra-judicial executions, custodial deaths, custodial torture, rapes, forced labour, including the Disappearances. As security forces suspect every Kashmiri so due to promiscuous arrests of the non-combatant Kashmiris and subsequent tortures has resulted in the disappearances from last 11 years. People from all spheres of life and different age groups, from 10 years to seventy years after their arrests have got disappeared. Militants, their sympathizers, political activists and large number of innocent persons have become the victims of Enforced Disappearances (APDP, n.d.).

The purpose of social work provides the vision, direction and motivation for addressing social problems for resolving interpersonal conflicts, and meeting human needs. Improvement of the quality of life in the human condition is envisioned as an explicit goal of the profession. Promoting adaptive functioning in the relationship between individuals and social institutions is central to the purpose of social work (Gulalia, 2008). The present chapter shows that the Half-widow face multidimensional problems which include social, economic, psychological and legal, and any social work intervention which is proposed to be done with these women should be able to take into account the various systems within the social environment of the Half-widows which have a direct or indirect bearing on their lives.

Methodology

In view of the complexity of the issue and respecting the uniqueness of every individual, qualitative methodology was adopted by the researcher to collect the data. The issue of Half-widows is very sensitive, their unending grief and continuous identity crisis cannot be measured in numbers. There is a need to understand the issue in a peculiar way seeking the uniqueness of each case within their context. Theoretical aspects of the study were very important to understand the issues and problems of Half-widows in a holistic manner. The issues of the Half-widows were studied by using secondary sources like books, reports, research papers, government reports etc. Based on the findings of the issues faced by Half-widows in Kashmir a Social Work Intervention programme was framed by the researcher in order to Alleviate the sufferings of Half-widows.

Objectives

- To explore the issues faced by Half-widows in Kashmir.
- To frame a Social Work intervention for Half-widows.

Half-widows as Single-parent Families in Kashmir

Kashmir is "estimated to have between 8,000 to 10,000 cases of politically motivated disappearance. Non-combatant Kashmiris account for the majority of the victims of custodial disappearances according to the Asian Human Rights Commission. Thousands of women in Kashmir are going through identity crisis owing to the phenomenon of enforced disappearances (Coalition of Civil Society, 2005). Kashmir conflict gave rise to a new section of society known as "Half-widows". Women are labelled as 'Half-widows' when their husbands have been disappeared but not yet been declared dead. As wives of 'disappeared', Half-widows occupy a precarious position, one of constant limbo, and face various economic, social, and emotional insecurities (Kaur, 2012). Half-widows experience many of the same problems as widows, but their situation bears some unique aspects. Besides the uncertainty about the existence of their loved one, they do not get official recognition of their status, as there is no proof of the husband's death. The struggle for survival with the sudden loss of the main breadwinner often pushes them to poverty and suffering. Under the circumstances, pressure mounts on the half-widows to assume the role of breadwinners for their households. In the process, they struggle between new roles and responsibilities, on one side, and their own vulnerabilities and deficiencies, on the other. Not being able to bury their loved ones and mourn properly adds to psychological trauma, as they do not get any closure. Death rituals like funerals for enabling the person or group to deal with loss and death and to start the process of reintegrating in the society (Bllauw and Lahteenmaki, 2002). Amidst the pain of losing their husbands, Half-widows endure the pain of searching often unsuccessfully for years for any word on the men's fates. In addition, Half-widows suffer as non-widows because they can't prove their husbands' deaths, they often face barriers to benefits like life insurance or government aid programmes. Some have no livelihood or education outside of their spouse, and certain fundamentalist cultures do not permit them to remarry without labeling the relationship adultery. Half-widows also run the same risks as any other impoverished, single females in a poor country. They have very little physical protection, if any, and run a high risk of losing their land (Caring for Half-widows, 2011). A half-widow assumes new roles and responsibilities, faces newer challenges, and in the process gets transformed in many ways. The society's attitude towards her also undergoes change (Qutub, 2012). The majority of the half-widows is illiterate and has no means of employment, some do menial jobs, like washing dishes and other kind of work which does not meet their financial needs (Kaur, 2004). In this context, it becomes common for the family unit to disintegrate as the Half-widows sometimes cannot afford to look after their children and they may get sent to live with other relatives or at an orphanage (Women's International League for Peace and Freedom, 2005). Some children are forced to engage in child labour out of necessity (Imroz, 2002). There have been reports of Half-widows facing domestic abuse in their in-laws' homes where they perceived to be an additional burden on the family (Women's International League for Peace and Freedom, 2005). Some return to their parents' homes, and others who are without parents become homeless after they are forced out of their in-laws' homes. This places the Half-widows in greater physical and economic insecurity (Kaur, 2004). Their forced status as 'single women' coupled with gender biases results in Half-widows facing social isolation, shaming, and physical vulnerability. Half-widows are at times senselessly blamed for their husbands' disappearances. For example, the women are told they are bad luck for the family or that they brought on tragedy due to their bad character or deeds. Furthermore, they are often watched with suspicion: being 'without a man', they are accused of trying to attract other men should they continue to dress as they did when married, or leave the house for work or everyday chores, or meet with lawyers or government officials. Some Half-widows have also reported becoming targets of sexual violence from those viewing them as defenseless without a partner (APDP, 2011). They faced threats to their life and harassment which sometimes made them regret the decision to follow their cases. Moreover, sexual harassment is a big issue facing these women. They not only find their life under threat in this process, but are also physically vulnerable in their encounters with the army, police and counter-insurgents (Zia, 2009). In addition to poverty, Half-widows face social stigma especially when it comes to remarriage. It is rare for Half-widows to remarry as it is a social taboo and they are often afraid of being ostracized by their communities if they marry again (Chuodhary and Moser, 2007). Half-widows on the one hand struggle for their identity and on the other hand child's self-esteem is wrapped in the identity of a missing father, a generation of children is now living through the confusion of broken dreams (Shukla, n.d.). A revision has been made to Islamic law which allows them to marry after four years which is largely underutilized by the Half-widows who prioritize raising their kids. Children of the disappeared have become half-orphans, undergoing a high level of psychiatric problems... the trauma of losing a family member along with the added stress of shouldering family responsibilities played havoc with the delicate equilibrium of many adolescents (Amnesty Report, 1999). For many Half-widows, the constant dilemma of whether or not to remarry is juggled with a sense of loyalty and the love for the missing husband. The considerations include children, too, whose very survival is a herculean task for single mothers struggling with life, education for their children and their own money making efforts (Shukla, n.d.). The Half-widows have often found themselves at the receiving end of the society. Scores of poor Half-widows, who do not come from wealthy families in Kashmir, are living in desolate conditions and suffering psychological illnesses connected to war conflict, including an inclination towards suicide. Many have fallen prey to psychological problems including depression, phobia, emotional instability and Post-Traumatic Stress Disorder (Shukla, n.d.). The various socio-economic pressures together have psychological effects on Half-widows that largely go unaddressed. Most of the Half-Widow reports anxiety (often described in terms of "speeding up" or palpitations), sleep disorders, and lack of interest in everyday activities. Many Half-widows would exhibit Post-Traumatic Stress Disorder (PTSD); Anxiety attacks may be triggered by memories of the disappearance or the disappeared (APDP, 2011). The findings gave a glimpse of the agonies of Half-widows. They are living a miserable life under the shadows of insecurity, helplessness and trauma.

Social Work Intervention for Half-widows

Social work services with single-parent families focus on both the broader social issues affecting these families and interpersonal issues presented by the families themselves (Strand, 1995). The social work profession pays particular attention to developing social policies that seek to ameliorate the poverty of single-parent families through income supports. Empowerment-based social work practice builds on the strengths of successful single parents. Olson and Haynes (1993) identify seven themes that accentuate single parents' competency:

- Accepting challenges.
- Making parenting tasks a priority.
- Disciplining children consistently with non-punitive actions.
- Developing open patterns of communication within their

families.
- Fostering individuality.
- Finding time for themselves.
- Creating distinctive family rituals and traditions.

Keeping in view the results of the present study, a comprehensive social work approach is needed to alleviate the sufferings of this section of society (Half-widows). The researcher has proposed following intervention models to deal with the issues and problems of Half-widows:

1. Generalist Approach.
2. Crisis Intervention Approach.
3. Psycho-Social Approach.
4. Integrated model of Practice.
5. Advocacy and Social Action.

Generalist Approach

Generalist social work provides an integrated and multilevelled approach for meeting the purposes of social work. Generalist practitioners work with a variety of human systems—societies, communities, neighbourhoods, complex organizations, formal groups, families, and individuals—to create changes that maximize human system functioning. This means that generalist social workers work directly with client systems at all levels, connect clients to available resources, intervene with organizations to enhance the responsiveness of resource systems, advocate just social policies to ensure the equitable distribution of resources, and research all aspects of social work practice. The generalist approach to social work practice rests on four major premises. First, human behaviour is inextricably connected to the social and physical environment. Second, based on this linkage among persons and environments, opportunities for enhancing the functioning of any human system include changing the system itself, modifying its interactions with the environment, and altering other systems within its environment. Generalist practitioners implement multilevel assessments and multi-method interventions in response to these possible avenues for change. Third, work with any level of a human system—from individual to society—uses similar social work processes. Social work intervention with all human systems requires an exchange of information through some form of dialogue, a process of discovery to locate resources for change, and a phase of development to accomplish the purposes of the work. Finally, generalist practitioners have responsibilities beyond direct practice to work toward just social policies as well as to conduct and apply research. For the present study Generalist Approach of social work is appropriate as the problems faced by Half-widows are multi-dimensional. With its wide scope of intervention, the problems of Half-widows and their dependent children can be addressed as it works with a variety of human-societies, communities, formal groups, family and individual level.

Levels of Intervention in Generalist Practice

Generalist social workers look at issues in context and find solutions within the interactions between people and their environments. The generalist approach moves beyond the confines of individually focused practice to the expanding sphere of intervention at multiple system levels. "In this process, all social work methods—traditional and innovative—are utilized, singly or in combination, to meet real needs and to alleviate stresses in ways that enhance or strengthen the inherent capacities of client systems" (Brown, 1982). In generalist social work, the nature of presenting situations, the particular systems involved, and potential solutions shape interventions, rather than a social worker's adherence to a particular method. The view of generalist social work is like the view through a wide-angle lens of a camera. It takes in the whole, even when focusing on an individual part. Workers assess people in the backdrop of their settings, and interventions unfold with an eye to outcomes at all system levels. Visualize potential clients and agents for change on a continuum ranging from micro- to mezzo- to macro-level interventions, small systems to large systems, including the system of the social work profession itself. Generalist social workers view problems in context, combine practice techniques to fit the situation, and implement skills to intervene at multiple system levels.

(a) Working with Micro-level systems

Micro-level intervention focuses on work with people individually, in families, or in small groups to foster changes in a personal functioning, in social relationships, and in the ways, people interact with social and institutional resources. Social workers draw on the knowledge and skills of clinical practice, including strategies such as crisis intervention, family therapy, linkage and referral, and the use of group process. Although micro-level interventions create changes in individual, familial, and interpersonal functioning, social workers do not necessarily direct all their efforts at changing individuals themselves. Often, workers target changes in other systems, including changes in the social and physical environments, to facilitate improvement in an individual's or family's social functioning. These activities involve work with systems at other levels. The psychological, physical and social problems of Half-widows can be addressed at the micro-level through social case work, counselling, social group work practice. Psychoanalytical and psychosocial approaches are widely used in addressing the problems of clients in this approach.

(b) Working with Mezzo-level systems

Mezzo-level intervention creates changes in task groups, teams, organizations, and the network of service delivery. In other words, the locus for change is within organizations and formal groups, including their structures, goals, or functions. Effecting change in organizations requires an understanding of group dynamics, skills in facilitating decision-making, and a proficiency in organizational planning. Working with agency structures and the social service delivery network is essential for developing quality resources and services. The mezzo-level of social work intervention represents work with formal groups and complex organizations. Various Governmental and Non-Governmental agencies come under this heading (Dubois, 1999). Work with formal groups includes working with teams and, interdisciplinary taskforces, service clubs etc. Effective mezzo-level work requires skills in organizational planning decision-making and conflict negotiation. The institutional intervention through services is done at this level.

(c) Working with Macro-level systems

The macro-level intervention addresses social problems in the community, institutional, and societal systems. At this level, generalist practitioners work to achieve social change through neighbourhood organizing, community planning, locality development, public education, policy development, and social action. A worker's testimony at a legislative hearing reflects a macro-level strategy to support a comprehensive national family welfare policy. Working with neighbourhood groups to lobby for increased city spending on police protection, street repair, and park maintenance is another example of a macro-level intervention. Social policy formulation and community development lead to macro system change. Macrosystems practice reflects the social reform—the pursuit of a desirable change to improve the quality of life. This approach believes more in activism—community mobilization, organization and social action are the key components of this approach. At macro-level, social workers help resolve intergroup tensions and community problems by initiating social action and social change. Their attitudes include activities such as economic development, legislative action and policy formulation. The socio-political problems of the Half-widows can be addressed through this approach. The community-based rehabilitation is important for the welfare of the Half-widows. The revival of local Mohalla (community) Committees is essential for the community rehabilitation Half-widows.

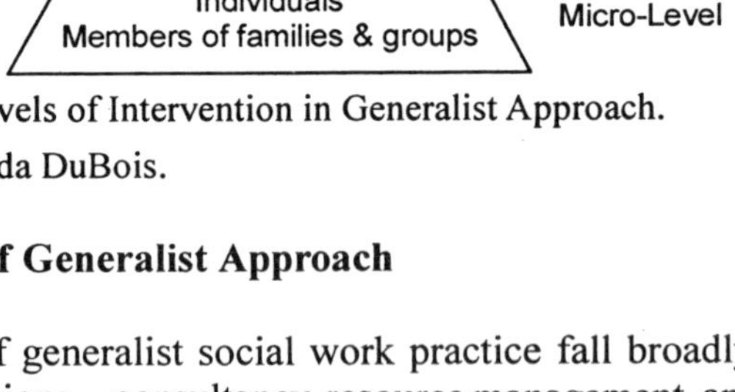

Fig. 15.1: Levels of Intervention in Generalist Approach.

Source: Brenda DuBois.

Activities of Generalist Approach

Activities of generalist social work practice fall broadly into three related functions—consultancy, resource management, and education (DuBois & Miley, 2008; Tracy & DuBois, 1987). Within each function are associated roles that explicate the nature of the interaction between clients and social workers at various system levels. These roles define responsibilities for both client systems and practitioners. Interventions designed within this model cover the range of issues presented to generalist social workers by clients at all system levels.

(A) Consultancy

Through consultancy, social workers seek to find solutions for challenges in social functioning with individuals, families, groups, organizations, and communities. Within the roles of the consultancy function of social work, workers and clients confer and deliberate together to develop plans for change. Practitioners and clients share their expertise with one another for the purpose of resolving personal, family, organizational, and societal problems. Consultancy acknowledges that both social workers and client systems bring information and resources, actual and potential that is vital for resolving the issue at hand. As a collaborative process, consultancy draws on the knowledge, values, and skills of social workers and clients to clarify issues, recognize strengths, discuss options, and identify potential courses of action. As consultants, social workers empower clients by respecting their competence, drawing on their strengths, and working with them collaboratively to discover solutions. These consultancy activities cast workers into the roles of an enabler, facilitator, planner, and colleague. In the present study, it has been observed that Half-widows are at a disadvantaged position, due to which their overall functioning is hampered, social workers as consultants can help in boosting their morale and involve them actively in finding solutions to their problems.

(a) Enabler Role

As enablers, social workers engage individuals, families, and small groups in counselling processes. An enabler encourages action by engaging in a helping relationship, framing solutions, and working for constructive and sustainable change. In other words, enablers are change agents who "use varying approaches in order to provide the conditions necessary for clients to achieve their purposes, meet life challenges, engage in their natural life development processes, and carry out their tasks" (Maluccio, 1981: 19). In the context of work with groups, social workers enable supportive interactions among group members to facilitate problem-solving. As enablers, practitioners consult with individual and family client systems to improve social functioning by modifying behaviours, relationship patterns, and social and physical environments. Half-widows face a lot of problems due to their physical and social environment in which they are living, relationships often sour up after the disappearance of their husbands they become a burden on the family.

(b) Facilitator Role

Facilitators activate the participation of organizational members in change efforts. By facilitating group processes, social workers encourage competent group functioning, stimulate intra-group support, observe group interaction, offer constructive feedback, and share information about group dynamics. As facilitators, social workers enhance linkages within organizations and help them counteract apathy and disorganization (Pincus & Minahan, 1973). In this role, practitioners may even target their own agency settings to increase the cooperation of staff and ensure the effectiveness of social service delivery. For the present study social workers as facilitators can bring all the Half-widows together and make them participate to bring an effective change.

(c) Planner Role

As social planners and community organizers, social workers understand community needs, recognize gaps and barriers to service delivery, and can facilitate a process for community-based or social change. Social planners use research and planning strategies to collect data systematically, explore alternative courses of action, and recommend changes to community leaders (Barker, 2003). Techniques for planning include needs assessments, service inventories, community profiles, community inventories, environmental scans, and field research to understand social problems and develop innovative solutions at the macro-level. The intervention involves social worker to assist communities in planning to resolve community problems and provide health and human services which are most required while dealing with the issues of Half-widows.

(B) Resource Management

In the resource management function, social workers stimulate exchanges with resources that client systems already use to some extent, access available resources that client systems are not using, and develop resources that are not currently available. Resources are sources of power and provide the impetus for change at any system level. Resources are found in individuals, in relationships, and in social institutions. Resources are not gifts bestowed by social workers. Instead, both social workers and clients play active roles in managing resources. Clients, as resource managers, take action to explore existing opportunities, activate dormant supports, and assert their rights to services. Social workers bring the resources of professional practice—the value imperative of equitable access to societal resources, the broad knowledge of the availability of resources, and a repertoire of skills to access and develop resources. Resource management is empowering when it increases the client system's own resourcefulness through coordinating, systematizing, and integrating rather than through controlling or directing. Social workers as resource managers function in the roles of advocate, convener, mediator, activist, and catalyst.

(a) Advocate Roles

The professional mandate of the social work profession, "to help people obtain resources", lays the foundation for the roles of an advocate. For the present study social workers as brokers, can link Half-widows with available resources by providing information about resource options and making appropriate referrals. Competent brokers assess situations, provide clients with choices among alternative resources, facilitate clients' connections with referral agencies, and follow up to evaluate their efforts. As advocates, social workers act as intermediaries between clients and other systems to protect clients' rights. Frequently, advocates function as spokespersons for clients in the bureaucratic maze of governmental structures. Advocates intervene with social service delivery systems or policy-makers on behalf of clients. Circumstances often press social workers to take on advocacy roles because the rights of social service clients have often been abridged.

(b) Convener and Mediator Roles

Social workers often serve as conveners and mediators with formal groups and organizations to coordinate resource distribution and development. Conveners promote interagency discussion and planning, mobilize coordinated networks for effective service delivery, and advocate policies that promote equitable funding and just service provisions. As conveners, social workers use networking strategies to bring together diverse representatives to address collective goals such as in the examples of community task groups, interagency committees, and United Way panels. When controversy or conflicts of interest arise, social workers as mediators use their skills for negotiating differences and resolving conflicts. Conveners-mediators ally service providers in identifying service delivery gaps and encouraging proactive interagency planning, activities that are central to prevention efforts in social work.

(c) Activist Role

Generalist social workers are in positions to identify societal conditions detrimental to the well-being of clients—a view that informs the social worker as an activist. According to Barker (2003), social activists alert the general public about social problems or injustices and garner support to alleviate these conditions. Social activists mobilize resources, build coalitions, take legal actions, and lobby for legislation. They create just social policies as well as initiate new funding or funding reallocations that address their identified priority issues. Engendering community support, activists empower community-based efforts to resolve community issues, redress social injustice, and generate social reform.

(d) Catalyst Role

As catalysts for change, social workers team with other professionals to develop humane service delivery, advocate just social and environmental policy, and support a worldview acknowledging global interdependence. Through professional organizations, social workers lobby at the state and federal levels and provide expert testimony. As catalysts, social workers initiate, foster, and sustain interdisciplinary cooperation to highlight client, local, national, and international issues.

(e) Education

The social work function of education requires an empowering information exchange between a client system and a social work practitioner. Mutual sharing of knowledge and ideas are central to the educational function. Educational processes at all system levels reflect partnerships of co-learners and co-teachers. Collaborative learning presumes that client systems are self-directing, possess reservoirs of experiences and resources on which to base educational experiences, and desire immediate applications of new learning. The education function of social work respects the knowledge and experience that all parties contribute. Functioning as educators involve social workers in the activities of teaching, training, outreach, and research and scholarship.

(a) Teacher Role

The teaching role in social work empowers client systems with information to stimulate competent functioning in all domains of living. Through teaching strategies, social workers strengthen clients with information to resolve current issues and to prevent other difficulties from emerging. To affirm clients' existing knowledge and skills, social workers select collaborative learning strategies to implement educational activities. Educational exchanges may occur in structured client-worker conferences, in formalized instructional settings, or in experiential exercises such as role plays. Social worker as a teacher helps in developing the client's interpersonal effectiveness, ability to access resources and make informed decisions, which are very important for improving the conditions of Half-widows.

(b) Trainer Role

As educational resource specialists for formal groups, trainers make presentations, serve as panelists at public forums, and conduct workshop sessions. Sometimes, trainers are organizational employees; at other times, organizations contract with social workers to provide specific training experiences. Effective trainers select methods and resource materials based on research about adult education, attitude change, and learning modalities. Successful training strategies require a careful assessment of staff-development needs, clear goals of what the organization seeks the ability to convey information through appropriate training formats, and a concrete evaluation process.

(c) Outreach Role

In outreach roles, social workers inform a variety of audiences about social problems, describe social injustices, and suggest services and policies to address these issues. Workers disseminate information to inform the community about public and private social service organizations, thereby enhancing service accessibility. At the macro-system level of community and society, the outreach role supports the prevention of problems. Increasing awareness of such issues as poverty, health care, disease control, stress, suicide, infant mortality, substance abuse, and family violence leads to early intervention and stimulates support for preventive actions. Using mass media, distributing posters and leaflets, conducting mailings, staffing information booths, and engaging in public speaking all bolster community members' awareness about programmes and services. Sensitive to the unique needs of potential clients, outreach social workers provide multilingual, signed, Braille, and large-print announcements.

(d) Researcher and Scholar Roles

The social work *Code of Ethics* (NASW, 1999a) specifically describes how professional knowledge and scientific research form the basis for practice. The *Code of Ethics* obligates social workers to contribute to the profession by conducting their own empirical research and sharing their findings with colleagues. Professionals also critically examine the social work literature to integrate research findings with their practice. Social workers contribute to and draw on research related to human behaviour and the social environment, service delivery, social welfare policy, and intervention methods.

In practice, social workers interweave the functions of consultancy, resource management, and education. For example, in addition to counselling, consultancy may involve linking clients with resources and teaching them new skills. Similarly, even though education is identified as a separate function, educational processes are inherent in all other social work activities as well. Rather than compartmentalizing these roles, this trilogy of social work functions provides an organizing schema for generalist social workers to construct and integrate multifaceted interventions.

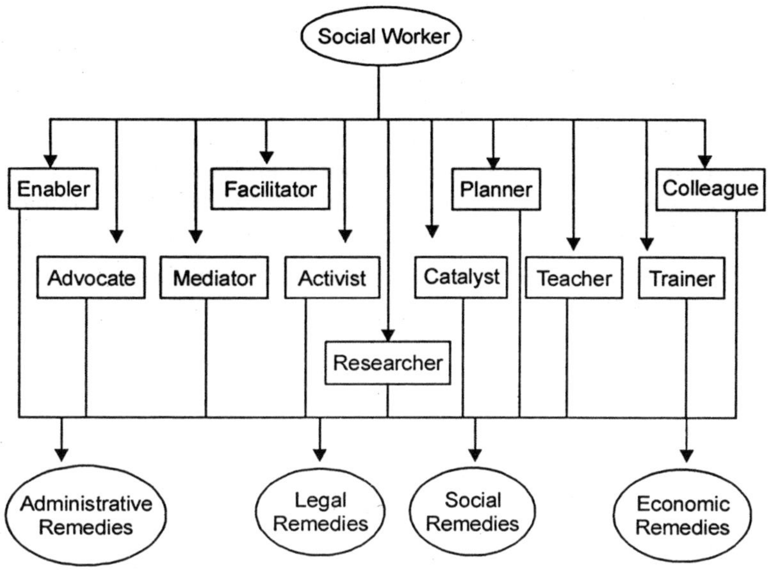

Fig. 15.2: Activities of Generalist Approach.

2. Crisis Intervention Approach

Crises intervention approach is to address the special needs and concerns of a client in an acute, psychological crisis. The intervention is applicable whenever the functioning of an individual or family has been suddenly or unexpectedly impacted by some personal loss or tragedy. The crisis theory states that it is important for people to resolve their crises situations and experiences in order to cope with new developments and crises (Aguilera, 1998). If individuals are unable to resolve their earlier crises, they become more vulnerable to the inability to resolve new crises. Individuals who learn new skills to resolve their crises are on the other hand strengthened in coping with future crisis situations (Aguilera, 1998). In the present study, Half-widows are facing an incessant crisis situation in their lives from the unexpected event of the disappearance of their husbands to the variety of changes that they experience in their daily lives. The social worker needs to understand the fact that when a member of any family is disappeared there is such a great shift in the family that they cease to focus on anything other than the disappearance and investigation. With no certainties and absolutes, the family loses its sense of control. The inability of the client system to cope with the issue of ambiguity and not knowing the fate of the disappeared person often land families in extreme conditions of stress. The unexpected event of disappearance is a situational crisis for the family which unexpected and unanticipated. Human beings have considerable capacities for handling or dealing with difficult situations. It is only when such difficulties assume significant proportions and people do not have appropriate resources, personal, emotional, social, spiritual or physical, to deal appropriately with stressful circumstances or events that they become involved in crises. Difficult or stressful events do not by themselves result in crisis situations (Aguilera, 1998). Crises are actually determined by the responses of individuals to specific stressful circumstances or events and their responses to them. Crises develop only when individuals perceive specific events to be significant and threatening, try to handle such events with their usual coping strategies without success, and are not able to use other alternatives (Aguilera, 1998).

Behavioural and psychological experts perceive crises to be akin to states of psychological disequilibrium. Individuals experiencing crises are likely to experience a range of emotions like feelings of apprehension, anxiety, fear, guilt and helplessness (Nash, *et al.*, 2005). Other indicators include alterations in eating and sleeping patterns, activity and energy levels and ability to concentrate. People in crises are also commonly known to suffer from depression and withdraw from social intervention (Nash, *et al.*, 2005). Social work experts argue that whilst the majority of crises run their course or reach some semblance of stability within one or two months, it is necessary for a skilled intervention to take place to strengthen the coping mechanisms of individuals. The failure to do so will result in the existence and continuance of crisis associated behaviours, even as the opportunity for change will be forgone (Nash, *et al.*, 2005).

People in crisis often have little by way of solutions and are receptive to external help and assistance (Roberts, 2000). The provisioning of skilled intervention by social work practitioners during the occurrence of the crises can result in opportunities for individuals experiencing crisis to learn new skills, achieve beneficial behavioural change, and regain stability. Individuals who have been able to successfully cope with crises are strengthened by such experiences and can use their skills in future times of difficulty (Roberts, 2000).

Crisis intervention is essentially a professional response that is limited in terms of time and is used to assist individuals, families, and groups (Hepworth, *et al.*, 2002). Social workers aim to assess the openness of individuals experiencing crises in learning of new skills and mechanisms for coping. They also help individuals in reducing their feelings of helplessness, isolation, and distress and use social resources to help in restoring individuals to their prior functional levels, as soon as practically possible (Hepworth, *et al.*, 2002). Such social work intervention is done through "listening, validation, acceptance, normalization, reassurance, education, advocacy and brokering resources" (Nash, *et al.*, 2005). Crisis intervention can be specifically segregated into 7 stages, namely (a) establishment of communication and development of feelings with individuals that circumstances can become better; (b) assessment of situation; (c) exploration of available strengths and resources; (d) goal setting with the use of such strengths and resources; (e) implementation of plan, teaching of new skills and mobilization of other support if required; (f) evaluation and adjustment of the plan; and (g) follow-up and termination of relationship (Hepworth, *et al.*, 2002).

3. Psycho-Social Approach

Glynis M. Breakwell and Collen Rowlett (1982) have presented social psychological approach. This emphasis perceiving and understanding the individual in her social context as is the problem of Half-widows. The problems of Half-widows are deep-rooted, complex and multilayered which categorically involves social and psychological aspects. This approach involves theories of social psychology. It involves analysis of problems, explanation of the problems, process of change and reflexivity. It is an attempt to mobilize the strengths of the personality and the resources of the environment at strategic points to improve the opportunities available to the individual and to develop more effective personal and interpersonal functioning (Hollis, 1997). The study shows that Half-widows are going through severe psychological imbalances due to the trauma they are facing every day. They are living in a constant limbo due to their ambiguous status which has a severe impact on her life. The social worker needs to work on enhancing the positive coping mechanisms of Half-widows and offer emotional support to them to alleviate their sufferings. Social workers can use counselling technique to provide psychological support to Half-widows and it can help in giving a vent to their colossal grief. Counselling is a process which takes place in a one-to-one relationship between an individual beset by problems with which he cannot cope alone and a professional worker whose trainings and experience have qualified him to help others reach solutions to various types of personal difficulties (Hahn and Maclean) (Nayak, 2002). The problems of Half-widows are multifarious and persistent, they are facing an unresolved loss and while working with them, a social worker should understand the fear of that phenomenon of having no answers. The Half-Widow of a disappeared person is not only facing the loss of her husband, but she has to deal with different issues. On the one hand, she is looking for her husband and the same she has to earn her livelihood, take care of her children, and accept the new role and to deal with demands of everyday life. In dealing with these events, a social worker can help the Half-widows through professional guidance. Communicating hope is very essential, hopeful attitude is an important element in responding to the client's issues.

4. Integrated Model of Practice

The integrated approach focuses on the transactions of individuals and their environment in the constant state of reciprocity with each shaping the other. This model is more consistent with an ecological approach. This model of social work involves casework, group work and community organization (Goldstein, 1973). It consists of role induction phase when the focus is directed towards the clarification, development and assumption of the client role concurrent with the identification and evaluation of the problem. Core phase is that juncture when the change system is stabilized, the emphasis is placed on problem-solving capabilities, and efforts are directed towards resolution and change. Ending phase is the terminal phase of service wherein resolution of the problem is achieved and evaluated. For the complex problems of Half-widows, the integrated approach is more advocated. Along with the community support model, the integrated model is expected to show some positive responses.

5. Advocacy and Social Action

Advocacy is defined as a key concept in social work practice. It is defined as exerting influence on behalf of organizations and groups within the legal power and political structure. Advocacy involves either an individual or group, or their representatives, pressing their case with influential others, about situations which either affect them directly or, and more usually, try to prevent proposed changes, which will leave them worse off (Soloman, 1985). The act of advocacy has a tremendous scope of helping the client system which has been neglected by anyways from receiving various services and amenities that are being withheld unfairly. The present study has strongly highlighted the various issues and concerns of the client system which it could not address on its own, for such issues the advocacy can play a very important role. While addressing the issues of Half-widows, advocacy as an intervention has a great scope as it involves all the aspect that are needed to be taken into consideration while addressing their problems most of them are not able to negotiate with the varied needs and resources that are to be addressed by the external institutions and the fact is that they do not have any control over them. Theorists like Gilbert and Specth (1976) have identified two types of advocacies one they refer to as case advocacy and the other is class advocacy. The type of advocacy which involves the social worker working with and on behalf of the individuals or families so as to assure that they are in receipt of services and benefits to which they are entitled and receive them in a dignified manner is a case advocacy. The class advocacy has a wider scope and involves the social worker to promote and induce changes in policies, practices, or laws that influence all persons in a specific class or group. Often this type of advocacy is referred to as a social action. In the context of the present study and the issues involved which demand social work intervention, both types of advocacies can be employed as the client system has a plethora of problems which require the integration of both types. The social worker while advocating for the client system needs to understand the importance of the target system of advocacy which may include, individuals, agencies, public officials, courts, legislatures and divisions of government. The tactics should also vary as per the targets of advocacy which, requires a thorough understanding of organizations structure and working and also the sound understanding of various policies (Rothman, 1991). It is also important that social workers should be able to understand whether the context and situations allow for advocacy or not and what is to be advocated and the strategy to be adopted (Sosin & Caulum, 1983). Therefore, this holds a very important place in the context of any place where the armed conflict has been going on, as the political situation might not allow for this action. Advocacy needs the full trust and faith of the client system on the social worker who is performing the role of an advocate for it. While considering advocacy interventions it is very important that the social workers should strictly observe the clients right to self-determination. If the client system does not wish to assert their rights, the social worker should respect their wishes. Similarly, when the social worker is implementing the advocacy actions he/she should bear in mind that it involves a certain amount of strain and tension, which can have a negative impact on the intervention. Social worker should discuss the possible outcomes and leave the final decision to the client. In the case of client system under in the present study which is very much prone to stress and other socio-economic burdens, the social worker should assess the situation and check whether it justifies the assertive action or not.

Social Action is the process of confrontation. It is used when other methods of social work like group work and community organization fail to meet the needs of the clientele group. When the resources are in the hands of a few people and they dictate their own terms and conditions, when power equation is imbalanced and rights are denied to a particular section of the community, the social action comes into play. It aims at equitable distribution of resources and power among different stakeholders. Social Action is used for mobilizing masses to bring about structural changes in the social system. It is an organized effort to change or improve social and economic institutions. It encompasses movements of political reform, industrial democracy, social legislation and social justice. The process of Social Action involves the following:

The first stage is **Developing Awareness.** It is the study of the social problem, its gravity, causes, impact on people etc. it involves understanding the socio-cultural milieu of the community and the pressing social problem affecting the well-being of a section of or the whole community. It also includes making people aware of the cause responsible for social problems.

The next stage would be **Organization.** It includes sharing the study results with the people concerned. The leaders of various groups and local leaders of the community are called for taking an integrated action. Awareness is created especially by using the means of mass communication. It is followed by efforts to mobilize people to organize for the given cause.

Next stage is **Making Strategies.** Goals are set on the basis of felt needs and strategies are developed to achieve them. The strategies could be negotiated with the authorities or if the need arises, there could be a direct confrontation.

The last stage is **Action** in which the implementation of the proposed intervention is done. This stage is more methodical and concrete as the final outcome largely depends on action.

Richard Bryant postulates two sets of strategies that are Bargaining and Confrontation. By Bargaining he means lobbying, submitting petitions, information and publicity campaigns etc. Whereas confrontation includes strikes, demonstrations and sit-ins. Singh adds another approach as an administrative approach. He mentions that most often than not any struggle or effort towards drastic or radical change is viewed by the establishment as a law and order problem and therefore, an administrative approach is adopted to deal with the situation. It includes persuasion, bargaining, pressure, coercion, infiltration, concession, co-option, splitting etc.

The techniques proposed by Hepworth and Larsen 1993 can be used for tackling the issues of Half-widows: Conferring with other agencies, Appeals to Review Boards, Initiating Legal Action, Forming Inter-agency Committees, Providing Expert Testimony, Gathering information through studies and surveys, Educating Relevant Segments of the Community, Contacting Public Officials and Legislators, Forming Agency Coalitions, Organizing Client groups, Developing Petitions and Making persistent Demands.

The present study shows that Half-widows are facing various social and economic problems, and there is a need to work on improving the socio-economic status of these women. Self-help groups (SHGs), vocational training, entrepreneurial activities and education programmes have been identified to address the rehabilitation of the Half-widows. Keeping in view the indigenous resources of Kashmir areas such as general artisanship, environmental management, agriculture, information technology, creative arts and entertainment, and tourism has been identified. It becomes obligatory for Governmental and Non-Governmental Institutions to set up training centres. The strategy that needs to be adopted in the rehabilitation programme is that the training institutions shall incorporate entrepreneurial skills for the various courses to give the Half-widows the option of self-employment after the completion of their training. The formal, as well as informal education needs to be imparted to the Half-widows. Identified vocational courses on the bases of interest of Half-widows are considered pertinent in the economic empowerment phase by setting Business Start-Up-Small & Medium Enterprises (SME).

The intervention approaches given for the present study can only alleviate the sufferings of the Half-widows to some extent only as they are going through a persistent grief. Nothing can compensate their loss, seeing the body of the deceased person helps to bring home the reality and finality of death and the person tries to move on, but for this section of society, the fate of their missing husbands is unknown. The present study reveals that the primary demand of Half-widows is to know the fate of their missing husbands.

Conclusion

In today's society, there are many different types of families. Some include intact, non-intact, single families, stepfamilies and a variety of others. Along with these different varieties of families, there is one common incident that can cause the family structure to change. One of the most striking changes in family structure over the last twenty years has been the increase in single-parent families. With the loss of a male breadwinner in the family, the poor woman faces difficulty in meeting the basic needs of children and other family members. Along with households duties, the women have to take other duties usually done by the male member. Moreover, these women tend to suffer from a lack of identity associated with their husband, feeling of isolation, anxiety about future, helplessness, lack of peace of mind, feeling of insecurity etc. most of the single mothers face the problem of lack of decision-making power regarding the future of children etc. Thus, financial problem and other stressful life event creates depressed mood and affect the psychological health. Single mothers in India are economically disadvantaged, many live at a bare subsistence level and face continuing difficulties in providing food, clothing and shelter for themselves and their children. Half-widows as single parents face a lot of problems due to their ambiguous status. They face multiple issues in the upbringing of their children. Social work as a helping profession can help in alleviating the sufferings of Half-widows.

References

Aguilera, D.C., Messick, J.M., and Farrell, M.S. (1970). *Crisis Intervention: Theory and Methodology* (p. 5). St. Louis: Cv Mosby.

American Psychiatric Association. (1994). *Diagnostic and Statistical Manual of Mental Disorders*. Washington DC.: American Psychological Association.

Barker, Robert. L. (1995). *The Social Work Dictionary* (3rd ed.). Washington DC: NASW Press.

Benokraitis, N. (2012, 2011, 2008). *Marriages and Families: Changes, Choices and Constraints.* New Jersey: Prentice-Hall.

Bllauw, M. and Lahteenmaki, V. (2002). *Denial and Silence "or" Acknowledgement and Disclosure*. IRRC (Denmark).

Choudhury, A. and Puangsuwan M.Y. (2007). *Justice Disappeared, Exploring the Links of Arms, Trade, Impunity and Political Disappearance in Asia.*

Crew, T. "IF THEY ARE DEAD, TELL US!" A Criminological Study of The "Disappearances" in Kashmir.

Dowd, N. E (1997). *In Defense of Single Families.* New York: New York University Press.

Dubois, Brenda, and Miley, Karla. Krogsrud. (1999). *Social Work an Empowering Profession* (3rd ed.). MA: Allyn & Bacon.

Goldstein, H. (1973). *Social Work Practice: A Unitary Approach.* University of South Carolina Press.

Gulalia, A. (2008). *Social Work Practice with Mobile Population Vulnerable to HIV/AIDS.* New Delhi: Mohit Publications.

Hepworth, D., Rooney, R., and Larson, J. (2002). *Direct Social Work Practice: Theory and Skills. (6th ed.).* Pacific Grove CA: Brooks/Cole.

Hepworth, D., Rooney, R.H., and Larsen, J.A. (1997). *Direct Social Work Practice (5th ed.).* Pacific Grove, CA: Brooks/Cole.

Hepworth, D.H., and Larsen, J.A. (1993). *Direct Social Work Practice Theory and Skills* (4th ed.). Pacific Grove CA: Brooks/Cole.

Hollis, F. (1997). *Casework: A Psychosocial Therapy.* McGraw-Hill.

Imroz, P. (2002). States Repression: Enforced or Involuntary Disappearances in Kashmir. *Combat Law, 1* (4).

Iqbal, A. (2005). *Principles and Practices of Social Work.* Jaipur: Sublime Publications India.

Jammu and Kashmir Coilition of Civil Societies (JKCSS). (2007). *Dead but not Forgotten: Survey of Death toll in District Baramulla,* Srinagar.

Kaur, R. (2004). Half-widows of Kashmir. *Institute of Peace and Conflict Studies.*

Kotwal, N., and Prabhakar, B. (2009). Problems faced by single mothers. *Journal of Social Science.*

Olson and Haynes, (1993). Towards a Resources and Stressors Model. *Journal of Divorce and Marriage.*

Pincus, A. and Minahan, A. (1973). *Social Work Practice: Model and Method.* Sage Publications.

Qutub, S. (2011). *Women Victims of Armed Conflict: A Study of Half-widows in Jammu & Kashmir. (M. Phil. Dissertation Social Work).* Mumbai: Tata Institute of Social Sciences.

Roberts, A.R. (Ed.). (2005). *Crisis Intervention Handbook: Assessment, Treatment, and Research.* Oxford University Press.

Rothman, Jack. (1991). A model of case management: Towards empirically based practice. *Social Work, 36* (6), 521-528.

Rothman, Jack. (1992). *Guidelines for Case Management.* Itasca IL: F.E Peacock.

Solomon, Z., Laror, N., and McFarlane, A. (1996). *Acute Post Traumatic Reactions in Soldiers and Civilians.* Guildford Press.

Sosin, M., and Caulum, S. (1983). Advocacy: A conceptualization for social work practice. *Social Work, 28*(1): 12-17.

Van der Kolk, B.A., and McFarlane, A.C. (Eds.). (1996). *Traumatic Stress: The Effects of Overwhelming Experience on Mind, Body, and Society.* Guilford Press.

Zia, A. (2009). *Women in Search for the Disappeared in Kashmir.* UC Irvine: Department of Anthropology.

16

Social Work Profession and its Feasibility in Agricultural Extension Services

Nayanjyoti Hazarika

Introduction

Indianisation of social work can be achieved through developing concepts which particularly deals with the issues concerning with Indian society, its values, culture and diversity. Agriculture is one field which gives humans an identity of their own. In India agriculture is not only the backbone of our economy, but it has cultural aspects that define the uniqueness of Indian society. Though we have learnt different ways and means to sustain our food, clothing and shelter, it is unfeasible to avoid the problems faced by agriculture in India.

Agriculture extension and professional social work primarily meant for empowering the community. Agriculture extension is concerned with assisting the economic and social aspects of people associated with agriculture, it also plays a crucial role in promoting agricultural productivity, increasing food security, improving rural livelihoods, and promoting agriculture as an engine of pro-poor economic growth whereas social work is a humanitarian approach dealing with all sections of the society including welfare of various stakeholders of agricultural sector. Social work facilitates individuals, families, groups and communities to enhance their individual and collective well-being. Over the years, social workers have developed scientific methods to address the shortcomings of the society, likewise agricultural extension have developed methods to ensure the overall development of the agricultural sector by improving the living standard of the people through transmission and practical application of latest agriculture technology.

Agricultural Extension has some core areas where it operates. It is concerned with agricultural education, assisting the economic and social aspects of people associated with agriculture, promoting agricultural productivity, increasing food security, improving rural livelihoods, promoting agriculture as an engine of economic growth and provides scientific and other factual information and training and guidance for the solution of problems of agriculture and rural life. Professional social work can play a significant role in enhancing the effectiveness of agricultural extension in these areas.

Amalgamation of social work methods with the agricultural extension will bring forth a new dimension to the traditional approaches of agricultural extension as well as professional social work. Social workers' community development skills can enable collaboration with extension agents to address issues, concerns in a neighbourhood or community setting, while the programme management and administrative skills developed by social workers can help create effective programmes that strive to address such needs in a holistic way. Social workers can also use their grant writing skills to help programmes generate funding to address the needs of communities. Lastly, social workers can apply their knowledge and training regarding policy writing and analysis to address issues on a broader level, leading to a sustainable and systemic change to ensure equal access for all citizens.

Agricultural Extension and Social Work

At the beginning of twentieth century, there was an inkling among the prominent social workers that various factors are devastating rural life, after this realisation they have started planning rural reconstruction to restore rural life. The social workers conducted several experiments which were beneficial for the area where it was undertaken. A close scrutiny of these efforts provided an insight into the background of the extension education approach adopted in the century (S.V. Supe, 1998).

The extension is an informal educational process directed toward the rural population. This process offers advice and information to help them solve their problems. The extension also aims to increase the efficiency of the family farm, increase production and generally increase the standard of living of the farm family. Extension mainly works with rural people. Rural people can make wise decisions about their problems if they are given full information including possible alternative solutions. By making decisions, people gain self-confidence. Extension, therefore, presents facts, helps people to solve problems and encourages farmers to make decisions. People have more confidence in programmes and decisions, which they have made themselves than in those which are imposed upon them similarly professional social work empower the client to help themselves instead of spoon feeding.

Agricultural extension is concerned with agricultural education aimed at assisting rural people to bring about continuous improvement in their physical, economic and social well-being through individual and cooperative efforts. It makes available scientific and other factual information, training and guidance for the solution of the problem of agriculture and rural life.

The likelihood of success in implementing a socially-just, sustainable, rural agriculture initiative through the utilisation of agricultural extension would be greatly enhanced with the participation of social work. Social work has never been singularly involved simply in the assessment, intervention, and treatment of individual psychological conditions. Indeed, the profession is not a monolithic undertaking but has been, rather, characterised by the evolution of multiple streams of both theory and practice (Coates & McKay, 1995; Day, 2000; Finn & Jacobson, 2003a; Mullaly, 1997; Reichert, 2003). For example, the profession has a long-standing tradition of critical theorising with respect to non-existent, unjust, or unsustainable social welfare policies and practices (Glicken, 2011; Wenocur & Reisch, 1989). It also has a historical legacy of advocacy for policy change and macro intervention within the context of community practice. Its early forbearers were often macro-level reformers, who sought change not only at the level of person but in the context of neighbourhood, community, state, and even national levels.

Given the richness and texture of its historical legacy with respect to both theory and practice, social work is in a unique position to consider multiple intersecting perspectives that serve the best interest of persons and communities in the context of their unique socio-cultural environments (Carrilio, 2007). For example, social workers can function as skilful members of interdisciplinary teams addressing issues of food access and sustainable production in low-income urban neighbourhoods. Sherriff (2009) studied a local food initiative in a low-income, racially-diverse urban area. The project integrated education and training for community members in the development of a sustainable food project. While the project sought to involve low-income community members and ethnic minority groups, in the end, the project was not successful in recruiting them. Sherriff (2009) found that this was likely due to a lack of cultural sensitivity on the part of the organisers. Cultural competence is one of the social work's core values, and sensitivity and skill with it would have greatly improved the results of this initiative. Social workers with a strong commitment to cultural competency are strategically placed to facilitate a relationship with community members and ethnically-diverse groups. As that relationship is developed, people are given a greater voice in the solution of their problems.

Another way in which social workers can contribute to agricultural extension initiatives would be in their ability to provide a comprehensive assessment of community needs, resources, and strengths. Social work's emerging emphasis on strengths-based approaches to practice could be applied to agriculture and used to determine what strengths and resources the residents already have that could be utilised in the implementation of an agricultural extension project. Social workers would also be able to use their community-based assessment skills to effectively discover what communities might want and need from the agricultural extension. For example, perhaps after holding focus groups with the residents of a neighbourhood, the planners of the agricultural extension project might discover that the residents would like access to foods that the developers had not considered. Because agricultural extension has the potential to facilitate the farm to grow nearly any kind of fruit or vegetable, the farm could be organised to cater to the ethnic food tastes of particular neighbourhoods. Perhaps they might also discover that many of the residents have difficulty finding the time to prepare healthy foods. After all, one of the incentives for people consuming fast food is that it is a warm meal that is prepared quickly and involves little effort on the part of the consumer. Perhaps planners would find that residents of a particular locale want on-site or nearby restaurants that serve healthy, organically-grown food. A professional social worker could include an on-site restaurant to supply those nearby so that they would have full access to freshly grown, healthy foods that accommodate the tastes of the neighbourhood or offer classes on the easy preparation of healthy, organically-grown foods.

Not only could social workers assess and communicate effectively with residents of the community or neighbourhood through deliberate integration and social investigation, they could also utilise their advocacy and policy skills to develop similar relationships with municipal governments and policy-makers. They could share their technical expertise to help city planners and lawmakers determine what the farmer community might want from them and what their concerns may be. Given the many ways in which a social worker could improve agriculture community resident's overall health and help alleviate psychological problems; perhaps agricultural extension planners, with the technical assistance that social work can provide, would be more willing to work in the planning and development projects which can address the psychological problems that various stakeholders of agricultural sector face. Social workers, working in concert with community members, may have knowledge of specific sites in neighbourhoods that would be optimal for the farm. If social workers were involved, the likelihood of a positive cooperative relationship between residents and agricultural extension workers would be greatly enhanced. Social workers may also be able to work with policy-makers to provide tax incentives and subsidies that would encourage the development of agriculture industry projects, especially within low-income and underserved neighbourhoods.

Social Work for Promoting Rural Development

Social work can make important contributions to rural development by supporting governments, employment and workers promote productive employment and decent work. Social work can draw on a vast array of rural relevant approaches and tools in core technical areas, long-time experiences, and a network of external partners to promote rural development. Social work can promote meaningful social development by capacity-building in a rural community. Education and training should be given the highest priority and investment in education should be increased so that socially distant and geographically remote population can have access to knowledge.

Intensive and low-cost training courses should be permanently available without regards to age, gender or level of previous studies.

The central problem of both the emigration from rural areas and repatriations inflows from the refugee camps should be tackled at their roots, particularly through education—both religious and secular in orientation—through promoting traditional studies, craftsmanship, farming skills and cultural tourism; encouraging the development of indigenous cultures and development of politics government; ensuring that everyone has access to shelter and other basics, and decentralizing education and social service at village level.

Combating socio-economic marginalization and exclusion to promote participation in rural life is a key indicator of sustainable development—respect for basic human rights and the forming of democratic attitudes and conflict resolution techniques must be promoted from early childhood. Social integration, tolerance, respect and non-violence should be encouraged by all possible means, as should intercultural dialogue and press freedom.

Efforts should be redoubled to promote environmental awareness. One extremely important goal is to reduce the debilitating impacts of natural hazards (especially recurrent ones, such as droughts and dust bowls).

To reduce isolation, to foster awareness and participation and to promote social integration, mass communication (private, community and alternative radio, and telecom) must be developed and existing system should be completely privatized, deregulated and improved within individual community, as well as between them and disparate regions, through the use of new communication and known information technologies. Regions and district should draw up overall information policies in these fields appropriate to their own needs and capabilities, but strictly owned by individuals and communities themselves.

Development must have a human face. Sustainable social development is only possible by way of tangible and steady improvement in quality of life: better security, better education, better health, respect for human rights, empowering women, popular democracy based on public and universal education, the rational use of resources through the application of advance in science and technology, and a universal commitment in the part of everyone to the culture of peace and national and international solidarity.

Implication of Social Work in Food Security

One of the prime concerns of agricultural extension is food security. Agricultural extension is working greatly towards increasing food security in the country. The definition of food security has evolved over a period of time. As a concept, food security originated in the mid-1970s, in the wake of the global food crisis. The initial focus of attention was assuring the availability and to some degree the price stability of basic foodstuffs at the international and national level. This was then broadened to incorporate the demand side of food security in the early eighties. During the nineties, issues such as food safety, nutrition, dietary needs and food preferences were also considered important ingredients of food security. In FAO report on, "The State of Food Insecurity, 2001", food security is defined as a "situation that exists when all people, at all times, have physical, social and economic access to sufficient, safe and nutritious food that meets their dietary needs and food preferences for an active and healthy life".

In the Indian context, the underpinnings for food security of the people can be found in the Constitution, though there is no explicit provision on right to food. The fundamental right to life enshrined in Article 21 of the Constitution has been interpreted by the Supreme Court and National Human Rights Commission to include right to live with human dignity, which includes the right to food and other basic necessities. Under Directive Principles of State Policy, it is provided under Article 47 that the State shall regard raising the level of nutrition and the standard of living of its people and the improvement of public health as among its primary duties.

Social worker's view on food security or insecurity is distinct than other professions like an agricultural extension. Food insecurity is the limited or uncertain availability of nutritionally adequate and safe foods or the ability to acquire acceptable foods in socially acceptable ways (Andersen, 1990). At the individual and household levels, food insecurity is characterized by four dimensions: (1) inadequate quantity of food; (2) inadequate quality of food, (3) psychological unacceptability of food and ways of obtaining food; and (4) social unacceptability of food and ways of obtaining food (Radimer, 2002).

Food insecurity is related to, yet distinct from, hunger and malnutrition. Hunger is usually understood as an uncomfortable or painful sensation caused by insufficient food energy consumption. Scientifically, hunger is referred to as food deprivation. Malnutrition results from deficiencies, excesses or imbalances in the consumption of macro- and/or micro-nutrients. Malnutrition may be an outcome of food insecurity, or it may be related to non-food factors, such as inadequate care practices for children; insufficient health services; and an unhealthy environment. Social workers can be involved in agricultural extension to prevent food insecurity.

Role of Social Worker in Agricultural Extension Services

It is a well-known fact that social work is a practice-based profession; social workers need to convey to the community the fact that social work is a valuable resource to every community member. Social workers have to build a relationship with farmers and other stakeholders of agriculture who need support, winning their trust and finding good ways of communicating with them, aiding farmers to assess their own needs, identify resources, make decisions, and arrange and manage their own support.

Farmers are facing various problems from government and corporates, social workers have to provide or arrange advocacy for the farmers who do not have a voice, and help them to be more in control of their own lives.

Social workers have to act as a broker to obtain the support people want, developing creative approaches to use of all available resources to extend individual choices, avoiding the trap of making people fit the agricultural service available, and being sensitive to unspoken needs. Helping farmers to develop the skills and understanding to be more effective in meeting their children's needs for care, development and control and supporting the physical, intellectual and emotional development of children and young people who belongs to agriculture-based communities and needs help, and helping disadvantaged people to improve their health and well-being, arranging good-quality alternative care for children and young people whose parents are agricultural labour.

It is very important to regularly review with farmers how well support fits their changing needs, involving them in co-recording progress and concerns, agreeing on adjustment and enabling people who are dissatisfied with the service they receive, including agricultural extension services, to make use of representations and complaints system to seek explanations, apologies and redress. Social workers have to encourage integrated working with extension workers, with other professionals and agencies, with networks run by people using services, and with community support group to improve the way services are coordinated in the agricultural sector.

Conclusion

If social work is to maintain relevancy and be part of global solutions "rather than an uninvolved bystander to the agricultural challenges" it is imperative for the profession to recognise the critical issue related to the agricultural sector. Scientific methods of social work such as case work, community development, social welfare administration, social work research and social action are imperative to agricultural extension. The gap between agricultural extension and social work are deeper structures of inequality along lines of race, gender, and socio-economic status of the agrarian community. "Social workers are uniquely equipped to address forces contributing to social and economic injustice as well as to the more personalised, specific needs of individuals, families and communities" (Carrilio, 2007: 528). Social work can make a significant contribution in enhancing agricultural extension for the greater well-being of the Agricultural sector.

References

Agricultural Technology Information Centre (ATIC), Retrieved from: http://www.aau.ac.in/directorate/extension-education/ATIC.

Agriculture Methods.GIF Retrieved from: http://www.fao.org/docrep/t0060e/T0060E08.GIF

Besthorn, F.H. (2013). Vertical farming: Social work and sustainable urban agriculture in an age of global food crises. *Australian Social Work, 66*(2): 187-203.

Bhattacharya, S. (2003). *Social Work: An Integrated Approach.* New Delhi: Deep and Deep Publication Pvt. Ltd.

Canadian Institute of Health Information (CA). Retrieved from: https://www.cihi.ca/en/social-workers.

Carrilio, T.E. (2007). Utilizing a social work perspective to enhance sustainable development efforts in Loreto, Mexico. *International Social Work, 50*(4): 528-538.

Coates, J., and McKay, M. (1995). Toward a new pedagogy for social transformation. *Journal of Progressive Human Services, 6*(1): 27-43.

Critical Issues for Agricultural Cooperatives. (2004). Retrieved from: http://farmdocdaily.illinois.edu/2011/11/critical-issues-for-agriculture-1.html.

Day, P. (2000). *A New History of Social Welfare* (3rd ed.). Boston: Allyn & Bacon.

Directorate of Agriculture. Retrieved from: http://www.aau.ac.in/directorate/extension-education.

Fernandez, A.B. and Geethakumari, K. (2014). *Social Work and Rural Development.* Delhi: Pacific Books International.

Finn, J.L., and Jacobson, M. (2003). Just practice: Steps toward a new social work paradigm. *Journal of Social Work Education, 39*(1): 57-78.

Glicken, M. (2011). *Social Work in the 21st Century: An Introduction to Social Welfare, Social Issues, and the Profession (2nd ed.).* Thousand Oaks: Sage Publication.

Krishi Vigyan Kendras (KVKs). Retrieved from: http://www.aau.ac.in/directorate/extension-education/kvks.

Mullaly, R. (1997). *Structural Social Work: Ideology, Theory, and Practice.* New York: Oxford University Press.

Reichert, E. (2003). *Social Work and Human Rights: A Foundation for Policy and Practice.* New York: Oxford University Press.

Sherriff, G. (2009). Towards healthy local food: issues in achieving just sustainability. *Local Environment, 14*(1): 73-92.

Singh, D., and Singh, B.K. (2011). *Agricultural Extension and Rural Developmen.* Delhi: Narendra Publication House.

Supe, S.V. (1998). *An Introduction to Extension Education.* New Delhi: Oxford & IBH Publishing Co. Pvt. Ltd.

The Role of Social Work in Mental Health, Retrieved from: https://www.casw-acts.ca/en/role-social-work-mental-health.

Wenocur, S., and Reisch, M. (1989). *From Charity to Enterprise: The Development of American Social Work in a Market Economy.* Chicago: University of Chicago Press.

What is Social Work? Retrieved from: https://www.casw-acts.ca/en/what-social-work.

Index